The Life of
Francis Thompson

Francis Thompson
in 1894

The Life of
Francis Thompson

By Everard Meynell

New York
Charles Scribner's Sons
597–599 Fifth Avenue
1913

Republished 1971
Scholarly Press, Inc., 22929 Industrial Drive East
St. Clair Shores, Michigan 48080

Library of Congress Catalog Card Number 75-145181
Standard Book Number 403-01107-8

To
Grazia

The Author's thanks are here tendered to Mother Austin of the Presentation Convent, Manchester, the Poet's sister; to Perceval Lucas and Father Austin Richmond for the fruits of research work; to Mrs. Coventry Patmore and Lewis Hind for letters and memories; and to many other kind helpers.

Contents

Illustrations

The Life of Francis Thompson

CHAPTER I: THE CHILD

"I WAS born in 1858 or 1859 (I never could remember and don't care which) at Preston in Lancashire. Residing there, my mother more than once pointed out to me, as we passed it, the house wherein I was born; and it seemed to me disappointingly like any other house."

The 16th of December 1859 was the day, 7 Winckley Street, a box of a house in a narrow road, the place of Francis Joseph Thompson's birth. He was the second son of Charles Thompson and his wife, Mary Turner Morton.[1] Charles Thompson's father (the poet's grandfather) was Robert Thompson, Surveyor of Taxes successively at Oakham in Rutlandshire, Bath, and Salisbury; he married Mary Costall, the daughter of a surgeon, at Oakham in 1812, and died at Tunbridge Wells in 1853. Charles, born in 1823, married Mary Morton in 1857.

Having first practised at Bristol and later been house-surgeon in the Homeopathic Dispensary in Manchester, he set up a practice in Winckley Street shortly after his marriage. Like his wife, his sisters, and the majority of his brothers, Dr. Thompson was a convert to the Catholic Church; but, unlike his brothers, he never

---

[1] Their first child, a son, lived only one day, and of the three daughters whose births followed Francis's, one, Helen, died in infancy. Of the other two, the elder, Mary, is a nun in Manchester, the other, Margaret Richardson, wife and mother in Canada.

A

The Child

committed himself to authorship, and is remembered only in the many good opinions of those who knew him. For his patients he had something of the pastoral feeling; his rounds were his diocese, and in the statistics of kindness which no man keeps—in deference perhaps to the thoroughness of the Recording Angel—his name is thought worthy to figure largely. Though he attended as many patients as the most successful members of his profession, his fees were smaller and fewer. He stood, like his clients of the poorer quarters, in fear of the Creator firstly, and of death secondly; and so it happened that, having ministered to mother and child, he would pour out the waters of baptism over infants who made as if to leave the world as soon as they had entered it. This much of his kindness will serve as a preface to the story of the part which, forced to a seeming severity, he played in the career of his son.

The verses of two of Charles Thompson's brothers (Francis's uncles [1]) supply no clue, not even a plebeian one, to the origin of Francis's muse. Edward Healy Thompson's sonnets and John Costall Thompson's *Vision of Liberty* show that not a dozen such rhyming uncles could endow a birth with poetry. Eugenists must accept an inexplicable hitch in the prosaic unfolding of the Thompson birth-roll. While there can be no chart made of Francis's intellectual lineage, it is not surprising that an occasional phrase in his uncle's *Vision of Liberty and other Poems*, privately printed in 1848, bears some resemblance to his form and diction.

[1] Edward Healy Thompson married Harriet Diana, daughter of Nicolson Calvert, sometime M.P. for Hertford, by Frances, co-heir of the 1st and last Viscount Pery. Another uncle of the poet was the Rev. Henry Thompson, who was educated at Magdalen Hall, Oxford; took clerical duty at Kirk Hammerton and at Greatham (Hants); published a sermon (1850) entitled *The New Birth by Water and the Spirit;* married Julia, daughter of Sir William Yea, Bart. A daughter by this union, Charlotte Anne Hechstetter Yea Thompson, married (1869) Ralph Abercrombie Cameron, elder son of the Rev. Alexander Cameron by Charlotte, daughter of the Hon. Edward Rice, D.D., Dean of Gloucester. A fourth uncle of the poet, James Thompson, lost his life in South Africa.

The Writing Uncles

A servant-maid destroyed John's autobiography—an unkind accident, since it left his career to be summed up by a relative in seven words : "An utter failure in life and literature." Gladstone and Sir Henry Taylor at one time interested themselves in his work, but neither so keenly nor so persistently as to secure his good fame with an exacting brother. Yet Edward Healy Thompson (born 1813, educated at Oakham and Emmanuel College, Cambridge) is duller in verse than John Costall. He never saw, or never used, even a second-rate vision. Before his conversion to Catholicism he was curate in the parish of Elia's "Sweet Calne in Wiltshire" from July 1838 to January 1840, and had for neighbour there the friend of Lamb and Wordsworth, to whom Coleridge, before a meeting, had written—

> My heart has thanked thee, Bowles, for those soft strains
> Whose sadness soothes the life with murmuring
> Of wild bees in the sunny showers of Spring.

But sweet Calne had its harsher properties : its human bees murmured in wrath, and had stings. Incumbent and curate both held a poet in disrespect. Coleridge and Francis Thompson, in whom may be traced in common the spoliations of opium, are linked by the coincidence that they were condemned by those Wiltshire associates —Coleridge by the rector in terms of high contempt, and Francis by the curate, who wrote in later days to warn Francis's London friends that he must be avoided as the writer of "erotic verse." Edward Healy Thompson afterwards admitted Francis's genius, but found no hereditary explanation of it in Francis's parents or any member of the family. On the other hand, Miss Agnes Martin, a cousin of Francis, writes : "From his father he inherited his passion for religion, and, from what I know of his poetry, I find he has expressed thoughts and yearnings habitual to other members of his father's family." It was Francis's custom to speak

3

The Child

of his mother as if it were from her at least as much as from his father that he derived certain mental and physical characteristics. Born in Manchester in 1822, she was daughter of Joseph Morton and Harriet Sigley. Her father, a clerk in the bank of Messrs. Jones, Lloyd and Co., was afterwards secretary to the newly-founded Manchester Assurance Co., and later lost money in a personal business enterprise. In 1851 her family left Manchester for Chelsea, and there in 1854 she was living with people who befriended her desire, frowned upon by her family, of becoming a Catholic. She became engaged to the son of the house, but he died, and before the close of the year she was received into the Church. In how far she was cast out by her own people I do not know, but to some degree she rehearsed the part to be played, after her death, in her own household by her own son. She set out to make a living, and took a position as governess at Sale, near Manchester, having failed—as he failed in his Ushaw days—in an attempt to enter the Religious Life.[1] In the following year, while still in the neighbourhood of Manchester, she met her future husband. She died December 19, 1880, at Stamford Street, Ashton-under-Lyne. Dr. Thompson married as his second wife Anne Richardson, in 1887.

The paternal relative (a cousin once removed) who finds in Francis thoughts and yearnings habitual to other members of his father's family, is better able to note them than he was. She tracks them in a girl (never seen by Francis) whose tragedy, since seeking admittance to a convent and failing to take final vows, is that she is not physically fit for the only life tolerable to her. She recognises the family mannerism in a relative who is famous in the suburban street of his choice for reciting the Psalms in a mighty voice in his sleep, so that no rest visits the guest new to the household noises.

[1] At the Convent of the Holy Child, St. Leonard's-on-Sea.

4

The Poet's Birthplace

No. 7, Winckley Street, Preston

Family Likenesses

She sees the family characters in Francis's niece who is about to end her noviciate and take vows in a Canadian community. She notes them in the two aunts, the sisters of Charles Thompson, who as Sister Mary of St. Jane Frances de Chantal of the Order of the Good Shepherd, and Sister Mary Ignatius of the Order of Mercy, lived and died as nuns ; of a third aunt nothing is known, but in a dozen other cases the inclination for a spiritual life or a disinclination for all the pleasures or successes of any other is apparent. She notes the same carelessness for worldly prosperity, the thoughtlessness for mundane concerns that goes with certain trains of spiritual speculation. In a family singularly scattered the family trait is for ever reappearing. The aloofness or vagueness that led Francis to lose himself in London was responsible for many lost addresses. As Francis wandered alone in the Strand, without knowing that he had relatives in Church Court within a stone's throw of his stony and uncovered bed, so do the brothers and sisters of the present generation inhabit London and its suburbs unknown to one another, but without real alienation or unkindness. She, the cousin here cited, has herself wished to enter a convent and failed, and knowing much of the family needs and inclinations, does not doubt that Francis's life-long trouble was that he failed in the attempt to be a priest. There is nothing to throw substantial discredit on such a reading of his career.

From Winckley Street, associated with none of Francis's conscious experiences of existence, the family moved to Winckley Square and to Lathom Street, Preston, and in 1864 to Ashton-under-Lyne, where they remained until Francis's flight to London twenty-one years later.

" KNOW you what it is to be a child ? " asks Thompson in his essay on Shelley; the answer tells us what it was

5

The Child

to be the child Francis : " It is to have a spirit yet stream-
ing from the waters of baptism ; it is to believe in love,
to believe in loveliness, to believe in belief ; it is to be so
little that the elves can reach to whisper in your ear ;
it is to turn pumpkins into coaches, and mice into
horses, lowness into loftiness, and nothing into everything, for each child has its fairy godmother in its own
soul ; it is to live in a nutshell and to count yourself the
king of infinite space ; it is

> To see a world in a grain of sand,
> And a heaven in a wild flower,
> Hold infinity in the palm of your hand,
> And eternity in an hour ;

it is to know not as yet that you are under sentence of
life, nor petition that it be commuted into death. When
we become conscious in dreaming that we dream, the
dream is on the point of breaking ; when we become
conscious in living that we live, the ill dream is but just
beginning." Francis was early alive. In a note-book
he says : "Yes, childhood is tragic to me. And then
critics complain that I do not write 'simply' about it.
O fools ! as if there was anything more complex, held
closer to the heart of mystery, than its contemplation."
He forgot perhaps that even fools have experienced the
dereliction and despair which catches at all children at
some time or another. It is improbable that he suffered,
but possible that he remembered, more than other
children.

Having attended for two months the school of the Nuns
of the Cross and the Passion—a name full of anticipa-
tions—he reached, in the cold phrase that admits to first
Confession and Communion, the " age of discretion."
At seven years he was reading poetry, and, overwhelmed
by feelings of which he knew not the meaning, had
found his way to the heart of Shakespeare and Coleridge : their three ages of discretion kept company.

6

He reaches the Age of Discretion

Already seeking the highway and the highway's seclusion, he would carry his book to the stairs, where, away from the constraint of chairs and tables and the unemotional flatness of the floor, his sister Mary remembers him. It is on that household highway, where the voices and noises of the house, and the footsteps of passengers on the pavement beyond the dark front door, come and pass quickly into other regions, that the child meditates and learns. There he may contract the habit of loneliness, populate his fancy with the creatures of fear; and gather about him a company of thoughts that will be his intimates until the end. And all the thronging personages of the boy's imagination are perhaps darkly arrayed against him. The crowd will be of tremors rather than of smiles, of secret rather than open-handed truths; the lessons learnt in that steep college of childhood are not joyful. The "long tragedy of early experiences" of which he spoke was a tragedy adventured upon alone. With his mother and his sisters, their toys, his books, and his own inventions he was happy. He would give entertainments to a more or less patient and tolerant audience of sisters; conjuror's tricks, and a model theatre on whose stage he would dangle marionettes, were the favourite performances, to one of which he was beholden for amusement and occupation till the end of his life. His early experience of the tragedy cannot be traced to the nursery. It was not there he built his barricade, or became in his own words "expert in concealment, not expression, of myself. Expression I reserved for my pen. My tongue was tenaciously disciplined in silence." There befell some share of accidental alarm. In a note-book that he had by him towards the end of his life and in which there are many allusions to its beginnings, he wrote of the "world-wide desolation and terror of for the first time, realising that the mother can lose you, or you her, and your own abysmal loneliness and helplessness without her." Such

7

The Child

a feeling he compares to that of first fearing yourself to be without God.

His toys he never quite relinquished; among the few possessions at his death was a cardboard theatre, wonderfully contrived, seeing that his fingers never learnt the ordinary tricks of usefulness, and with this his play was very earnest, as is attested in a note-book query— "Sylvia's hairs shall work the figures (?)." That he was content with his childhood, its toys, and even its troubles, he has particularly asserted. "I did not want responsibility, did not want to be a man. Toys I could surrender, with chagrin, so I had my great toy of imagination whereby the world became to me my box of toys." It is remembered by a visitor to the Thompson household that at meal times the father would call upon the children to come out of their rooms. But they, for answer, would lock their doors against the dinner hour : they were playing with the toy theatre. Francis went on playing all his life; his sister has kept her heart young in a convent. And there is no discontent in this particular memory of early loneliness :—

"There is a sense in which I have always been and even now remain a child. But in another sense I never was a child, never shared children's thoughts, ways, tastes, manner of life, and outlook of life. I played, but my sport was solitary sport, even when I played with my sisters ; from the time I began to read (about my sixth year) the game often (I think) meant one thing to me and another (quite another) to them—my side of the game was part of a dream-scheme invisible to them. And from boys, with their hard practical objectivity of play, I was tenfold wider apart than from girls with their partial capacity and habit of make-believe."

Crosses he also experienced, and the sense of injustice was awakened early. He lost the prize—a clockwork mouse, no less!—offered by his governess.

He has Plevna by Heart

Although first in lessons, his brisker, punctual-footed sisters and governess would have to wait many times during a walk for him to come up with them. And so the mouse went to a sister. "I remembered the prize," she writes, "but had forgotten the reason of my luck. But Francis *never* forgot it; he could never see the justice of it, he said—and no wonder!" His tremulous, sudden "not ready!" jerked out at the beginning of a game of cards, is still heard in the same sister's memory, and also the leverage of calls and knockings that was required to get him from the house for church or a train; and his unrecognising progress in the street. Every detail of the boy recalls the man to one who had to get him forth from his chamber when he was a grown traveller, and has often seen him oblivious in the streets, and has heard his imperative appeals for "ten minutes more" in all the small businesses of his later life. His toys he could surrender, but he played the same games without them. As a youth during the Russo-Turkish war he built a city of chairs with a plank for drawbridge; "Plevna," his father said, would be found written in his heart for the interest he had in the siege. If Plevna was written there, then so was Ladysmith. He had no plank drawbridge during the Boer war, but he was none the less excited on that account.

He knew little of the technique of being a boy; childhood was an easier rôle. Brothers would have told him it was bad form to care for dolls. He writes, in "The Fourth Order of Humanity," that he was "withheld even in childhood from the youthful male's contempt for these short-lived parasites of the nursery. I questioned, with wounded feelings, the straitened feminine intolerance which said to the boy: 'Thou shalt not hold a baby; thou shalt not possess a doll.' In the matter of babies, I was hopeless to shake the illiberal prejudice; in the matter of dolls, I essayed to confound it. By eloquence and fine diplomacy I wrung from

9

The Child

my sisters a concession of dolls; whence I date my knowledge of the kind. But ineluctable sex declared itself. I dramatized them, I fell in love with them; I did not father them; intolerance was justified of her children. One in particular I selected, one with surpassing fairness crowned, and bowed before the fourteen inches of her skirt. She was beautiful. She was one of Shakespeare's heroines. She was an amity of inter-removed miracles; all wrangling excellencies at pact in one sole doll; the frontiers of jealous virtues marched in her, yet trespassed not against her peace; and her gracious gift of silence I have not known in woman. I desired for her some worthy name; and asked of my mother: Who was the fairest among living women? Laughingly was I answered that I was a hard questioner, but that perhaps the Empress of the French bore the bell for beauty. Hence, accordingly, my Princess of puppetdom received her style; and at this hour, though she has long since vanished to some realm where all sawdust is wiped for ever from dolls' wounds, I cannot hear that name but the Past touches me with a rigid agglomeration of small china fingers."

A housemaid remembers Francis on the top of the ladder in the book-cupboard, oblivious of her call to meals. Of this early reading he writes :—

"I read certain poetry—Shakespeare, Scott, the two chief poems of Coleridge, the ballads of Macaulay—mainly for its dramatic or narrative power. No doubt—especially in the case of Shakespeare, and (to a less extent) Coleridge — I had a certain sublatent, subconscious, elementary sense of poetry as I read. But this was, for the more part, scarce explicit; and was largely confined to the atmosphere, the exhalation of the work. To give some concrete instance of what I mean. In the 'Midsummer Night's Dream' I experienced profoundly

that sense of trance, of dream-like dimness, the moonlight glimmer and sleep-walking enchantment, embodied
in that wonderful fairy epilogue 'Now the cat' &c.,
and suggested by Shakespeare in the lines, 'These
things seem small and undistinguishable, like far off
mountains turned into clouds.' I did indeed, as I
read the last words of Puck, feel as if I were waking
from a dream and rub my mental eyes. No doubt the
sense of the lines 'These things' &c., was quickened
(it may be created—I will not at this distance say) by
an excellent note on them in the edition I read. But
the effect on me of the close was beyond and independent of all notes. So, in truth, was it with the play as a
whole. So, again, I profoundly experienced the atmos-
pheric effect of 'Macbeth,' 'Lear,' 'The Tempest,'
'Coriolanus,' of all the plays in various degree. Never
again have I sensed so exquisitely, so virginally, the *aura*
of the plays as I sensed it then. Less often I may have
drunk the effluence of particular passages, as in the case
already instanced. But never, in any individual passage,
did I sense the poetry of the poetry, the poetry as poetry.
To express it differently, I was over young to have
awakened to the poetry of words, the beauty of language
which is the true flower of poetry, the sense of magic in
diction, of words suddenly becoming a marvel and quick
with a preternatural life. It is the opening of the eyes
to that wonder which signalises the puberty of poetry.
I was, in fact, as a child, where most men remain all
their lives. Nay, they are not so far, for my elemental
perception, my dawn before sunrise, had a passion and
prophetic intensity which they (with rare exceptions)
lack. It was not stunted, it was only nascent."

Another recollection :—

" I understood love in Shakespeare and Scott, which
I connected with the lovely, long-tressed women of
F. C. Selous' illustrations to Cassell's Shakespeare, my

The Child

childish introduction to the supreme poet.[1] Those girls of floating hair I loved ; and admired the long-haired, beautiful youths whom I met in these pictures, and the illustrations of early English History. Shakespeare I had already tried to read for the benefit of my sisters and the servants ; but both kicked against ' Julius Cæsar ' as dry—though they diplomatically refrained from saying so. Comparing the pictures of mediæval women with the crinolined and chignoned girls of my own day, I embraced the fatal but undoubting conviction that beauty expired somewhere about the time of Henry VIII. I believe I connected that awful catastrophe with the Reformation (merely because, from the pictures, and to my taste, they seemed to have taken place about the same time)."

He "first beheld the ocean" at Colwyn Bay when he was five years old. It was there that the Thompsons spent their holidays, several excursions there during a year keeping them in touch with the sea. Its sunsets are still remembered by Mother Austin, his sister, in her convent in black Manchester, where her skies are for the most part locked behind bricks or otherwise tampered with. Remembered by this sister as particularly attracting Francis is "the phosphorescence on the crest of the waves at dusk." Her memory is good, for I find in a long mislaid note-book the following verse of an early epithalamium :—

> The mighty waters of his soul
> Beat on her strand and break in fire ;
> Her spirit's shore, on which they roll,
> Bursts into answering desire
> From all its trembling depths together,
> Till their encountering souls illume
> The nuptial curtaining of gloom.

[1] A photograph (now missing), taken at the age of eleven or twelve, shows Francis with a small bust of Shakespeare—the treasured gift of his mother. In all the early photographs he conforms to one early description—" a boy known for his piety, obedience, and truthfulness "—and he is tidy, too !

Francis, his sisters, and their dolls
1870
("The Fourth Order of Humanity")

He beholds the Ocean

He adds, "I do not know whether the image is altogether clear to the ordinary reader, as it was in my own mind. Anyone, however, who has ever seen on a dark night a phosphorescent sea breaking in long billows of light on the viewless beach, while, as the hidden pools and recessed waters of the strand are stirred by the onrush, they respond through the darkness in swarms of jewel-like flashes, will understand the image at once."

The sea was there, and Francis bathed, timidly and always with the consecrated medal that was still round his neck when he died. He would not strip it from its place, and his sister, only less pious, would laugh at his anxiety concerning it. On the beach brother and sister would score Hornby's centuries. That was the chief use and joy of the sands to the enthusiasts; the whole series of triumphs would be thus shiftingly writ in full particularity. To Colwyn Bay he went before Ushaw, during the holidays and after he left college, and he went also to Kent's Bank, near Ulverstone, to Holyhead and New Brighton, so that it may be wondered why his poetry harbours so few seas. Topographically, his verse is very bare of allusion. The chapter of his childhood must close without the benefits of such witness, unless, as indeed it should be, the whole body of his poetry is taken as the evidence of his teeming experiences. Only in a nonsense verse found in his note-book (where doggerel keeps close, as the grave-digger to Hamlet, to the exquisite fragments of his poetry, so that strings of puns must be disentangled from chains of images) does he confess the place-names of his childhood. Runs the doggerel :—

> All along the gliding Lyne
> They told the nymphs of mislaid wine,
> And only by the mooney Med
> They found it had got in the driver's head.

But even early experiences are rare. In "Dream

13

The Child

Tryst " one is employed. He was eleven, older by two years than Dante smitten with love in Florence, when he met the Lucidé of that poem in Ashton-under-Lyne. She was a school-friend of his sister, and tells me she had no knowledge of Francis's admiration.[1]

It may not be supposed that Francis was too busy collecting lore of Hornby's centuries or other boyish excitements to be moved by nature ; he tells little of his early childhood's experiences because he was moved only to meditative dumbness, whereas later, when he knew he was a poet, each experience, however fleeting, smote upon his heart as a hammer on an anvil, and the words flew from each immediate stroke. He was too full of emotional adventures when he was sent, after his trials, to Storrington and Pantasaph to need to ransack the unmeaning confusion of his early impressions. Childhood proper was snatched from him when he became a schoolboy. His childhood he had called the true Paradisus Vitæ, and he would have combated the convention that school-days are the happiest of one's life. In an essay on his own childhood it had been his intention to include an account of his first year at Ushaw for the sake of contrast with his home existence, telling of the " refugium or sanctuary of fairy-tales, and dream of flying to the fairies for shelter " that he made there.

---

[1] " Dream Tryst " was afterwards alluded to by Mr. Edward Healy Thompson as " erotic "—a poem, explained Francis, " addressed to a child. Nay, hardly that—to the memory only of a child known but once when I was eleven years old."

CHAPTER II: THE BOY

IN 1870, after the summer vacation, Francis was sent to Ushaw College, four miles from Durham. By the kind fate that has kept many memories of him alive, his journey thither is remembered by Bishop Casartelli, who wrote to my father at the time of the poet's death :—

"I doubt if I ever saw F. Thompson since his boyhood. I well remember taking him up to Ushaw as a timid, shrinking little boy when he was first sent to college in the late sixties; and how the other boys in the carriage teased and frightened him—for 'tis their nature to—and how the bag of jam tarts in his pocket got hopelessly squashed in the process! I never thought there were the germs of divine poesy in him then. Strange that about the same time (but I think earlier) my classmate at Ushaw was the future Lafcadio Hearn—in those days he was ' Jack ' or ' Paddy ' Hearn ; I never heard the Greek forename till the days of his fame."

Timid his journey must have been, for all the crises of his life were timidly and doubtfully encountered. Dr. Mann gives some account of the event and of his first impressions of the new boy :—

" Canon Henry Gillow—the Prefect of that time in the Seminary—assigned him his bedplace, and gave to him two ministering angels in the guise of play-fellows. Then, for initiation, a whinbush probably occupied his undivided attention, and he would emerge from it with a variant on his patronymic appellation! ' Tommy ' was he then known to those amongst whom he lived for the next seven years.

" His mode of procedure along the ambulacrum was quite his own, and you might know at the furthest point from him that

The Boy

you had 'Tommy' in perspective. He sidled along the wall, and every now and then he would hitch up the collar of his coat as though it were slipping off his none too thickly covered shoulder-blades. He early evinced a love for books, and many an hour, when his schoolfellows were far afield, would he spend in the well-stocked juvenile library. His tastes were not as ours. Of history he was very fond, and particularly of wars and battles. Having read much of Cooper, Marryat, Ballantyne, he sought to put some of their episodes into the concrete, and he organised a piratical band."

Another impression comes from Father George Phillips :—

" I was his master in Lower Figures, and remember him very well as a delicate-looking boy with a somewhat pinched expression of face, very quiet and unobtrusive, and perhaps a little melancholy. He always showed himself a good boy, and, I think, gave no one any trouble."

From Dr. Mann's description, too, you get glimpses of the man. Those shoulder-blades were always ill-covered. The plucking-up of the coat behind was, after the lighting of matches, always the most familiar action of the man we remember ; while the tragedy of the tarts seems strangely familiar to one who later had a thousand meals with him. Fires he always haunted, and his clothes were burnt on sundry occasions, as we are told they were before the class-room fire. But of the piracy what shall we say ? Why, if he did not lose that habit of the collar and never shook off the crumbs of those tarts, why did he forget the way to be a pirate ? There was no rollick in Francis, and his own talk of his childhood showed him to have always been a youth of most undaring exploits. A good picture of his person is to be had from his schoolfellows' recollections ; for his mood we must go to his own recollections. In writing of Shelley he builds up a poet's boyhood from his own experience ; there is no speculation here :—

16

Grief and the Child

"Now Shelley never could have been a man, for he never was a boy," is the argument. "And the reason lay in the persecution which overclouded his school-days. Of that persecution's effect upon him he has left us, in 'The Revolt of Islam,' a picture which to many or most people very probably seems a poetical exaggeration; partly because Shelley appears to have escaped physical brutality, partly because adults are inclined to smile tenderly at childish sorrows which are not caused by physical suffering. That he escaped for the most part bodily violence is nothing to the purpose. It is the petty malignant annoyance recurring hour by hour, day by day, month by month, until its accumulation becomes an agony; it is this which is the most terrible weapon that boys have against their fellow boy, who is powerless to shun it because, unlike the man, he has virtually no privacy. His is the torture which the ancients used, when they anointed their victim with honey and exposed him naked to the restless fever of the flies. He is a little St. Sebastian, sinking under the incessant flight of shafts which skilfully avoid the vital parts. We do not, therefore, suspect Shelley of exaggeration: he was, no doubt, in terrible misery. Those who think otherwise must forget their own past. Most people, we suppose, *must* forget what they were like when they were children: otherwise they would know that the griefs of their childhood were passionate abandonment, *déchirants* (to use a characteristically favourite phrase of modern French literature) as the griefs of their maturity. Children's griefs are little, certainly; but so is the child, so is its endurance, so is its field of vision, while its nervous impressionability is keener than ours. Grief is a matter of relativity: the sorrow should be estimated by its proportion to the sorrower; a gash is as painful to one as an amputation to another. Pour a puddle into a thimble, or an Atlantic into Etna; both thimble and mountain overflow. Adult fools! would not the angels smile at *our* griefs, were not angels too wise to smile at them? So beset, the child fled into the tower of his own soul, and raised the drawbridge. He threw out a reserve, encysted in which he grew to maturity unaffected by the intercourses that modify the maturity of others into the thing we call a man."

When he recalls in a note-book his own first impressions of school he could not write as a boy, or of boys:

"The malignity of my tormentors was more heart-lacerating than the pain itself. It seemed to me—virginal to the world's ferocity—a hideous thing that strangers should dislike me, should delight and triumph in pain to me, though I had done them no ill and bore them no malice; that malice should be without provocative malice. *That* seemed to me dreadful, and a veritable demoniac revelation. Fresh from my tender home, and my circle of just-judging friends, these malignant school-mates who danced round me with mocking evil distortion of laughter—God's good laughter, gift of all things that look back the sun—were to me devilish apparitions of a hate now first known; hate for hate's sake, cruelty for cruelty's sake. And as such they live in my memory, testimonies to the murky aboriginal demon in man."

The word "reserve" is written large across the history of the schoolboy and the man; that he laid it aside in his poetry and with the rare friend only made its habitual observance the more marked. He was safest and happiest alone at Ushaw, and little would his schoolfellows understand the distresses of his mind there. One at least I know who could not recognise Thompson's painful memories as being conceivably based on actual experience. Teasing, at best, is an ignorant

Teasing, and a Punishment

occupation; at worst, not meant to inflict lasting wrong.

I have in mind two gay and gentle men, once his class-fellows, who are unfailingly merry at the mention of college hardships; they are now priests, whose profession and desires are to do kindness to their fellow-men, and I do not suspect them of ever having done a living creature an intentional hurt. Thompson's poetry they can understand, but not his unhappiness at school.

Nor does your normal boy, of Ushaw or any other school, admit that wrong is done him by the rod. The rod bears blossoms, says the schoolboy grown up; and the convention which makes men call their school-days the happiest of their lives likewise makes them smile at the punishments in the prefect's study. For the average schoolboy this attitude is perhaps an honest one. His school-days are happy; the cane is only an inconvenience to be avoided, or, if impossible of avoidance, to be grimaced at and tolerated. But every boy at school is not a school-boy, and the boy at school has to suffer general-isations about the school-boy and the rod. The commonweal spells some individual's woe, and doubtless the discipline proper for the normal child was hard for the abnormal. The boy at school, unlike the school-boy, is not brave, or, if he is brave, his courage is of a tragic quality that should not be required of him. The school-boy's account of the punishment of the boy at school illustrates the difference between the two; for the one it is fit matter for an anecdote, for Francis it was an episode never to be alluded to. Dr. Mann writes :—

"Some old Ushaw men may wonder whether, in his passage through the Seminary, he ever fell into the hands of retributive justice. To the best of his schoolfellows' recollections he did. It fell on a certain day during our drilling-hour that Sergeant Railton dropt into confidential tones, and we had grouped round him to drink in his memories of the Indian Mutiny. 'Tommy,'

·19

The Boy

who scented a battle from afar, was with us. All went well until the steps of authority were heard coming round the corner near the music rooms, and with well-simulated sternness our Sergeant ordered us back into our ranks. 'Tommy,' who, doubtless, was already making pictures of Lucknow or Cawnpore on his mental canvas, was last to dress up, and was summarily taken off to Dr. Wilkinson's Court of Petty Sessions, where, without privilege of jury or advocate, he paid his penalty. He was indignant, naturally, not to say sore, over this treatment."

Such is the gallant and approved vein of school reminiscence, of which one of the classics is the jest about the Rev. James Boyer, the terror of Christ's Hospital : "It was lucky the cherubim who took him to Heaven were nothing but wings and faces, or he would infallibly have flogged them by the way." [1]

But Francis was neither cheerful, nor mock-heroic, like Lafcadio Hearn, whose "The boy stood on the bloody floor where many oft had stood" was conned by his class-mates at Ushaw. Nor did a sense of the grotesque assuage the sense of injury, as in the Daumier drawing of a small boy's agonised contortions under the stroke of a wooden spoon upon the palm of the hand. He did not join his past school-mates in the brave bursts and claps of laughter and winking silences that I have known break in upon the narration of ancient floggings. Says Lamb, in describing Mr. Bird's blister-raising ferule, "The idea of a rod is accompanied with something of the ludicrous" : with Francis's school-mates it provokes a gaiety almost beyond the requirements of priestly light-heartedness. I am reluctant and ashamed to be less brave on the poet's behalf—to be out of the joke; and yet I find it difficult to put a better face on it. To remember Thompson's own extreme gentleness is to be intolerant of a small but over-early injury.

[1] Lamb's jest was perhaps remembered when F. T. wrote: "If a boy were let into Heaven, he would chase the little angels to pluck the feathers out of their wings "—a justification of Boyer rather than the Boy.

Henry Patmore

Being no observer, Francis failed to find the friends he might have found at Ushaw. Vernon Blackburn was his friend, but not till after-life. Henry Patmore, son of the poet, in a class above him, was as little known to him as he to Henry Patmore. Those who remember Francis as a shy and unusual boy, remember Henry Patmore — "Skinny" Patmore — in much the same terms. These two unusual boys had no more than the acquaintance of sight that is common in a school of over three hundred strong. Another school-fellow was Mr. Augustine Watts, who married Gertrude Patmore, Henry's sister. It was from Ushaw, where he went in 1870 (Thompson's year), that Henry Patmore wrote to his step-mother :—

" I will begin by telling you I am very happy. I have been much happier during these last two or three months than ever before. . . My bump of poetry is developing rapidly. For now poetry seems to me to be the noblest and greatest thing, after religion, on earth. . . . But what I mean by the development of my poetic bump is that I can now see the poetry in Milton, Wordsworth, Papa, and Dante as I never could till quite lately ; and I really think that being able to enjoy poetry is a new source of happiness added to my life."

At Ushaw, then, were two readers in the conspiracy of spacious song. But Francis wrote no tidings of happiness home. Of schoolboys in general Henry Patmore wrote, and, in writing, disproved his belief :—

" It is quite sickening, after reading the ' Apologia,' to turn to those around me and to myself, and see how very frivolous and aimless and selfish our lives are ; how we go on living from day to day for the day, as if we were animals put here to make the best of our time, and then ' go off the hooks ' to make way for others. Of course, grown-up people often live for God, but I think nearly all my ' compeers ' here (myself included) are animals."

Paddy Hearn (referred to before)—the Lafcadio of later life—was an older schoolfellow. College can be all things to all boys; some may find there a genial scene and cordial entertainment; others unfriendly and frightening surroundings. The case of Lafcadio Hearn, who arrived in Ushaw in 1863, a boy of thirteen, is not comparable to Thompson's, for Hearn mixed a strong rebelliousness with his nervousness; and he was neither unhappy nor unpopular, although peculiar, and even "undesirable" from the principal's point of view. Sent there, like Thompson, that he might discover if his inclination lay in the direction of the priesthood, like Thompson he drifted, after Ushaw, to London, and suffered there. The circumstances are strangely like those of Francis's case. But the invitation of the road and sea maintained Lafcadio's spirits. He endured his poverty mostly near the docks: "When the city roars around you, and your heart is full of the bitterness of the struggle for life, there comes to you at long intervals in the dingy garret or the crowded street some memory of white breakers and vast stretches of wrinkled sand, and far fluttering breezes that seem to whisper 'come.'" Thereafter the scope of his thought and action, with murder-case reporting in New York, with his unconfined sympathies for rebel blood, and contempt for "Anglo-Saxon prudery," might most easily be described as the opposite of Thompson's. A closer observer marks something more remarkable than dissimilarity. His Japanese biographer says of him that "he laughed with the flowers and the birds, and cried with the dying trees" — words which have an accidental likeness to "Heaven and I wept together."

Hearn's own words, in a letter to Krehbeil, the musician, show a much more deeply-rooted likeness. He says:—

"What you say about the disinclination to work for years upon a theme for pure love's sake touches me, because I have felt that despair so long and so often. And yet I believe that all the world's art-work—all that is eternal—was thus wrought. And I also believe that no work made perfect for the pure love of art can perish, save by strange and rare accident. Yet the hardest of all sacrifices for the artist is this sacrifice to art, this trampling of self underfoot. It is the supreme test for admission into the ranks of the eternal priests. It is the bitter and fruitless sacrifice which the artist's soul is bound to make. But without the sacrifice, can we hope for the grace of heaven? What is the reward? the consciousness of inspiration only? I think art gives a new faith. I think, all jesting aside, that could I create something I felt to be sublime, I should feel also that the Unknowable had selected me for a mouthpiece, for a medium of utterance, in the holy cycling of its eternal purpose, and I should know the pride of the prophet that has seen the face of God."

Thompson's "The conduit running wine of song" exactly matches the last of Hearn's sentences. Is that the Ushaw spirit? Probably Hearn was too little in touch with the school to have taken away such aspirations, even had they been in the air. But it is noteworthy that when the time came for him to choose a school for his own son he wrote :—

"What shall I do with him? I am beginning to think that really much of the ecclesiastical education (bad and cruel as I used to imagine it) is founded on the best experience of man under civilisation ; and I understand lots of things I used to think superstitious bosh, and now think solid wisdom."

When an enthusiastic critic said, at the time Thompson's first book was published, that Ushaw would be chiefly remembered in the future for her connexion with the poet, Ushaw smiled, counting the host of canons of the Church whom she had reared, her bishops, her archbishops, and her cardinals. Ushaw remembered, too, Cardinal Wiseman's saying : " Ushaw's sons are known not by words, but by deeds." But a few college friends did their best to keep Francis in sight during his early years in London, and if they did not help him, it was because he effectively hid himself among his adversities. It would have been more pain to brook the conditions of assistance, more impossible to follow a régime of rescue than to shiver unobserved on the Embankment, or starve, with no invitation or punctuality to observe save the long and silent appeals of an empty stomach, in the Strand. He had privacies to keep intact, aloofness that made a law to him, and these he never abused, even in a doss-house. "What right have you to ask me that question?" he said to the gentleman who accosted him in the street, asking him if he were saved. He had then been fifteen nights upon the streets, a torture insufficient to curb the spirit.

Dr. Carroll, Bishop of Shrewsbury, Fr. Adam Wilkinson, and Dr. Mann were of the few who remembered or sought to renew acquaintance. It is said that Bishop Carroll, when he came to London, would search "with unaccustomed glance" the ranks of the sandwich-men for his face. And when later the poet had a friend, and was to be found at his house, Bishop Carroll sought him there in London, and at Pantasaph from time to time, and had the poet, if not in his diocese, almost within his fold. We have Dr. Mann's record of a visit to London and a meal with Francis at Palace Court, but I know of no other meeting with a college friend. Thompson had never been a schoolboy, nor did he grow into an "old boy."

Applicable to him are the words of Hawthorne, of which he was fond :—"Lingering always so near his childhood, he had sympathies with children, and kept his heart the fresher thereby like a reservoir into which rivulets are flowing, not far from the fountain-head."

The distractions of his imagination were the most pertinent to his needs at Ushaw. Some scraps from his class compositions and his note-books do not sufficiently illustrate the sway that literature already held in his heart and brain, for they are but exercises in expression, stiff words on parade, rather than the natural swinging

publication of his thoughts.   A writer in the Ushaw
magazine lends us some knowledge of his literary and
other recreations :—

" He never fretted his hour upon the stage when our annual ' Sem
play ' delighted the senior house.   A pity that was, for such an appearance might have helped to remove some of the awkward shyness
which characterised him to the end.   His recreation, as a rule, did
not assume a vigorous form, though in the racquet houses he
showed that at hand-ball he attained a proficiency above the
average.   At ' cat ' his services were at times enlisted to make up
the full complement of players.   But here his muse was his undoing, for a ball sharply sent out in his direction would find him
absent.   He does not therefore figure as a party-game player.   He
seldom handled a bat or trundled a ball.   Most of his leisure hours
were spent in our small reading-room amongst the shades of dead
and gone authors.   It says a good deal for his perseverance and
patience that he sometimes read and wrote when all around him
was strife and turmoil of miniature battle.   Thompson would be
there, and pause was given to his dreamings ; he was rudely
brought down from his own peculiar empyrean.   After the vacation of 1874 he automatically changes his surroundings, going from
Seminary to College.   The master who had then care of him
exerted much influence over him ; he was a man of reading and
a rare discriminating taste.   In Grammar Francis had a still
larger selection of books, and many of his beloved poets were
well represented."

Books that were not school-books compelled his
attention in other places and at other times.   It is
remembered that

" He would deliberately take up his seat opposite Mr. F. S.,
who presided at the cross-table near the door, and, after erecting
a pile of books in front of him, would devote his whole soul to a
volume of poetry.   But Mr. F. S. was not of a restless, suspicious
nature.   Or it may be that he saw out of his spectacles more
than we supposed, and of set purpose did not interfere with the
broodings of genius."   •

Glimpses of Francis in the social life of the college
are few.   He was not so social but that somebody

The Boy

else sang his songs for him. Dr. Mann describes a picnic :—

" After regaling ourselves at Cornsay with tea, coffee, and toast, we did not leave the board till the old songs had been sung. I remember only the refrain. The first verse told of the virtues of our President (Dr. Tate), the second of the Vice (Dr. Gillow), the third of the Procurator (Mr. Croskell), and so on, each verse ending with—

> Fill up your glass, here's to the ass
> Who fancies his coffee is wine in a glass."

Somebody else, too, recited his prose for him, declaiming " The Storming of the Bridge of Lodi " amid applause in the Hall on a College-Speaking Day. It is the fourteen year essay of a schoolboy, and a fair specimen of the stuff that put him head of his English class. The piece took the ears of his schoolfellows ; it was recited by his particular class friend in the school debating-room, and thence, having been heard by the class-master of elocution, was promoted to the Hall, in the company of passages from Macaulay and Gibbon.[1]

---

[1] Prowess in English was officially reported. From Father Nowlan, a friend of the family, to Doctor Thompson, Easter, 1872 :—" You will be anxious to hear how Frank has passed at the last examinations. They have been very satisfactory indeed—second in Latin and first in English. His master was speaking to me about him yesterday, and said that his English composition was the best production from a lad of his age which he had ever seen in this seminary. His improvement in Latin is also remarkable, and his steady improvement in this subject will depend in a great measure upon a cure of that absent-mindedness which certainly, at the very outset, threatened to prove a great obstacle to his application to study. This, I am happy to tell you, has disappeared in a great measure, and in a little time we may be quite sure of its entire disappearance."

To the late Monsignor Corbishly I am indebted for the following record of the place Francis held in the compositions set three times a year :—

" In Latin he was first six times, second three times, and twice he was third. The lowest place was 6th, except when he composed in so-called Latin verse, when he got 23rd. His muse could not get going in a dead language. In Greek his place ran from 2nd to 10th. In French, average place about 8th. In English, 1st sixteen times ; of his Arithmetic, Algebra, and Geometry the less said the better. He was a good, quiet, shy lad. Physically, a weakling : he had a halting way of walking, and gave the impression that physical existence would be rather a struggle for him. He did practically nothing at the games. Haec habeo quae dicam de nostro poeta praeclarissimo."

St. Cuthbert's College, Ushaw
in Francis Thompson's time

The Greek of Dreams

For such warlike enterprises in prose and a certain occasional straightening of the back and assumption of soldierly bearing the name of "Tommy" was sometimes abandoned for "l'homme militaire."

Another witness, in the *Ushaw Magazine* of March 1894, remembers Francis on one occasion himself speaking his composition, but it is said by some that he never put such a trial upon his courage :—

"During his later years at College his literary gifts were well known. He declaimed some of his own compositions—written in a clear, rich, vigorous prose—at the public exhibitions in the Hall for the 'speaking playday.' His verse we never heard, except a skit in Latin rhyme, bidding farewell to work before the vacation, and beginning :

> Nunc relinquemus in oblivium
> Cæsarem et Titum Livium.   ;

We have, however, a vivid recollection of him as he was accustomed to come into the Reading-room, on the long dim half-playday afternoons, with a thick manuscript book under his arm, and there sit reading and copying poetry, nervously running one hand through his hair."

While Dr. Whiteside (later Archbishop of Liverpool) was Minor Professor at the College he had charge of Francis's dormitory. One night after lights were out he heard the sound of strictly forbidden talk. Searching for the offender, he found Francis reciting Latin poetry in his sleep. The Minor Professor awakened him and told him he was disturbing the dormitory. Ten minutes later he heard more noise, and found Francis, again asleep, reciting Greek poetry! I doubt if Francis's Greek, save in dream or anecdote, was fluent enough to waken his fellows.

The habit of humorous verse was already on him, and argues that he was light-hearted at school, even as the note-books, filled at the time of his greatest depression in after years, argue that he never wholly lacked

The Boy

relief.   His joke showed his independence; he was not under the thumb of his distresses.   He could put them aside, or accept, or forget, or forbid, or do to them whatever may have been the armouring process.

Of all the essays, in verse or prose, of his Ushaw days, the verses aimed at an invalid master had caught out of the future the most characteristic note.   I can hear him say his "Lamente Forre Stephanon" in the deep tremulous voice that he affected for reading, and it hardly comes amiss from the mature tongue :—

Come listen to mie roundelaie,
    Come droppe the brinie tear with me.
Forre Stephanon is gone awaye,
    And long away perchance wille be !
       Our friendde hee is sicke,
       Gone to takke physicke,
       Al in the infirmarie.

Swart was hys dresse as the blacke, blacke nyghte
    Whenne the moon dothe not lyghte uppe the waye,
And hys voice was hoarse as the gruffe Northe winde
    Whenne he swirleth the snowe awaye.
       Our friendde hee is sicke,
       Gone to takke physicke,
       Al in the infirmarie.

Eyn hee hadde lyke to a hawke,
    Soothe I saye, so sharpe was hee
That hee e'en mought see you talke
    Whenne you talkynge did not bee.
      ·Our friendde hee is sick,
       Gone to takke physicke,
       Al in the infirmarie.

We ne'er schalle see hys lyke agenne,
    We ne'er agenne hys lyke schalle see,
Searche amonge al Englyshe menne,
    You ne'er will fynde the lyke of hee.
       Our friendde hee is sicke,
       Gone to takke physicke,
       Al in the infirmarie.

The First Verses

A copy of the verses fell into the hands of Stephanon, without ill effects; his mighty laugh is still raised when he remembers them. The resolve to be a poet is in some of the college verses; the word has not been made poetry, but the spirit is willing and anxious. "Yet, my Soul, we have a treasure not the banded world can take," was the stuff to fill the manuscript book he clutched in recreation hours :—

Think, my Soul, how we were happy with it in the days of yore,
    When upon the golden mountains we saw throned the mighty Sun,
When the gracious Moon at night-time taught us deep and mystic lore,
    And the holy, wise old forests spoke to us and us alone.

Yes, I loved them ! And not least I loved to look on Ocean's face,
    When he lay in peace sublime and evening's shades were stealing on,
When his child, the King of Light, from Heaven stooped to his embrace,
    And his locks were tangled with the golden tresses of the Sun.

And much more; in that last he is feeling his way toward the line, to be written in maturity, "Tangle the tresses of a phantom wind." He was already on nodding terms with nodding laburnum :—

    The laden laburnum stoops
        In clusters gold as thy hair,
    The maiden lily droops
        The fairest where all are fair,
    The thick-massed fuchsias show
        In red and in white—thy hue !
    In a pendant cloud they spread and glow
        Of crimson, and white, and blue,
    In hanging showers they droop their flowers
        Of crimson and white, and crimson and blue.

Pan was not yet done to death, nor did Francis know that he, of all poets, would most searchingly chase the

god from his lairs, and give over the forests of poetry
to Him of the Rood, proving

> the Crucifix may be
> Carven from the laurel-tree.

The schoolboy's invocation is :—

> And thou, O Pan, whose dwelling must be sought
> Deep in some vast grown forest, where the trees
> Are wet with cold large dew drops in the breeze,
> Where hangs dark moss in rain-steeped tresses long,
> Aid me, O aid, to body forth in song
> A scene as fair as thou in all thy days
> Hast gazed upon, or ever yet wilt gaze.

Of Ushaw walks, another recreation fit for Francis,
a companion writes : " In all weathers we tramped the
roads, and it must have been at these times (for after
he left college he saw little of meadows and hedgerows),
that he unconsciously imbibed his wonderful knowledge
of the flowers of the field."

It was sowing-time and the soil rich, but an observer,
in the exact sense, Francis never was. He would make
any layman appear a botanist with easy questions about
the commonplaces of the hedges, and a flowered dinner-
table in London always kept him wondering, fork in air,
as to kinds and names. On the other hand, he was
essentially an observer : let him see but one sunset and
the daily mystery of that going down would companion
him for a life-time ; let him see but one daisy, and all
his paths would be strewn with white and gold. He
had the inner eye, which when it lifts heavy lashes lets
in immutable memories.

And of Religion : more pressing than the invitation
to the northern road would be the invitation to Ushaw's
Chapel. His lessons in ceremonial were not the least
he was taught. Eton could have given him his Latin,
but his Liturgy was more important. His singing-gown

was a vestment, and he learnt its fashioning at college. He learnt the hymns of the Church and became her hymn-writer; he learnt his way in the missal, and came to write his meditation in "The Hound of Heaven." A priest, who was his schoolfellow, writes:

" No Ushaw man need be told how eagerly all, both young and old, hailed the coming of the 1st of May. For that day, in the Seminary, was erected a colossal altar at the end of the ambulacrum nearest the belfry, fitted and adorned by loving zeal. Before this, after solemn procession from St. Aloysius', with lighted tapers, all assembled, Professors and students, and sang a Marian hymn. In the College no less solemnity was observed. At a quarter past nine the whole house, from President downwards, assembled in the ante-chapel before our favourite statue. A hymn, selected and practised with great care, was sung in alternate verses by the choir in harmony, and the whole house in unison. ' Dignare me laudare, te, Virgo Sacrata,' was intoned by the Cantor; ' Da mihi virtutem contra hostes tuos ' thundered back the whole congregation; and the priest, robed already for Benediction, sang the prayer ' Concede, misericors Deus,' etc. Singing Our Lady's *Magnificat*, we filed into St. Cuthbert's, and then, as in the Seminary, Benediction of the Blessed Sacrament followed. For thirty-one days, excepting Sundays and holy days, this inspiring ceremonial took place—its memory can never be effaced."

Although it is somewhere affirmed that Francis betrayed no singular piety, we know how devout was his young heart. It was intended for him that he should enter the Church, and he studied for the priesthood. Letters written to his parents by those who had him under observation go to make the history of the case; on September 6, 1871, Father Yatlock wrote:—

" I am sure, dear Mrs. Thompson, that it will be a pleasure and a consolation to you and Dr. Thompson that Frank gives the greatest satisfaction in every way; and I sincerely trust, as you said the other evening, that he will become one day a good and holy priest."

But at the last his ghostly advisers found him unfitted. They held his absent-mindedness to be too grave a disability, and in his nineteenth year he was advised to relinquish all idea of the priesthood. In June 1877 the President wrote a letter proving the good will, a quality that may easily collapse before a silent, strange, evasive child, which was felt for Francis.

The President wrote :—

" With regard to Frank, I can well appreciate the regret and disappointment which you and his mother must feel. Frank has always been a great favourite of mine ever since he came as a child to the Seminary. He has always been a remarkably docile and obedient boy, and certainly one of the cleverest boys in his class. Still, his strong, nervous timidity has increased to such an extent that I have been most reluctantly compelled to concur in the opinion of his Director and others that it is not the holy will of God that he should go on for the Priesthood. It is only after much thought, and after some long and confidential conversations with Frank himself, that I have come to this conclusion : and most unwillingly, for I feel, as I said, a very strong regard and affection for your boy. I earnestly pray God to bless him, and to enable you to bear for His sake the disappointment this has caused. I quite agree with you in thinking that it is quite time that he should begin to prepare for some other career. If he can shake off a natural *indolence* which has always been an obstacle with him, he has ability to succeed in any career."

Indolence is one name of many for the abstraction of Francis's mind and the inactivities of his body. He was not of the stuff to " break ice in his basin by candle-light," and no doves fluttered against his lodging window to wake him in summer, but he was not indolent in the struggle against indolence. Not a life-time of mornings spent in bed killed the desire to be up and doing. In the trembling hand of his last months he wrote out in big capitals on pages torn from exercise books such texts as were calculated to frighten him into his clothes. " Thou wilt not lie a-bed when the last trump blows "; " Thy sleep with the worms will be long enough," and so on. They were ineffectual. His was a long series of broken

The Disappointment

trysts—trysts with the sunrise, trysts with Sunday mass, obligatory but impossible; trysts with friends. Whether it was indolence or, as he explained it, an insurmountable series of detaining accidents, it is certain that he, captain of his soul, was not captain of his hours. They played him false at every stroke of the clock, mutinied with such cunning that he would keep an appointment in all good faith six hours after it was past. Dismayed, he would emerge from his room upon a household preparing for dinner, when he had lain listening to sounds he thought betokened breakfast. He was always behindhand with punctual eve, and in trouble with strict noon.

And yet there were the makings of the parish priest, or the hint of them, in his demeanour. "Is that the Frank Thompson I quarrelled about with my neighbouring bishop?" asked Cardinal Vaughan (then Bishop of Salford) when many years later he heard the name of the poet from my father; "each of us wanted him for his own diocese."

The ritual of the Church ordered his unorderly life; he was priestly in that he preached her faith and practised her austerities. Nature he ignored till she spoke the language of religion; and he, though secretly much engrossed in his own spiritual welfare, was, priest-like, audible at his prayers—or poetry. His muse was obedient and circumspect as the voice that proclaims the rubrics. He was often merely in Roman orders, so to say, when the critics accused him of breaking the laws of English and common-sense. At the same time he failed signally in the practical service of his fellows. His rhymes were the only alms he gave; but annoyances he seemed at times to distribute as lavishly as St. Anthony his loaves.

Having done no wrong, he bore home a disappointment for his parents. It is no light thing to have a son, destined for the sheltered rallying-place of the Church, thrust back into a world he had been well rid of. Nor

33   c

The Boy

did his indifference as to his prospects (the disguise, perhaps, of his own disappointment) inspire them with confidence.   I have already mentioned that it is thought by many persons well-versed in the spiritual affairs of the family that his failure in the Seminary was with him an acute and lasting grief.

On the other hand, he was from his childhood a prophet in his own strange land, and it is probable that while his family were solicitous for him to enter the Church, he recognised the justice of his confessor's opinion.   The "A.M.D.G." inscribed in his exercise books was none the less the perfect dedication.   "To the Greater Glory of God" was already his pen's motto.   He saw "all the world for cell," and he made much of the pains he thought necessary for his poetry.

Francis Thompson
in 1894

CHAPTER III: MANCHESTER AND MEDICINE

An awed, awkward youth, Francis had yet, before the age of eighteen, experience enough to know how futile for him was the study of medicine. A career in medicine, a career in anything, made no appeal to one who saw himself a man spoiled for the world. Home from his daily lectures, he would, not seldom, shut himself up in his room. His cloister was solitude, and in that painful sanctuary he hid himself from success. He made a pretence of study, and for six years was a medical student.

He had been seven years at Ushaw when he left in July 1877. The photographs of the time show him to have arrived at the most robust and perhaps most normal period of his life. But awaiting him at home were the traps of personality. There the opportunity to be himself set on foot and gave courage to all the essential peculiarities of his character. If he had evaded at Ushaw the claims of the community, he now evaded them much more. Although he resumed his play and make-believe with his sisters, he was growing further and further apart from a good understanding with any of his fellow-creatures. Holding himself little bounden to his duties, he soon started on a career of evasion and silence. After a pause of some more months he was examined, and passed with distinction in Greek, for admission as a student of medicine to Owens College. For six years he studied or attempted to study in Manchester, making the journey from Ashton-under-Lyne under the compulsion of the family eye. But once round the corner he was safe from the too strict inquiry by a

35

father never stern. The hours of his actual attendance at lectures were comparatively few. "I hated my scientific and medical studies, and learned them badly. Now even that bad and reluctant knowledge has grown priceless to me," he wrote in after life.

The Manchester of his studies had little hold of him, and keeps few memories of him. In the wide but mean street leading to Owens College you may, it is true, picture him making a late and lingering way to work, or entering the cook-shops which even then had initiated him in the consumption of bad food (but he long remembered the excellence of one underground restaurant for modest commercial classes), or nervously awaiting the offer of the bookseller for some volume superfluous to a truant student's needs. The thoroughfare is so busy as to disregard the abstracted walk and expression of an eccentric wayfarer. Francis soon learned the art of being lonely in a multitude, and would only occasionally perceive one of the passers who turned and looked after him. Boys provoked to jeer at him he met to his own satisfaction, sometimes with a complete disregard, sometimes with a threatening show of anger. He would congratulate himself upon his tactics, not knowing that he, a young man, was more timid and abashed than any seven-year-old rough of the pavement. The college building, oppressive and awesome in its arches, halls, and corridors, is difficult to reconcile with the timidity with which Francis faced it. Your footsteps "hullo!" at you in the passages, and must ring with self assurance or with carelessness if they are not to echo and exaggerate your doubtful mood. Laughter, the ungentle laughter of medical students—whither, asked Stevenson, go all unpleasant medical students, whence come all worthy doctors?—swings down on you or bars you from a corner that you must needs pass. Among the sheltering cases of the deserted museum there is more room for the would-be solitary. Silent mineralogies,

The Doctor's Son

fragments, fossils, tell the poet more than the boisterous tongues of the young men. Yorkshire delivered up to the museum a vast saurian and other creatures of the past of whom we hear in the "Anthem of Earth."

Those were years of anything but the making of a doctor. To have conformed so little to the style of the medical student promised little for the expected practitioner. He would even leave his father's reputable doorstep with untied laces, dragging their length on the pavement past the windows of curious and critical neighbours. He did not work, and his idleness was all unlike the idleness proper to his class. He read poetry in the public library. One sort of idleness, an idleness that gave business to his thoughts for all his life, took him to the museums and galleries. In an essay of the 'nineties he remembers.

"The statue which thralled my youth in a passion such as feminine mortality was skill-less to instigate. Nor at this let any boggle; for *she* was a goddess. Statue I have called her; but indeed she was a bust, a head, a face—and who that saw that face could have thought to regard further? She stood nameless in the gallery of sculptural casts which she strangely deigned to inhabit; but I have since learned that men call her the Vatican Melpomene. Rightly stood she nameless, for Melpomene she never was: never went words of hers from bronzèd lyre in tragic order; never through *her* enspelled lips moaned any syllables of woe. Rather, with her leaf-twined locks, she seems some strayed Bacchante, indissolubly filmed in secular reverie. The expression which gave her divinity resistless I have always suspected for an accident of the cast; since in frequent engravings of her prototype I never met any such aspect. The secret of this indecipherable significance, I slowly discerned, lurked in the singularly diverse set of the two corners of the mouth; so that her profile wholly shifted its meaning according as it was viewed from the right or left. In one corner of her mouth the little languorous firstling of a smile had gone to sleep ; as if she had fallen a-dream, and forgotten that it was there. The other had drooped, as of its own listless weight, into a something which guessed at sadness ; guessed, but so as indolent lids are easily grieved by the prick of the slate-blue dawn. And on the full countenance these two expressions blended to a single expression inexpressible ; as if pensiveness had played the Maenad, and now her arms grew heavy under the cymbals. Thither each evening, as twilight fell, I stole to meditate and worship the baffling mysteries of her meaning : as twilight fell, and the blank noon surceased arrest upon her life, and in the vaguening countenance the eyes broke out from their day-long ambuscade. Eyes of violet blue, drowsed-amorous, which surveyed me not, but looked ever beyond, where a spell enfixed them,

> Waiting for something, not for me.

And I was content. Content ; for by such tenure of unnoticedness I knew that I held my privilege to worship : had she beheld me, she would have denied, have contemned my gaze. Between us, now, are years and tears ; but the years waste her not, and the tears wet her not ; neither misses she me or any man. There, I think, she is standing yet ; there, I think, she will stand for ever : the divinity of an accident, awaiting a divine thing impossible, which can never come to her, and she knows this not. For I reject the vain fable that the ambrosial creature is really an unspiritual compound of lime, which the gross ignorant call plaster of Paris. If Paris indeed had to do with her, it was he of Ida. And for him, perchance, she waits."

Here already was the artist, the actor in unreal realities. Already he had been thrice in love—with the heroines of Selous' Shakespeare, with a doll, with a statue.

Cricket

Before he knew that his lot was to be more chipped
and filled with blanks than the ladies of the Parthenon,
he had set about furnishing the gaps with complementing
fragments of fancy.   He was winning consolation prizes
before any races had been lost.   "No youth expects to
get a heroine of romance for a mistress," he avers, but
I doubt if many youths court woodcut and wax on
that account.   They look for their heroines in living
replica ; Francis, the artist, went to book and toy-box.
And he went walking often to the accompaniment of his
father's talk of buds, and trees, and flowers.   Mr. J.
Saxon Mills, his neighbour, writes :—

"Some few may remember him when, a good many years ago,
he used to take his walks up Stalybridge Road, and in the semi-
rural outskirts of Ashton.   They will recall the quick short step, the
sudden and apparently causeless hesitation or full stop, then the
old quick pace again, the continued muttered soliloquy, the frail
and slight figure.   Such was the poet during his studentship at
Owens College.   An intellectual temperament less adapted to the
career of a doctor and surgeon could not be imagined.   To such
a profession, however, Frank was destined by a careful and practical father."

Besides the public galleries, the libraries, and the
roads, he had the cricket-field.   From the writing of
his own and his sister's heroes' scores upon the sands
at Colwyn Bay, he and she had taken to back-garden
practice of the game.   At school he had not played, but
neither had he lost his enthusiasm there.   Returning
from Ushaw, he would, his sister tells me, go to a friend's
garden and play for hours by himself, and bowl for
hours at the net, which meant that he had, after each
delivery, to retrieve his own ball.   He was much at the
Old Trafford ground, and there he stored memories that
would topple out one over another in his talk at the end
of his life.   The most historic of the matches he wit-
nessed was that between Lancashire and Gloucestershire
in 1878.   His sister remembers it, and he celebrates it

39

Manchester and Medicine

in the following poem, written in the clear but tragic
light that his devotion to the game shed upon the distant
scene of whites and greens :—

It is little I repair to the matches of the Southron folk,
    Though my own red roses there may blow ;
It is little I repair to the matches of the Southron folk,
    Though the red roses crest the caps, I know.
For the field is full of shades as I near the shadowy coast,
And a ghostly batsman plays to the bowling of a ghost,
And I look through my tears on a soundless-clapping host
    As the run-stealers flicker to and fro,
        To and fro :—
    O my Hornby and my Barlow long ago !

It is Glo'ster coming North, the irresistible,
    The Shire of the Graces, long ago !
It is Gloucestershire up North, the irresistible,
    And new-risen Lancashire the foe !
A Shire so young that has scarce impressed its traces,
Ah, how shall it stand before all resistless Graces ?
O, little red rose, their bats are as maces
    To beat thee down, this summer long ago !

This day of seventy-eight they are come up North against thee,
    This day of seventy-eight, long ago !
The champion of the centuries, he cometh up against thee,
    With his brethren, every one a famous foe !
The long-whiskered Doctor, that laugheth rules to scorn,
While the bowler, pitched against him, bans the day that he
        was born ;
And G. F. with his science makes the fairest length forlorn ;
    They are come from the West to work thee woe !

Nor did Francis's cloistered sister forget. On reading
Mr. E. V. Lucas's criticisms on her brother's cricket verses
(*Cornhill Magazine*, 1907) she wrote to me :—" The article
stirred up many old memories, thank God. I can
remember seven names out of the Lancashire XI of that
match." For thirty years she remembered the seven
jolly cricketers, with the seven joyful mysteries of the
Rosary, to keep her young.

The Red Rose

Francis in 1900 could draw up the whole of the Lancs. XI and name eight of the other XI, with a guess at a ninth man. Mr. E. V. Lucas knows all about the match. " It was an historic contest, for the two counties had never met before, and was played on July 25, 26, 27, 1878, when the poet was eighteen. The fame of the Graces was such that 16,000 people were present on the Saturday, the third day—of whom, by the way, 2000 did not pay but took the ground by storm. The result was a draw a little in Lancashire's favour. It was eminently Hornby's and Barlow's match. In the first innings the amateur made only five, but Barlow went right through it, his wicket falling last for 40. In the second innings Hornby was at his best, making with incredible dash 100 out of 156 while he was in, Barlow supporting him while he made eighty of them. The note-book in which these verses are written contains numberless variations upon several of the lines. 'O my Hornby and my Barlow long ago!' becomes in one case 'O my Monkey and Stone-Waller long ago!' Monkey was, of course, Mr. Hornby's nickname. 'First he runs you out of breath,' said the professional, possibly Barlow himself, 'then he runs you out, and then he gives you a sovereign!' A brave summary!"

Other Lancashire heroes and other worship were here recorded :—

Sons, who have sucked stern nature forth
From the milk of our firm-breasted north !
Stubborn and stark, in whatever field,
Stand, Sons of the Red Rose, who may not yield !

Gone is Pattison's lovely style,
Not the name of him lingers awhile.
O Lancashire Red Rose, O Lancashire Red Rose !
The men who fostered thee, no man knows.
Many bow to thy present shows,
But greater far have I seen thee, my Rose !

41

Manchester and Medicine

Thy batting Steels, D. G., H. B.,
Dost thou forget ? And him, A. G.,
Bat superb, of slows the prince,
Father of all slow bowlers since ?

Yet, though Sugg, Eccles, Ward, Tyldesley play
The part of a great, a vanished day,
By this may ye know, and long may ye know,
Our Rose ; it is greatest when hope is low.

The Lancashire Red Rose, O the Lancashire Red Rose !
We love the hue on her cheek that shows :
And it never shall blanch, come the world as foes,
For dipt in our hearts is the Lancashire Red Rose !

Vernon Royle, says the sister, was one of them ; nor did the brother forget him. I quote from his review of Ranjitsinhji's *Jubilee Book of Cricket* (*The Academy*, September 4, 1897) :—

"'From what one hears,' Prince Ranjitsinhji says, 'Vernon Royle must have been a magnificent fielder.' He was. A ball for which hardly another cover-point would think of trying he flashed upon, and with a single action stopped it and returned it to the wicket. So placed that only a single stump was visible to him, he would throw that down with unfailing accuracy, and without the slightest pause for aim. One of the members of the Australian team in Royle's era, playing against Lancashire, shaped to start for a hit wide of cover-point. 'No, no !' cried his partner, 'the policeman is there !' There were no short runs anywhere in the neighbourhood of Royle. He simply terrorised the batsmen. In addition to his swiftness and sureness, his style was a miracle of grace. Slender and symmetrical, he moved with the lightness of a young roe, the flexuous elegance of a leopard. . . . To be a fielder like Vernon Royle is as much worth any youth's endeavours as to be a batsman like Ranjitsinhji or a bowler like Richardson."

Old Trafford

The cricket verses are all lamentations for the dead. I doubt if he was ever so happy as when mourning his heroes. To decorate his boyish memories of the departed with rhymed requiems and mature rhythms was one of his few luxuries. The note-books were full of fragments : —

> He that flashed from wicket to wicket
> Like flash of a lighted powder-train ;
> Where is that thunderbolt of cricket ?
> And where are the peers of Charlemain ?
> With this, with this, for an undersong,—
> " But where are the peers of Charlemain ? "

He had projects beyond cricket verses and reviewing. At a late London period he proposed to write his cricket memories, gravely justifying his connoisseurship and his qualifications :—

" For several years, living within distance of the O. T. Ground, where successively played each year the chief cricketers of England, where the chief cricketers of Australia played in their periodic visits, and where one of the three Australian test-matches was latterly decided, I saw all the great cricketers of that day, and it was a very rich day. Naturally, I have a few things to say about cricket now and then. . . . Thousands of others have the same basis, but it happens that I have what they have not—some trained faculty of expression. The few remarks that follow carefully avoid the province of purely technical criticism, which is rightly engrossed by those who are themselves great cricketers. The only technical criticism worth having in poetry is that of poets, and the same is true of cricket."

Of the true historian of the game he writes : " Nyren— at once the Herodotus and Homer of cricket—an epic writer if ever there was one."

His Lancastrian ardour had suffered no diminution

Manchester and Medicine

when, after an absence from the north and from cricket fields of twenty years, he and I talked cricket. There was a well-established understanding between us that he was for the red rose, I for the white. It was make-believe, but served during many seasons and in many letters. More chivalrous than a knight of Arthur in rivalry he would write thus :—

"Well done, Yorkshire! your county is coming up hand over hand I see by the placards. I said how it would be, so I am not surprised. Our tail is not plucky. Love to all, dear Ev.   F. T."

That was about a match lost by Lancashire in 1905. The year before, Thompson's fellow-lodgers, with an eye to comedy as much as to cricket, had persuaded him to meet them at a cricket-net near Wormwood Scrubbs. Of seven men and boys who met there, six had made some compromise with the conventional costume of the game ; they could boast a flannelled leg, soft collar, or at least a stud unfastened in deference to a splendid sun ; and they were active, and their shadows on the green quite playful. But he was dingy from boot laces to hat band. Timorously excited and wonderfully intent upon all the preparations, he stiffly waited his turn to bat. When it came he remembered he had no pads on and stayed to strap them with fingers so weak that they were hurt by the buckle with which they fumbled. And then, supremely grave, he batted for the first time since he had faced his sister's bowling on the sands of Colwyn Bay.

I was never at Lord's or the Oval with him, in spite of many plans, and he himself passed the turn-stile on very few occasions. But he was always thinking of the cricket he would see, and always for some good reason postponing the day, as for instance in a note written in 1905 :—

Lord's

"I did not go to Lord's. Could not get there before lunch ; and getting a paper at Baker Street saw Lancashire had collapsed and Middlesex were in again. So turned back without getting my ticket—luckily kept from another disappointing day."

Mr. E. V. Lucas has written of the incongruity of Thompson's appearance and his enthusiasm :—

"If ever a figure seemed to say, ' Take me anywhere in the world so long as it is not to a cricket match,' that figure was Francis Thompson's. And his eye supported it. His eye had no brightness : it swung laboriously upon its object ; whereas the enthusiasts of St. John's Wood dart their glances like birds. But Francis Thompson was born to baffle the glib inference."

It was his unpromising figure that, making its way late at night from Granville Place to Brondesbury, would pass through St. John's Wood and be stirred with thoughts of the game. Had his mutterings reached the ear of the policeman on the Lord's beat, it would have been known that they were not always so tragically engendered as his mien suggested. The following lines he wrote out for me and posted in the early hours after such a journey :—

The little Red Rose shall be pale at last.
　　What made it red but the June Wind's sigh ?
And Brearley's ball that he bowls so fast ?
　　It shall sink in the dust of the late July !

The pride of the North shall droop at last ;
　　What made her proud but the Tyl-des-lie ?
An Austral ball shall be bowled full fast,
　　And baffle his bat and pass it by.

The Rose once wounded shall snap at last.
　　The Rose long bleeding it shall not die.
This song is secret. Mine ear it passed
　　In a wind from the field of Le-bone-Marie.

Manchester and Medicine

At the end of two years at Owens College he went to London for the first time, staying with his cousin, Mr. May, in Tregunter Road, Fulham.[1] The trials of examination were partly compensated for by a visit to the opera.

In 1879 Francis fell ill, and did not recover until after a long bout of fever. He looks stricken and thin in photographs taken at his recovery, and it is probably at this time that he first tasted laudanum. It was at this time too, during his early courses at Owens College, that Mrs. Thompson, without any known cause or purpose, gave her son a copy of *The Confessions of an English Opium Eater*.[2] It was a last gift, for she died December 19, 1880. Apart from the immediate consequences of this momentous introduction, fraught with suggestions and sympathies for which there was a gaping readiness in the young man, it greatly serves in the understanding of the opium-eater in general, of the Manchester opium-eater in particular, and of Francis Thompson, to make or renew acquaintance with de Quincey. Indeed if there is one favour that must be asked by the biographer of Francis Thompson, it is that his readers should also be readers of the *Confessions*, for, without the mighty initiation of that masterly prose, the gateways into the strange and tortuous landscape of dreams can hardly be forced, nor half the thickets and valleys be conquered, of the poet's intellectual history.

---

[1] It pleases the idle mind of the present writer to find that Francis visited Tregunter Road when my mother, who was years later to be the lady of " Love in Dian's Lap," was staying there, unknown to him.

[2] His uncle, Edward Healy Thompson, afterwards remembered that *The Opium Eater* was his favourite book at home : " We had often said his experiences would surpass those of de Quincey."

At the same time the family noted other influences ; it was a tradition of theirs that " On the 3rd Sunday of September, 1885, Fr. Richardson of St. Mary's, Ashton-under Lyne, delivered a sermon on ' Our Lady of Sorrows,' which, Francis hearing, was the subject of his meditation, and, two years later, of his poem ' The Passion of Mary.' It is thought that he did not make any notes on the sermon in church, but in the drawing-room at home in Stamford Street he made use that same night of pencil and paper."

46

A de Quincey Parallel

As a sight of the pictures of Tintoretto would serve to make known, to one entirely ignorant of the style, the possibilities and achievements of the Venetian School; would serve to make known, not Titian, but the possibility of a Titian, so the style of de Quincey, the habit of his mind, the manner of his confessing, his concealments and sincerities, his association of passion and idleness, his fretfulness and his habit of presaging dole, his manner of complaining of being cold a-bed, his bulletins, his conscious style and repetitions, serve to bring the personality of Thompson to the memory of those who knew him and into the ken of those who did not. For the family likeness, for the school manner, there are passages, too, in the history of Coleridge that will be found suggestive and explanatory. In knowing these cousins of the habit, you come, as you cannot come by any single and uncorroborated experience, into very convincing touch with him whom you are seeking. If, apart from the special significance of Francis's communion with de Quincey, these two are linked, and in them the family likeness is apparent, what of the likeness and the linking when we find how strong was the allegiance sworn by Francis to the spirit of de Quincey; when we track allusions and words and mannerisms in the "Anthem of Earth" back to the *Confessions;* when coincidence of actualities as well as the coincidence of intellect, such as the two flights from Manchester and the two lives in the streets of London, clashed upon the attention of the young man who was withdrawn from the companionship of contemporaries?

De Quincey, like Francis, had spent much time in the Manchester library. There both made their vocabularies robust and rare from the same Elizabethans, both fattened to the marrow the bones of their English from Sir Thomas Browne. And both stumbled headlong down a precipice of despondency. De Quincey has said many things on his own behalf, in that despondency and in the recourse to opium, that may well be said on Thompson's.

It happened as if in giving Francis the *Confessions* Mrs. Thompson had found for him a guardian, a spokesman, as if she had borne to him an elder brother. For Francis's feeling for de Quincey soon came to be that of a younger for an elder brother who has braved a hazardous road, shown the way, conquered, and left it strewn with consolations and palliations. From de Quincey he received the passport, the royal introduction set forth in Sir Walter Raleigh-like language ringing with at least the assurance of its own stateliness and power :—

" O just, subtle, and all-conquering opium ! that to the hearts of rich and poor alike, for the wounds that will never heal and for the pangs of grief that ' tempt the spirit to rebel,' bringest an assuaging balm :—eloquent opium ! that with thy potent rhetoric stealest away the purposes of wrath, pleadest effectually for relenting pity, and through one night's heavenly sleep callest back to the guilty man the visions of his infancy, and hands washed pure from blood ;—O just and righteous opium ! that to the chancery of dreams summonest for the triumphs of despairing innocence false witnesses, confoundest perjury, and dost reverse the sentences of unrighteous judges ; then buildest upon the bosom of darkness, out of the fastastic imagery of the brain, cities and temples, beyond the art of Phidias and Praxiteles—beyond the splendours of Babylon and Hekatòmpylos ; and, ' from the anarchy of dreaming sleep ' cullest into sunny light the faces of long-buried beauties, and the blessed household countenances, cleansed from the ' dishonours of the grave.' Thou only givest those gifts to man ; and thou hast the keys to Paradise, O just, subtle, and mighty opium ! "

Opium indeed was in the air of Manchester, the cotton - spinners being much addicted to its use. And it called aloud to Francis in these words of de Quincey. Damnable things become reasonable or tolerable in a city. It harbours such a multitude of distresses,

The Confessions

such a conflict of right and wrong — the purposes
of nature stand confused, instincts go haltingly along the
streets, conscience and reasonings are stunned between
stone walls. In one thing, then, did Francis mishear
the edict of lawfulness. He took opium — a very
pitiful and, surely, very excusable misunderstanding.
Constitutionally he was a target for the temptation of
the drug ; doubly a target when set up in the mis-fitting
guise of a medical student, and sent about his work in
the middle of the city of Manchester, long, according to
de Quincey, a dingy den of opium, with every facility of
access, and all the pains that were de Quincey's excuse.
He took opium at the hands of de Quincey and his
mother. That she, "giver of life, death, peace, distress,"
should thus have confirmed and renewed her gifts was a
strange thing to befall. From her copy of the *Confessions
of an English Opium Eater* he learnt a new existence at
her hands. That the life that opium conserved in
him triumphed over the death that opium dealt out to
him shall be part argument of this book. 'On the one
hand, it staved off the assaults of tuberculosis ; it gave
him the wavering strength that made life just possible
for him, whether on the streets or through all those
other distresses and discomforts that it was his character
deeply to resent but not to remove by any normal
courses ; if it could threaten physical degradation he
was able by conquest to tower in moral and mental
glory. It made doctoring or any sober course of life
even more impractical than it was already rendered by
native incapacities, and to his failure in such careers we
owe his poetry. On the other hand, it dealt with him
remorselessly as it dealt with Coleridge and all its con-
sumers. It put him in such constant strife with his
own conscience that he had ever to hide himself from
himself, and for concealment he fled to that which made
him ashamed, until it was as if the fig-leaf were of necessity plucked from the Tree of the Fall. It killed in him

the capacity for acknowledging those duties to his family and friends which, had his heart not been in shackles, he would have owned with no ordinary ardour.

It is on account of a hundred passages of the *Confessions* that the friendship was established. What solace of companionship must Francis have discovered when de Quincey told him, "But alas! my eye is quick to value the logic of evil chances. Prophet of evil I ever am to myself; forced for ever into sorrowful auguries that I have no power to hide from my own heart, no, not through one night's solitary dreams." Here was a boon though sorrowful companion. For here was one who could translate his distresses into a brave art; one who could extract good writing out of his disabilities. Doubtless it was he who first showed to Francis the profitableness of bitter experiences, and that, if gallant prose might come of weakness, poetry might be sown in the fields of failure, and the crown of thorns be turned to the chaplet of laurel. As it serves us in following the friendship that Francis had imagined for himself, a passage in which no immediate relation to him can be traced may perhaps be pardoned on this page. It is necessary inasmuch as it shows the equal ground trodden by the two men; they were going the same road, the stride of their thoughts was equal. It occurs in the part of the *Confessions* telling of the eve of de Quincey's flight from school. Evening prayers are being said, and with nerves highly strung by the responsibilities of the morrow there comes to de Quincey the higher meanings and motives of the school devotions. He feels how "the marvellous magnetism of Christianity" has gathered into her service the wonders of nature, and builded her temple with the bricks of Creation :—

"Flowers, for example, that are so pathetic in their beauty, frail as the clouds, and in their colouring as gorgeous as the heavens, had through thousands of years been the heritage of children—

The School of Opium

honoured as the jewellery of God only by *them*—when suddenly the voice of Christianity, countersigning the voice of infancy, raised them to a grandeur transcending the Hebrew throne, although founded by God Himself, and pronounced Solomon in all his glory not to be arrayed like one of these. Winds again, hurricanes, the eternal breathings, soft or loud, of Æolian power, wherefore had they, raving or sleeping, escaped all moral arrest and detention? Simply because vain it were to offer a nest for the reception of some new moral birth whilst no religion is yet moving amongst men that can furnish such a birth. Vain is the image that should illustrate a heavenly sentiment, if the sentiment is yet unborn. Then, first, when it had become necessary to the purposes of a spiritual religion that the spirit of man, as the fountain of all religion, should in some commensurate reflex image have its grandeur and its mysteriousness emblazoned, suddenly the pomp and mysterious paths of winds and tempests, blowing whither they list, and from what fountains no man knows, are cited from darkness and neglect, to give and to receive reciprocally an impassioned glorification, where the lower mystery enshrines and illustrates the higher. Call for the grandest of all earthly spectacles, what is *that?* It is the sun going to his rest. Call for the grandest of all human sentiments, what is *that?* It is that man should forget his anger before he lies down to sleep. And these two grandeurs, the mighty sentiment and the mighty spectacle, are by Christianity married together."

Is that, then, a Manchester school of thought, or no more than an accident? These two men, singularly conscious of nature's liturgy, one of whom wrote this passage, and the other of "pontifical death," had both been forced to dodge the cotton warehouses that they might see their sunsets; both had to fly from the normal liturgy of life and be estranged from themselves and their fellow-creatures by those qualities and sensitivenesses of the intellect which best enabled them to see in themselves and in their fellow-men the symbols and instruments of the Almighty.

Very like de Quincey's repudiation of guilt would have been Francis's :—

" Infirmity and misery do not, of necessity, imply guilt. They approach, or recede from, the shades of that dark alliance in

Manchester and Medicine

proportion of the probable motives and prospects of the offender, and to the palliations, known or secret, of the offence ; in proportion as the temptations to it were potent from the first, and as the resistance to it, in act or in effort, were earnest to the last."

Through what complication of persuasion by weakness and pain, impulse and even reason, the other Manchester boy passed may be guessed at through the more palpable screen of de Quincey's prose. De Quincey published his offences and defences, prosecuted, summed up, and reported in his own case; and it was upon his ruling that Francis built up his own subtler arguments, advanced and judged *in camera*.

Unlike de Quincey, he had no burning desire to justify himself ; his own private excuse he had no desire to strengthen with the written and published word, or by seeking the corroborating content of others. He was consistently silent and secret on the point, and, if his silence did not avail to hide his secret, he was still silent in the manner of the lover who stole a kiss in the "Angel in the House": we knew that he knew we knew about his drug. His pleading was not before man's tribunal, but before the higher courts of conscience and of poetry. During his first experiences of the opium he had not the consolatory knowledge of his genius, for it was only in later years when he was delivered of his poetry and beheld it emerge unmarred by his former surrender to the drug, that he found peace of mind.

De Quincey, while he averred that the object of his confessions "was to emblazon the power of opium—not over bodily disease and pain, but over the grander and more shadowy world of dreams," did nevertheless owe his initial experience of the drug to the prompting and searching of frantic toothache. Nor was his object merely an emblazoning. On one page it is denunciation of an intolerable burden—the "accursed chain"; on another his motive seemed to him to be to give to opium-eaters

52

"The Saving of my Life"

the consolation and encouragement of the knowledge that the habit may be put off, "without greater suffering than an ordinary resolution may support, and by a pretty rapid course of descent." He sets up his admirable argument in the midst of contradictions : he is positive of his own attitude even while he does not know which way to face, whether towards dreams, or towards the harsher fields of actuality. Under the generalship of his prose his reader may be marshalled into toleration and acceptance, or sent hurrying away from the contemplation of a dreadful enemy. De Quincey's two minds are apparent, too, in the history of his case. At times he turned upon himself and mastered the habit to which at others he was obedient, and even reverent.

How weak the prop, as weak as broken poppies ; its very praises fade on the page, like water thrown on sand, in the setting forth. De Quincey writes that the opium-eater never finishes his work, that Coleridge's contributions to literature were made in spite of opium, that it killed him as a poet, that the leaving off of this—his mighty opium—creates a new heaven and a new earth.

"Opium, the saving of my life," is one of Thompson's own most rare allusions to it. For de Quincey he never abated his old ardour of respect. The heat of his partisanship may be sufficiently measured in a letter, dated 1900, in which he falls upon some critic of his Manchester master :—

"Read the essay on D. Q.—read—read, and if you ever meet the writer, kick him till he roar at the squeak of a boot and snuffle at the whiff of a leather shop for the rest of his life ! Yet canst thou not kick to the measure of his deserts, wert thou Polypheme with earthquake on thy feet. Shall such monstrous fellows live and publish their villainous mismeasurement of great literature, and be hailed 'sane critics' by the muddy clappers-on of mediocrity ? I am whipped out of my patience that

Manchester and Medicine

I cannot call these scullions in good print 'ass un-
paralleled,' but must mince and fine my phrases to a
smooth and customed censure."

Only those who know how well his mental matched
his physical inability in assault and battery can be
certain of the utter artifice of this exercise in petulance.
He could be angry only when his anger was safely
out of range of giving pain. He would kick in the
closet of his note-books, but would ever be nearer kissing
when his action came to be communicated. And even
in his note-books he would seldom indulge personal
spite ; his unkind entries are sheathed in blanks, so that
no accident of perusal could hurt the feelings of the
censured.

It has been doubted whether he actually " sat " for his
medical examination, but considering how little bold he
was among strangers and in a strange town, it is unlikely that on this first occasion he summoned enough
courage to play truant. In all probability he was con-
ducted to the place of examination, but one can only
conjecture his behaviour as he was more than usually
silent on his return. " I have not passed " is all the information he vouchsafed when, some little time after,
he is supposed to have received notice of his failure.
Two years more of pretended study followed, with some
real reading at home in the evenings. It was Francis's
quickness of intelligence during these extra hours of
more congenial research that enabled him to appear
in conversation with his father as one moderately well
equipped in the knowledge of medicine. But after
Francis again visited London in 1882, after four years
in all of study, and again returned with the formula of " I
have not passed," his father called upon the authorities at
Owens College, and learnt that Francis's non-attendances
were far in advance of his attendances. During two
more years of preparation he read less and less at home.

Francis Thompson
in 1877

The Examinations

He would come in late in the evening, declaring that a professor or a lecturer had taken him to give him extra instruction, and not till some time afterwards was it discovered that the house he visited was the home of a musician, and the instruction that of listening to music performed upon the piano. Of music he was extremely fond : his interest in it would be passionate or else totally obscured when, in later years, there was music going forward in his presence.

Calling it his chief recreation, he continued for years without it. For Berlioz he kept the excited enthusiasm of a child, childish memory doing the trick. He would often tell of music (Berlioz, Beethoven, Chopin) heard in Manchester, where he attended concerts with his mother. He himself could no more than strike a sequence of chords upon the piano, which he would do with so much earnestness that I, as a child, was impressed by his performance. In listening to music his emotion was equally manifest. Standing at the piano, he would gaze at the performer, his body wavering to and fro in tremulous pleasure ; or, as often, he would not heed at all.

It was decided that his third attempt upon the profession of medicine should be made at Glasgow, where degrees were more easily, if less honourably, to be obtained. But the examination, if indeed it was actually accepted, was approached with no endeavour or even anxiety, except on the father's part, for success. Indeed, failure must have been very frankly courted by Francis, whose main fault was that he had not the courage openly to dispute his father's decision in regard to a career. Never once did he intimate that his heart was set on poetry, although from sixteen, as he afterwards said, he studied and practised metre ; it is not unlikely that to have been told to go and make a business of literature would have been more irksome to him than passing the years in the evasion of medicine. His secret absorption in his own interests was, after all, not uncomfortably

55

circumstanced during all these years, for it is certain that literature was a second life to Francis which could be lived alone most happily. After failure in Glasgow, Francis met with a severe show of impatience and disappointment from his father. Many trials had been tolerated at the son's hands, hundreds of pounds had been expended, and the son's future was less secure than ever. Dr. Thompson determined on such courses as he thought would compel Francis to some undertaking of the responsibilities of life.

No little money had been spent on examination fees to examiners who probably had no papers to examine; on dissecting fees which did not once compel Francis's presence at the dissecting-table. He was already spending money on opium.

After many leniencies, such as accepting Francis's own account of his studies at Owens College and all his excuses for absences from home in the evening, Dr. Thompson put Francis to such obviously uncongenial tasks as were to be found in the establishment of a surgical instrument maker, whom he served for two weeks only, and as the purveyor of an encyclopædia.

At neither of these businesses did Francis succeed; it took him two months to read the encyclopædia, and then he discarded it, unsold. Nor was there any possibility of success. In reviewing his prospects at this time his father warned him, among other things, that he would have to enlist if he found no other means of support. Without a word, Francis went, like Coleridge, for a soldier. With what hopes or intentions it is difficult to conceive, but obviously still with that desire of obeying, so far as he was able, his father's instructions. It seems he did not suffer himself merely to be measured by the recruiting examiners, but also to be marched and drilled in the attempt to expand his chest to the necessary inches. He spoke in later years of the weariness it was to march, and of the barrack yard, and even maintained that his

He Enlists

upright bearing had been learnt at that time. But as his upright bearing is exactly the upright bearing of a brave figure (his sister's), stiffer than the starched gear about her face and throat in the habit and convent of her order in Manchester, it does not follow that Francis's recruiting counts for very much. He returned from it late one night, silent as when he returned from the examinations in London and Glasgow. I do not think he even told the family as much as he told my father in later years— that he was not " Private Thompson " only because he failed to pass the army physical examination.

On the second Sunday (day of rest and the turmoil bred of rest) in November, 1885, Francis was forced to find time for the discussion of his prospects with his father, and with it he found a certain energy of failure and despair. His demeanour gave rise to the notion in his family that he was in the habit of drinking. His father taxed him with it, but was mystified by Francis's strenuous denials ; opium, not alcohol, was the cause of his flushes. Here was yet another point of difficulty and trial.

The next day (Monday, November 9, 1885), his sister found on her dressing-table a note from Francis saying that he had gone to London. It was a hopeless note ; his mood was hopeless. He later described his flight thus : " The peculiarity in my case is that I made the journey to the Capital without hope, and with the gloomiest forebodings, in the desperate spirit of an *enfant perdu.*" But in hopelessness, as in all his moods, he hesitated. He did not want to leave home. " To stay under happy parental supervision, to work because I must, but to make my delight of the exercise of the imagination " was his ambition. Parental supervision had not prevented the shutting of his door. So closely did he fasten it that he had never told his father of his exercises, or his sisters, who, according to an uncle, eschewed poetry as if it were a snare ; " both have

57

character, but both are very reserved, indeed impenetrable." Small wonder there had been silence in the house, save about cricket and wars. "What does one want with a tongue when one has silence?"

For a week he lingered in Manchester, living on the proceeds of the sale of his books and other possessions. It had been his habit to obey the command of the drug by the disposal of his books and medical instruments. His microscope had gone, and been replaced— no light task for his father—and now, at the crisis, he had to go bare even of poetry books. Ninety-five would he sell, but to the remnant of a library he would cling with a persistence that defied even the terrific imp of the laudanum bottle.

For a week Francis hesitated and then wrote home, dating his letter from the Post Office, for his fare to London. It was sent, and he made the journey. Whatever its discouragement, it must yet have been something added to the little sum of hopefulness to leave Manchester. London, of conjectural disaster, drew him from the Manchester of tried and proved failure. His luggage, scanty enough in itself, was weighted with no regrets. He was going to new possibilities. But he carried Blake and Aeschylus in his pocket. Thus had de Quincey gone, content with the same bodily starvation and mental food—"carrying a small parcel with some articles of dress under my arm; a favourite English poet in one pocket, and an odd volume, containing one-half of Canter's *Euripides* in the other."

Of the father and the fugitive the poet's uncle afterwards wrote to my father :—

" He has been a great trouble and sorrow to his father from his want of ballast. He started with every advantage, but has come to nothing. At last he went to London, where he seems to have led a sort of Bohemian life. There does not appear to have been anything of what is usually termed immorality ; but he was never to be depended on, and I fear he indulged in drink. As his

His Father

father expresses it in a letter to me this morning, he likes to lead a dawdling, sauntering sort of life. . . . There was nothing in his home life to lead him to divulge himself, no encouragement and no sympathy with his ambitions. His sisters, who might have been of use in expounding him—if I may use such a phrase— have so little of the poetical element in them that they seem on principle to have eschewed all poetry as if it were a temptation and a snare. . . . This I believe to be the key to, and so far an excuse for, his deceitful proceedings and his apparent callousness and ingratitude. I wish I were in a position to help him pecuniarily, but at present I am not. However, I can show him sympathy and approbation. It is years since any communication took place between us, and in my last letter I ventured to give him some advice as to his hypercritical tendencies, and he never wrote to me again. So I suspect he did not relish my animadversions."

Another Manchester letter from a close friend of his family runs :—

" To begin with, young Thompson was not brought up amongst ' gallipots ' ; no son could have been more kindly or more generously treated, and it was not until this genius was gone utterly to the bad that his father lost sight of him. He was most carefully educated, and no young man has ever had a better or a kinder mother or father. I don't think Dr. Thompson is destitute of the poetic imagination, and I think he might have been excused if he did not perceive at once that poetry which differs from all which has delighted the world for three thousand years was, of all poetry, the most to be admired. . . . The way in which you have compared the coming of Frank Thompson to the Messiah is approaching the profane."

But Francis had another opinion of the poetic influence of his home ; and to see his sister and read in her eyes the new and more explicit version of the household spirituality, is to credit his own view. His statement that "the spirit of such poems as ' The Making of Viola' and ' The Judgement in Heaven ' is no mere mediæval imitation, but the natural temper of my Catholic training in a simple provincial home" is easily believed. It is

59

not generally understood, he says, that the " irreverence " (so called) of mediæval poetry and drama is not merely primitive but Catholic. He quotes, as quite within his comprehension, the remark of Miss L. that, if she saw Our Lord, the first thing she would be impelled to do would be to put her arms about Him—a remark prompted by a hostile comment on a Christ and St. Francis (in statuary) with their arms about each other.

The father's own comment, when he found his son welcomed as a poet, was : " If the lad had but told me ! " Mr. J. Saxon Mills says :—

" The doctor was even more amused than gratified at seeing his son's name suddenly coupled with those of Shelley or Keats or Tennyson. He admitted, moreover, that Frank's productions were quite beyond his own comprehension, and I am not sure that the worthy doctor regarded the greenest of poetic laurels as a fair exchange for a thriving medical practice."

CHAPTER IV: LONDON STREETS

To him who had during that last week fathomed the abysses of Manchester, the "unfathomable abyss" of London was hardly more black. It might be supposed that the city of Manchester was as good as another in which to be destitute; poverty in modern streets is a mean and dirty business at its best as at its worst. But in London a staggering part is played on a great stage haunted with great presences. There is a literary grandiloquence about the capital's rags that Manchester's do not own: for the time it takes for the fraying of a pair of cuffs, we may suppose, this glamour has effect. It was something to tread the pavements of Oxford Street, something to despair, if despair one must, where Chatterton despaired ; fitting, in a poetic sense, as Francis had discovered when he wrote " In no Strange Land," to have your Christ walking on the dark waters of the Thames, and to rear your Jacob's ladder from Charing Cross.

But if there is a ghostly companionship in the capital, it was mightily empty of the real solace of friendly presences. "The only fostering soil for genius" Lamb called the Metropolis. But Francis did not so regard it. The writing of the first poems and prose, the whole acceptance of a vocation, were undertaken in complete isolation. It was a hard soil, bare as the pavement. There were no allurements of companionship, no excitements or encouragements of example and emulation. He knew no laughing bookseller in St. Martin's Court. A poet, he knew no poet, save a formidable uncle, in the flesh ; no writer, save the reputed " noted authors " whom he came to serve with slippers at a shop in Panton Street. Without friends or courage, Francis found no better job than that of a " collector " of books. Thus his first efforts for a livelihood in London were made with a sackful of literature upon his shoulders, the day's " orders " of a general bookseller. His journeys would be laborious and slowly accomplished, and his turn in all probability the last served at the wholesale counters where he called out the list. Unlike his fellow-collectors, he would have an additional stock in his private pocket—his own library—and his interest would be in this rather than in the bundle on his back; he might bend under works on cookery, sport, Methodism, and social reform, but Blake and Aeschylus would buoy him up.

That he found no work commensurate with his attainments is but another item in the whole sequence of circumstances that liken his case to de Quincey's. De Quincey tells of difficulties imagined and real that kept him from applying to the friends of his father for assistance. Another mode of livelihood, " that of turning any talents or knowledge that I might possess to a lucrative use—I now feel half inclined to join my reader in wondering why I overlooked it. As a corrector of Greek proofs (if in no other way), I might surely have gained enough for my slender wants. . . . But why talk of my qualifications ? Qualified or not, where could I obtain such an office ? For it must not be forgotten that even a diabolic appointment requires interest. Towards *that* I must first of all have an introduction to some respectable publisher ; and this I had no means of obtaining. To say the truth, however, it had never once occurred to me to think of literary labours as a source of profit." With arguments as lengthy as those, Francis would often expound excellent reasons for not doing that which it had never occurred to him to undertake. The truth was that he came to London that he might exist and no more.

A desire of observing the town was de Quincey's excuse for his wanderings over London. Francis made no such plea, but wandered the same gait. Market-place and an occasional theatre ; door-step consolation and porch shelter ; the absorption in the things of the spirit and the stifling of the interruptions of material things with opium ; the momentary fears of bodily privation, succumbing to fortunate forgetfulness and numbness, the intellectual realisation of the awfulness of their surroundings tempered by physical indifference ; and the admixture with this same physical indifference of an extreme bodily frailty and susceptibility to suffering—all the contradictions found in the one man are confirmed in the other. That each was befriended by an unfortunate girl of the streets was a continuation of the duality of contradictions. Two outcast women were to these two outcast men the sole ambassadors of the world's gentleness and generosity. More of Francis's " brave, sad, lovingest, tender thing " will be set down on a later page.

He was quick to lose his " book-collecting," slow to find other work. He liked the Guildhall Library better than " situations," and while he had seven shillings a week from home, he managed to be there a good deal. He spoke of having clung to outward respectability, and told that on the streets rags are no necessary accompaniment to destitution. But his rags came quickly enough ; within a few weeks he was below the standards set by the employers of casual labour. He now began to learn something of his companions, of their slang, of their ways and means. It was not always amongst the lowest grades of the poor that he met the people he could most dislike. He notes that the street-outcast is generally opposed to Atheism ; that he is often nameless, often kind, always honest with his fellows (" only once did any one try to cheat me""). Generosity he noticed

particularly in the readiness of beggars to pay each
other's lodgings. Once a policeman aided him, but that
aid was unexpected and unrepeated. Of the men he
met at common lodging-houses, or in whose company
he slept in archways, or with whom he entered into
partnership in the business of fetching cabs or selling
matches, he names but very few : "The actor, poor
Kelsall, 'Newcastle,'" is one entry in a note-book. The
murderer to whom he makes several allusions, he disguises
under the initials D. I. From one friend he had practical
lessons in the arts of confinement, so that he could say
to his editor in later years, when a review-book was lost :
" You can either let me replace it, or put me in gaol.
I know how to pick oakum." But there were some
companions to disgust him : "Their conversation is impossible of report. If you want to know it (and you
are every way a gainer by not knowing it, while you
lose what can never be regained by knowing it) go to
Rabelais and his like, where you will find a very faint
image of it. Nearer you may get by reading 'Westminster Drolleries' and other eighteenth century collec-
tions of swine-trough hoggery. For naked bestiality you
must go to the modern *bête humaine*." He learnt enough
of their slang to be amused at the unreality of language
put into the mouths of the thieves of fiction ; and in
any case the foulness of the real thing is irreproducible.
He learned, too, of the workhouse, of homes of refuge ;
that prison is held to be no disgrace ; and above all, as
month succeeded month, that death is surprisingly slow
on a shilling a day.

His bed was made according to his fortune. If he had
no money, it was the Embankment; if he had a shilling,
he could choose his lodging ; if he had fourpence, he
was obliged to tramp to Blackfriars. Something of his
manner of spending his money he told me : "No, Evie,
you do not spend your penny on a mug of tea. That
will be gone very quickly. You spend it, Evie, not on

Boot-black

a mug of tea; not, I say, on a *mug* of tea, but on the
tea itself. You buy a pennyworth and make it with
the boiling water from the common kettle in the doss-
house. You get several cups that way instead of one."
It was at lodging-houses that he would lie watching the
beetles crawling on the ceiling—that was the exchange
he made for "the abashless inquisition of each star" of
the nights when he had no pennies and so no bed; and
it is the image he used afterwards in a Tom-o'-Bedlam's
song :—

> As a burst and blood-blown insect
> Cleaves to the wall it dies on,
> The smearéd sun
> Doth clot upon
> A heaven without horizon.[1]

In a common lodging-house he met and had talk with
the man who was supposed by the group about the fire
to be a murderer uncaught. And when it was not in
a common lodging-house, it was at a Shelter or Refuge
that he would lie in one of the oblong boxes without
lids, containing a mattress and a leathern apron or
coverlet, that are the fashion, he says, in all Refuges.
The time came when for a week his only earning was
sixpence got for holding a horse's head. That was after
he had made an attempt to establish himself with a
boot-black stand, and failed because of the interference
of the police, who moved him on at the request of the
shopkeeper at his chosen street-corner.

His way home in later years was always northwards,
along the Edgware Road. It is a thoroughfare that keeps
late hours, crossing the highway between Paddington

---

[1] There is some parallel for this image (Tom-o'-Bedlam's, be it remembered)
in Rossetti's—

> But the sea stands spread
> As one wall with the flat skies,
> Where the lean black craft, like flies,
> Seem well-nigh stagnated,
> Soon to drop off dead.

and King's Cross ; it makes southwards towards Victoria and the town ; it has its music-halls, and, after they are closed, its coffee-stalls, tiny centres of distressed humanity waiting for the dawn. They are the pickets set up against the enemy Night, in a campaign which, on the whole, is less sullenly undertaken than the campaign of the day. There is much companionship along the pavements in the night watches : the regiment of the poor falls into some sort of rank, and whether a man's business is merely to keep moving till the park-gates are opened in the morning, or to reach some distant lodging, some favourite shelter, or a point of vantage for the coming day, he need never be com-panionless on this road. And seldom, unless he be very new to the manner of life or very old, does the poor man not fall in with the conviviality that is within his reach. Be he so stupid that he has failed in the meanest ambitions, yet he will be able to establish himself in this society, and be a man of affairs among beggars.

Every man, and every woman however grossly she has fallen, acquires a certain aptitude in the University of the Last Resort. Some sort of shrewdness, entirely above the scullery pitch, has become a necessity by the time the pavement is the Home. And even the poet came, like the outcast ostler, or matchmaker, or scullery-maid, to possess a small share of this lower-worldliness. When it was a matter, during the day, of collecting coppers sufficient for the day and spending them in the pinched markets of poverty, he had perforce to be alive to the world about him. Later on, when there was no necessity, I could observe in him a certain flickering pride of experience : occasionally he would exert him-self to show that he knew how to pass the time of day with a man upon the street, how to invest in a pipe, a kettle, or in oddments of cheap food. Ordering his meal at a coffee-house, he would pretend to a certain acumen in the matter of dishes or of waitresses, adjusting his tie and his expression. But who can ever have been deceived that here was any one save a timorous defaulter in the matter of *savoir-faire*? Not, certainly, an A.B.C. girl or an observant tramp.

Among the miracles is that of The Golden Halfpennies. They came to him on a day when he had not even the penny to invest in matches that might bring him interest on his money. He was, he told me, walking, vacant with desperation, along a crowded pavement, when he heard the clink of a coin and saw something bright rolling towards the gutter. He stooped, picked it up, looked around, found no claimant, and put into his waistcoat pocket, as he affirmed with the many repetitions that characterised his anecdotes, a bright new halfpenny. He proceeded some distance on his way, pondering the things he could or could not procure with his money, when it struck him that the other direction would lead him to a shop with such wares as he had decided on. As he neared the place where he had found the first coin he saw another glittering in the road. This, too, he picked up, and again thought he held a halfpenny. But looking closer he discovered it to be golden and a sovereign, and only after much persuasion of his senses would he believe the first-found one to be likewise gold. " That was a sovereign too, Evie ; I looked and I saw it was a sovereign too!" he ended, with rising voice and tremulous laughter. One who heard him tell his tale held strictly that he should have delivered the money to the nearest police-station to await the inquiry of its owner ; but that, surely, were an ill economy, to look after the farthings of scrupulousness at the cost of the pounds of Providence. Thompson, half suspicious of a miracle, made a shrewd guess that no angel would apply at Marlborough Street.

At another time he did have scruples. One of the Rothschilds, buying a paper from him at the Piccadilly end of Park Lane, put a florin into his hand. " I was worried," said Francis, " lest he thought it was a penny, and tried to catch him up in the street crowd. But he was gone, and it worried me." Years later the news of that Rothschild's death was read out at a meal at our house in Palace Court. Francis heard, and dropped his spoon, aghast. "Then I can never repay him!" he cried.

For a time a few shillings might have been his each week for the fetching; but he did not fetch them. An allowance, sufficient to lodge and feed him, and insufficient to do either fully, was sent to him by his father at a reading-room called, it is thought, the "Clarendon," in the Strand. The more he needed it the greater worry would it seem to collect it. Fear lest it were not there; fear lest he should be refused it because of his rags, and, finally, an illusory certainty— the certainty of dejection—that it had been discontinued, prevented him, until at last, through his default, it did really cease.

He had the words of the Proverb by heart—" Give me neither poverty nor riches; feed me with the food convenient for me "—but he would rather say his prayer in the street than ask for his allowance in the " Clarendon." He was willing to starve both ways: he wrote out for his comfort : " Even in the night-time of the soul wisdom remains."

In addition to the allowance there were relatives and friends to whom Francis might have gone, if assistance in his need had been part of his scheme. Besides those with whom he stayed during his examinations in London, there was a Catholic relative who had an establishment for stationery off the Strand (he was not asked for so much as a pencil), and who died in Church Passage, Chancery Lane, about 1891 ; his paternal grandmother, then an old lady, lived in City Road, and Edward Healy Thompson had resided in Hinde Street, Manchester Square, and made many town friends.

Delirium

The time came when he had no lodging ; when the nights were an agony of prevented sleep, and the days long blanks of half-warmth and half-ease. After seven nights and days of this kind he is deep immersed in insensibility. Pain, its own narcotic, throbs to painlessness. Touch and sight and hearing are brokenly and dimly experienced, save when some unknown touch switches on the lights of full consciousness. Sensation is still painful, but disjointedly, impotently. When a cart jolts by the noise of its wheels comes to him long after—or before—he troubles to move out of reach of the shafts—the yell of the driver seems to have no part in the incident. He knows not if it came from that or from another quarter. He sees things pass as silently as the figures on a cinematograph screen ; one set of nerves, out of time and on another plane, respond to things heard. The boys now running at one end of the alley, in front of him, are behind him the next, and their cries seem to come from any quarter and at random. Is it that they move too quickly for him or that he unknowingly is wheeling about in his walk, or that London herself spins round him ? For hours he has stood in one place, or paced one patch of pavement, as if his feet were trapped in the lines between the stones. He remembers that, as a child, he had made rules, treading only on the spaces, or only on the line of the pattern ; now they make much stricter bounds. He is tied to the few slabs of stone that fill the space beneath his archway. It seems dreadfully perilous to move beyond them, and he sways within their territory as if they edged a precipice. And then, he knows not how or why, his weakness has passed, and he is drifting along the streets, not wearily, but with dreadful ease, with no hope of having sufficient resolution to halt. Time matters as little to him as the names of the streets, and the very faces of the clocks present, to his thinking, not pictures of time and motion, but stationary, dead countenances. Noting that the hands of one have moved, he wonders at it only because its view of the passage of time is so laughably at variance with his own. Had it marked a minute since he had last looked, or a whole day, he would not have been surprised, but the foolish half-hour it told of is absurd. His time leaped or paused, while the clock went with lying regularity. The street-names, too, deceived him; they were unfamiliar in most familiar places; or they showed well-known names on impossible corners. He seemed to be spinning, like a falling leaf, and tossed by unseen winds of direction. Oxford Street was short and narrow; Wardour Street big enough to hold the tribes of Israel, and the houses of it as high, he guessed, though he dared not lift his head to see, as the divided waves of the Red Sea. Out of confusion came a voice, "Is your soul saved?" It broke in upon his half-consciousness as the school gong wakes the boy. The mantle of protecting delirium fell away; the voice broke in upon his privacy, threatening his reserves, seeking the confidences of the confessional. "What right have you to ask me that question?" he replied.

To one who had spent a fortnight of nights on the streets, Mr. McMaster and family, standing forth against the comfortable background of shop, work-rooms, and parlour, should have loomed large. But what the rescued man thought worth telling of the incident of rescue was that in Wardour Street some one approached and asked him, in the resented voice of the intruder, if his soul were saved, and that he, clothed in the regimentals of the ragged, and with as much military sternness of voice and gesture as might be, made answer. Nothing seemed so important to him as the rebuff he imagined he had administered to a stranger threatening his privacy. He also recounted that the other then said: "If you won't let me save your soul, let me save your body," and a compact was made on terms agreeable to his dignity. But it is probable that it was entered upon with greater zest by Mr. McMaster the enthusiast, churchwarden, and boot-maker, than by the indifferent poet, to whom it seemed to matter little whether he were rescued or not rescued. Francis was as little eager for this help as he was, two years later, for my father's.

Francis recounted little more than the reproof and the fact that his new master was kind to him. But did he forget, do you think, the least detail of the shop in Panton Street,[1] or his companions there? Did he forget Mr. McMaster the elder, or Mr. McMaster the brother, or the nieces, or the assistants, or Lucy? It is because he could not forget that one must accept his account of the first encounter. The rescuer remembers it as happening in the Strand, but Thompson, who says Wardour Street, seems the surer witness.

Before taking him into his employ at his bootmaker's shop, No. 14 Panton Street, Mr. McMaster wrote in August, 1886, to the Superintendent of Police at Ashton-under-Lyne asking if Francis Joseph was, as he stated, the son of a Dr. Charles Thompson of that place. Finding this to be the case, he secured a lodging for Francis in Southampton Row, clothed him, and with some hope, at first, set him to work. It was rather later that he communicated with Francis's father, who had been absent from Ashton on a holiday.

I learn that Mr. McMaster was much interested in

---

[1] Here is a minor clue to the region of London best mapped out in his mind. From the *Academy*, 1900, he tore Mr. Whitten's review of an atlas of London, in which a comment is made on the restrictions of the scale—three inches to the mile ; so that " York Street, Covent Garden, is merged in Tavistock Street ; and Panton Street, Haymarket, and its short continuation, Spur Street,are marked but not named." When Francis does not dog de Quincey he is at the heel of Coleridge. Each had gone for a soldier; both were accosted with friendship in London. The Strand is remembered as the place where Coleridge was, as a youth, once walking in abstraction with waving arms, to find himself with his hand in a pedestrian's pocket and accused of attempted thieving. " I thought, sir, I was swimming in the Hellespont," he explained, and made a friend only less valuable than Mr. McMaster.

assisting the unfortunate. If he says "Thompson was my only failure," it means that he was careful and useful in the rescuing of young men, particular in awarding his charity, and strict in enforcing reform. The men he cared for learned the trade of boot-making, possibly, and had been known to sing in the choir of St. Martin's Church, or to do other reputable deeds. They were civil-spoken men, or learnt to be, and tidy, whereas Francis would raise his voice, Mr. McMaster remembers—would shout, as his only breach of good manners—in medical and other arguments ; was a Catholic, and therefore not a church-goer in the ordinary sense, and was, of course, incapable of work. How did Mr. McMaster succeed so well with his only failure ? It is to his exceeding credit that he accepted Francis on the terms that were inevitable in accepting a waif subject to accidents and unpunctual. Francis would discuss literature and medicine, or be silent, or write, always in sight of the hammering and sewing group in the workroom behind the shop. In the delivery of goods and the general running of messages he did ill the duties of a boy of twelve. And yet he was liked, and respected as well as pitied. His dignity and gentleness gave him the name of a gentleman among friends where the title is a talisman.

It did not take long to discover that Francis could neither make boots nor sell them. He ran messages, and still in the make-believe of earning his food and lodging and the five shillings a week that were his wages, put up the shutters, as H. M. Stanley, whose back still ached with the memory when he came to write his autobiography, had done as a boy. It is incredible, to one who knew the hours Francis favoured, that he was present at their taking down.

His master has interesting memories. He remembers the meeting in the street ; he remembers that he was informed immediately that Francis was a Catholic,

The Outcast's Devotions

and he remembers the crucifix upon the wall of the bedroom in Southampton Row, and the medal round the collarless neck. "I knew he was of another belief—not a bit of difference! I am a Church of England man myself—Churchwarden, and on the Council—an average Church of England man, I trust. But not a bit of difference!" he repeats, and has it too that Francis "said his Mass—always said his Mass—at night." About Sunday church-goings he is uncertain, having the impression that Francis no longer held with the priests of his Church. "There was something between him and the priests. Perhaps I ought not to tell you (I take it you are Catholics), but I fancy there was something." Mr. McMaster's narrative is here interrupted, not by the poet's shout, but by the poet's record of his habit of prayer. Francis writes, in a note to the following poem, composed years later: "It was my practice from the time I left college to pray for the lady whom I was destined to love—the unknown She. It is curious that even then I did not dream of praying for her whom I was destined to marry; and yet not curious: for already I previsioned that with me it would be to love, not to be loved."

With dawn and children risen would he run,
  Which knew not the fool's wisdom to be sad,
  He that had childhood sometimes to be glad,
Before her window with the co-mate sun.
At night his angel's wing before the Throne
  Dropped (and God smiled) the unnamed name of Her:
  Nor did she feel her destinate poet's prayer
Asperse her from her angel's pinion.

So strangely near! So far, that ere they meet,
The boy shall traverse with his bloody feet
  The mired and hungered ways, three sullen years,
Of the fell city: and those feet shall ooze
Crueller blood through ruinous avenues
  Of shattered youth, made plashy with his tears!

London Streets

As full of love as scant of poetry ;
Ah ! in the verses but the sender see,
And in the sender, but his heart, lady !

Mr. McMaster continues :—"Mr. Thompson was a great talker. I remember him asking me questions. My father, a University man—or rather a Scottish College man . . . would talk to him, very interested." And his employer lent him books and discussed them, and had, as he remembers it, some hand in the making of an author. It was in his shop and on his paper that Thompson wrote continually. Bulwer Lytton was devoured, then as in later years, and Francis took Mr. McMaster's Iliad even as far as Southampton Row along with Josephus and Huxley. "My Josephus and my Huxley," remembers his friend, who recalls, too, that he was "always reading the *Standard Book of British Poetry*." Francis did not know then that the "little obscure room in my father's poor house," where Traherne learnt, as a child of four, to be a poet, was also at the back of a shoemaker's. Children were of the Panton Street household, and Mr. McMaster remembers Francis's awed but gentle ways with them. A niece, called Rosie Violet or Rosebud by the family, and Flower or Little Flower, as Mr. McMaster remembers, by Francis, was his particular friend, and used to take his tea to him and walk with him in the park. That there was "another lady who helped him" may be an allusion to the friendship of the streets.

After rather more than three months' service in the shop, it was arranged that Francis should go home for the Christmas of 1886. There is not much to tell of his home-coming. Other members of the Thompson family were adepts, like Francis, in reserve, and it was practised rigorously during his holiday. It was known that he had suffered ; and his sufferings, or the occasion of them, were no more to be spoken of than misdeeds that had had

74

He leaves the Boot-shop

their punishment. He volunteered no account of himself and was asked for none, it being supposed that he had found a settled though humble way of life which allowed the past to fall back into the past. From his sister I learn that he filled his place in the family saddened, perhaps, but yet much as he had filled it before he left it : affection was there, on his side and on hers.

On his return from Manchester, where he lingered—or was delayed—longer than had been expected, the shop was even less well served than before. He returned as from a bout of drinking, and with no regard for the things around him. He had periodic visitations of much more than customary uselessness; they were such as Mr. McMaster observed in their approach. He would grow very restless and flushed, and then retire into an equally disconcerting satisfaction and peace of mind. These, of course, were the workings of opium, although Mr. McMaster mistook them, as Dr. Thompson had done previously, for those of alcohol. "There were accidents," says Mr. McMaster, with some horror of details. It seems Francis had let the shutter slip on a certain evening of delirium, and, it is gathered, a foot— the foot of a customer, no less—had been hurt. Whatever the immediate cause, Francis had to leave Panton Street in the middle of January 1887. Mr. McMaster stands an example. His charity was of such exceptional fortune as commends mankind to daily good works lest great benefits be left unperformed, lest our omissions starve a Francis Thompson. The persuasion of "Ye did it unto Me" may be varied by "Perhaps ye did it unto a Poet."

Before he left, Francis had sent manuscripts, Mr. McMaster avers, to more than one magazine ; for the discarded McMaster account-books had all the while been as freely covered with poetry and prose as had been the bulky business folios of Mme. Corot, Marchande de Modes, with Jean Baptiste Camille's landscapes of pen and ink. But Francis left Panton Street unanswered; he left Panton Street for less kindly thoroughfares. Nor did he ever return, though immediately after his dismissal he came to be in desperate need of any charity. How little he felt himself bounden by the ties of gratitude or kindly feeling, both of which he felt strongly in an inactive manner, is shown in this as in all his negotiations with his family and friends. He never forgot a kindness or an injury (nor failed to forgive either). Both meant too much to him. If he neglected the obligations of gratitude, he also, by a hard habit of constraint and a close conscience, kept his tongue consistently innocent of recriminations, so that I have never heard him use really hard words of any man. Mr. McMaster was never told till after his assistant's death that Francis came to find success as a writer of books and a journalist. That Francis was fond of him might be gathered in the few words in which he mentioned him no less than in Mr. McMaster's own account, and in his brother's, who says that Francis's eyes would follow the boot-maker round the room with a persistence that made him, seemingly, entirely like a fawn. " I can only compare him to a fawn," declared the brother; and he " not the only one to notice it ! "

As he stood on the threshold of the shop—"Still, as I turned inwards to the echoing chambers, or outwards to the wild, wild night, I saw London extending her visionary gate to receive me, like some dreadful mouth of Acheron " (de Quincey's words became his own by right of succession)—he was in no mood to fight for existence. He gave himself to Covent Garden, the archways and more desperate straits—" a flood-tide of disaster "—than he had known before.

Jane Eyre, while she felt the vulture, hunger, sinking beak and talons in her side, knew that solitude was no solitude, rest no rest, and instinct kept her roaming round the village and its store of food, even while she

He returns to the Streets

dared not ask for it. But that you are in a city of larders, and that you sleep in Covent Garden, the pulse of London's kitchens, does not scare the vulture; it is a town-bird, a cockney like the sparrow. I know that Thompson suffered hunger; so much he told me. But he found no simile for his pain, and perhaps Charlotte Brontë, in that she did find one, was as deeply scarred. Misery is a bottle-imp which you may put to your lips without going through the swing-doors of experience. Francis came back through them with a light heart, while Charlotte Brontë's was heavy with inexperience. Many of the horrors of the street Francis knew only in later years, when the bandages with which nature covers the eyes of those whom she condemns were removed. He had walked the battle-field among bullets and not known that one nestled in his heart, another in his brain, another in his flesh; only twenty years later did he grow weak with their poison, and develop a delirium of fear of the sights and sounds of London. It was in later years that he wrote : " The very streets weigh upon me. Those horrible streets, with their gangrenous multitude blackening ever into lower mortifications of humanity. . . . These lads who have almost lost the faculty of human speech : these girls whose very utterance is a hideous blasphemy against the sacrosanctity of lover's language. . . . We lament the smoke of London :—it were nothing without the fumes of congregated evil." [1] It was later, too, that he wrote of

> the places infamous to tell,
> Where God wipes not the tears from any eyes.

---

[1] Of the despoiling of the Lady Poverty he writes in an unpublished poem :—

DEGRADED POOR

> Lo, at the first, Lord, Satan took from Thee
> Wealth, Beauty, Honour, World's Felicity.
> Then didst Thou say : " Let be ;
> For with his leavings and neglects will I

77

London Streets

There is more in the same strain of heated hate and distress, but I quote no more, in the belief that it is far from illustrating his mood when he was actually on the streets. He had realised what the inexperienced does not, that "in suffering, intensity has not long duration; long duration has not intensity," or again: "Beyond the maximum point of a delicate nature you can no more get increase of agony by increasing its suffering than you can get increase of tone from a piano by stamping on it. It would be an executioner's trick of God if he made the poet-nature not only capable of a pang where others feel a prick, but of hell where others feel purgatory." One learns from almost the same page of his contradictory notes that he knew suffering beyond the range of other men's knowledge, but that, knowing it, he also knew the narrow limits of suffering.

Above all things, he learnt that lack of the world's goods is small lack, that to lose everything is no great loss—a proposition easily proved by analogy to those who have gained everything and found it small gain. While in the streets he had his tea to drink and his murderer to think about. It was in retrospect that he beheld misery incarnate in the outcast, and it was

Please Me, which he sets by,—
Of all disvalued, thence which all will leave Me,
And fair to none but Me, will not deceive Me."
My simple Lord! so deeming erringly,
Thou tookest Poverty;
Who, beautified with Thy Kiss, laved in Thy streams,
'Gan then to cast forth gleams,
That all men did admire
Her modest looks, her ragged sweet attire
In which the ribboned shoe could not compete
With her clear simple feet.
But Satan, envying Thee Thy one ewe-lamb,
With Wealth, World's Beauty and Felicity
Was not content, till last unthought-of she
Was his to damn.
Thine ingrate ignorant lamb
He won from Thee; kissed, spurned, and made of her
This thing which qualms the air—
Vile, terrible, old,
Whereat the red blood of the Day runs cold.

In Darkest London

through the sheltering pane of a window in a lodging that he saw :—

"A region whose hedgerows have set to brick, whose soil is chilled to stone; where flowers are sold and women; where the men wither and the stars; whose streets to me on the most glittering day are black. For I unveil their secret meanings. I read their human hieroglyphs. I diagnose from a hundred occult signs the disease which perturbs their populous pulses. Misery cries out to me from the kerb-stone, despair passes me by in the ways; I discern limbs laden with fetters impalpable, but not imponderable; I hear the shaking of invisible lashes, I see men dabbled with their own oozing life. This contrast rises before me; and I ask myself whether there be indeed an Ormuzd and an Ahriman, and whether Ahriman be the stronger of the twain. From the claws of the sphinx my eyes have risen to her countenance which no eyes read.

"Because, therefore, I have these thoughts; and because also I have knowledge, not indeed great or wide, but within certain narrow limits more intimate than most men's, of this life which is not a life; to which food is as the fuel of hunger; sleep, our common sleep, precious, costly, and fallible, as water in a wilderness; in which men rob and women vend themselves— for fourpence; because I have such thoughts and such knowledge, I needed not the words of our great Cardinal to read with painful sympathy the book just put forward by a singular personality."[1]

Of the things he heard—and misery, he says, cries out from the kerbstone—the laugh, not the cry, of the children familiar with all evil was what appalled him most. Appalling, too, was the unuttered cry of children who knew not how to cry nor why they had cause. Among the notes are many jottings of a resolve to write on the

---

[1] F. T.'s review of Booth's *In Darkest England*.

young of the town, but these were used only incidentally in essays or letters. Such a one is found in the passage, of his study of Blessed John Baptist de la Salle, in which he states the case for Free Education :—

"Think of it. If Christ stood amidst your London slums, He could not say : 'Except ye become as one of *these* little children.' Far better your children were cast from the bridges of London, than they should become as one of those little ones. Could they be gathered together and educated in the truest sense of the word ; could the children of the nation at large be so educated as to cut off future recruits to the ranks of Darkest England ; then it would need no astrology to cast the horoscope of to-morrow. *La tête de l'homme du peuple*, nay rather *de l'enfant du peuple*—around *that* sways the conflict. Who grasps the child grasps the future."

He writes there at the high pressure of one who sees the tragedy and must shout "Help !"

"Let those who are robust enough not to take injury from the terrible directness with which things are stated read the chapter entitled 'The Children of the Lost.'[1] For it drives home a truth which I fear the English public, with all its compassion for our destitute children, scarcely realises, knows but in a vague, general way ; namely, that they are brought up in sin from their cradles, that they know evil before they know good, that the boys are ruffians and profligates, the girls harlots, in the mother's womb. This, to me the most nightmarish idea in all the nightmare of those poor little lives, I have never been able to perceive that people had any true grasp on. And having mentioned it, though it is a subject very near my heart, I will say no more ; nor enforce it, as I might well do, from my own sad knowledge."

[1] In Booth's *In Darkest England*.

His Friend

To the juvenilia of the London period belongs a poem
on an allied problem of the streets :—

> Hell's gates revolve upon her yet alive ;
> To her no Christ the beautiful is nigh :
> The stony world has daffed His teaching by ;
> " Go ! " saith it ; " sin on still that you may thrive,
> Let one sin be as queen for all the hive
> Of sins to swarm around ; "
>
> .   .   .   .   .
>
> The gates of Hell have shut her in alive.

It was not improbably written while he was befriended
by the girl who, having noticed his forlorn state, did all
in her power to assist him.

A monastic segregation of the sexes is often the hard
rule of the outcast's road.   Francis had no other friends
among the women-folk or children of London, and often
passed months without having speech of any save men.
When he was again among friends and knew the children
of *Sister Songs* he wrote :—

> All vanished hopes, and all most hopeless bliss
>   Came with thee to my kiss.
> And ah ! so long myself had strayed afar
> From child, and woman, and the boon earth's green,
> And all wherewith life's face is fair beseen ;
>   Journeying its journey bare
> Five suns, except of the all-kissing sun
>   Unkissed of one ;
>   Almost I had forgot
>   The healing harms,
> And whitest witchery, a-lurk in that
> Authentic cestus of two girdling arms.

This girl gave out of her scant and pitiable opulence,
consisting of a room, warmth, and food, and a cab thereto.
When the streets were no longer crowded with shameful
possibilities she would think of the only tryst that
her heart regarded and, a sister of charity, would take
her beggar into her vehicle at the appointed place and
cherish him with an affection maidenly and motherly,

London Streets

and passionate in both these capacities. Two outcasts,
they sat marvelling that there were joys for them to
unbury and to share. Then, in a Chelsea room such
as that of Rossetti's poem would they sit :—

> Your lamp, my Jenny, kept alight,
> Like a wise virgin's, all one night !
> And in the alcove coolly spread
> Glimmers with dawn your empty bed.

Weakness and confidence, humility and reverence,
were gifts unknown to her except at his hands, and she
repaid them with graces as lovely as a child's, and as
unhesitating as a saint's. In his address to a child, in a
later year, he remembers this poor girl's childishness :—

> Forlorn, and faint, and stark
> I had endured through watches of the dark
> The abashless inquisition of each star,
> Yea, was the outcast mark
> Of all those heavenly passers' scrutiny ;
> Stood bound and helplessly
> For Time to shoot his barbéd minutes at me ;
> Suffered the trampling hoof of every hour
> In night's slow-wheeléd car ;
> Until the tardy dawn dragged me at length
> From under those dread wheels ; and, bled of strength,
> I waited the inevitable last.
> Then there came past
> A child ; like thee, a spring-flower ; but a flower
> Fallen from the budded coronal of Spring,
> And through the city-streets blown withering.
> She .passed,—O brave, sad, lovingest, tender thing !
> And of her own scant pittance did she give,
> That I might eat and live :
> Then fled, a swift and trackless fugitive.
> Therefore I kissed in thee
> The heart of Childhood, so divine for me ;
> And her, through what sore ways
> And what unchildish days.
> Borne from me now, as then, a trackless fugitive.
> Therefore I kissed in thee
> Her, child ! and innocency.

"Swift and Trackless Fugitive"

Her sacrifice was to fly from him: learning he had found friends, she said that he must go to them and leave her. After his first interview with my father he had taken her his news. "They will not understand our friendship," she said, and then, "I always knew you were a genius." And so she strangled the opportunity; she killed again the child, the sister; the mother had come to life within her—she went away. Without warning she went to unknown lodgings and was lost to him. In "the mighty labyrinths of London" he lay in wait for her, nor would he leave the streets, thinking that in doing so he would make a final severance. Like de Quincey's Ann, she was sought, but never found, along the pavements at the place where she had been used to find him.

With de Quincey Thompson could have said, "During some years I hoped that she did live; and I suppose in the literal and unrhetorical use of the word myriad, I must, on my visits to London, have looked at myriads of female faces, in the hope of meeting Ann." And, again, that this incident of friendship "more than any other, coloured, or (more truly I should say) shaped, moulded and remoulded, composed and decomposed, the great body of opium dreams." Pursuit and search have been matters of much nocturnal and poetic moment; such was Patmore's recurring dream of the dead whom—

> I, dreaming, night by night seek now to see,
> And, in a mortal sorrow, still pursue
> Through sordid streets and lanes,
> And houses brown and bare,
> And many a haggard stair,
> Ochrous with ancient stains,
> And infamous doors, opening on hapless rooms,
> In whose unhaunted glooms
> Dead pauper generations, witless of the sun,
> Their course have run.

London Streets

As with de Quincey, so with Patmore, so with Francis. To the dream, or sense, of pursuit, was added the suspicion of balking interference. De Quincey says that throughout his dreams he was conscious "of some shadowy malice which withdrew her, or attempted to withdraw her, from restoration and from hope." And Patmore :—

> And ofttimes my pursuit
> Is check'd of its dear fruit
> By things brimful of hate, my kith and kin,
> Furious that I should keep
> Their forfeit power to weep.

Pursuit circles after flight, and flight circles before pursuit, and they go about and meet and are confounded —as when children play round a tree—in the dreams that were common to de Quincey and Thompson, in the "Daughter of Lebanon" of the one and "The Hound of Heaven" of the other.

It was loyalty, the loyalty of one who knew what benefits he bestowed in receiving the alms of his forlorn friend, rather than love, that kept him so fast to his tryst with her that even when the chance offered for him to leave the streets, he refused at first to do that which would put an end to the possibility of their meetings. But he had not yet loved, nor met her whom he was destined to love—the unknown She for whom in Manchester he had prayed every night.

In an account of charities among the outcasts he quotes : "To be nameless in worthy deeds exceeds an infamous history. The Canaanitish woman lives more happily without a name than Herodias with one."

CHAPTER V: THE DISCOVERY

A RALLY, probably the result of a gift from Manchester, came about in the latter half of February 1887. I quote his own words : " With a few shillings to give me breathing space, I began to decipher and put together the half-obliterated manuscript of ' Paganism.' I came simultaneously to my last page and my last halfpenny ; and went forth to drop the MS. in the letter-box of *Merry England*.[1] Next day I spent the halfpenny on two boxes of matches, and began the struggle for life."

This was the covering letter to my father, its editor :—

" *Feb.* 23*rd*, '87.—Dear Sir,—In enclosing the accompanying article for your inspection I must ask pardon for the soiled state of the manuscript. It is due, not to slovenliness, but to the strange places and circumstances under which it has been written. For me, no less than Parolles, the dirty nurse experience has something fouled. I enclose stamped envelope for a reply, since I do not desire the return of the manuscript, regarding your judgment of its worthlessness as quite final. I can hardly expect that where my prose fails my verse will succeed. Nevertheless, on the principle of ' Yet will I try the last,' I have added a few specimens of it, with

---

[1] *Merry England* was a magazine he had known in Manchester, and noted especially during his Christmas holiday at home. His uncle, Edward Healy Thompson, was already a contributor, and among others were Cardinal Manning, Lionel Johnson, Hilaire Belloc, May Probyn, St. John Adcock, Sir William Butler, Coulson Kernahan, Alice Corkran, Coventry Patmore, W. H. Hudson, Katharine Tynan, J. G. Snead Cox, Aubrey de Vere, Wilfrid Scawen Blunt, Father R. F. Clark, J. Eastwood Kidson, and Bernard Whelan.

The Discovery

the off chance that one may be less poor than the rest. Apologising very sincerely for any intrusion on your valuable time, I remain yours with little hope,

FRANCIS THOMPSON.

Kindly address your rejection to the Charing Cross Post Office."

Francis had more than remembered the existence of the magazine and its editor. " I was myself virtually his pupil and his wife's long before I knew him. He has in my opinion—an opinion of long standing—done more than any man in these latter days to educate Catholic literary opinion," he wrote to Manchester soon after his first appearance in the magazine. He knew the target at which he aimed.

"Paganism Old and New" is written in the un-harassed manner of a man whose style, and cuffs, had been kept in order at the Savile Club. But he had no backing of library and chef to give him the courage of his fine sentences ; he was the man selling matches in the gutter and sharpening his pencil on the kerb-stone. The beauty of the circumstances of Pagan life, its pro-cessional maidens, " shaking a most divine dance from their feet," its theatres unroofed to the smokeless sky— with these, he says, the advocates of a revived Paganism contrast the conditions of to-day : "the cold formalities of an outworn worship ; our *ne plus ultra* of pageantry, a Lord Mayor's show ; the dryadless woods regarded chiefly as potential timber ; the grimy streets, the grimy air, the disfiguring statues, the Stygian crowd ; the temple to the reigning goddess Gelasma, which mocks the name of theatre ; last and worst, the fatal degrada-tion of popular perception which has gazed so long on ugliness that it takes her to its bosom. In our capitals the very heavens have lost their innocence. Aurora may rise over our cities, but she has forgotten how to blush." From the pavement where the East sweeps the

Dead-letter Office

soot in eddies round his ankles, he protests : " Pagan Paganism was not poetical. No pagan eye ever visioned the nymphs of Shelley." " In the name of all the Muses, what treason against Love and Beauty ! " he cries against Catullus, Propertius, and Ovid, for the arid eroticism that was satisfied to write of love without tribute to the colour of a lady's eyes. For contrast, he quotes Rossetti's—

> Her eyes were deeper than the depth
> Of waters stilled at even ;

Wordsworth's " Eyes like stars of twilight fair " ; Collins's Pity " with eyes of dewy light " ; Shelley's " Thy sweet-child sleep, the filmy-eyed." And of the fair love of Dante and other Christian poets he makes sweet and loyal praises. He was the lover to write an essay in defence of the social order that denied him love, sleep, pity, and the eyes of any lady. It was the essay, too, of a man physically hungry. He supped full, but with fancies.

Thompson's manuscripts, most uninviting in outward aspect, were pigeon-holed, unread by a much-occupied editor for six months—were then released, read, and estimated at their worth. The sanity of the essay was proof enough of the genius of Thompson's inspiration against the evidence in some of the poems of another inspiration—that of drugs. My father and mother (the A. M. and W. M. of following pages) decided to accept the essay and a poem, and to seek the author. To this end my father wrote a letter addressed to Charing Cross Post Office, stating the intention of printing some of the manuscript, and asking Francis to call for a proof and to discuss the chances of future work. To that letter came no reply and publication was postponed, but when at last his letter was returned through the dead-letter office, he printed the " Passion of Mary " as the best way of getting into communication with the author. The poem

The Discovery

appeared in *Merry England* for April 1888, and on the 14th my father received the following letter :—

"*April 14th*, 1888.—DEAR SIR,—In the last days of February or the first days of March, 1887 (my memory fails me as to the exact date), I forwarded to you for your magazine a prose article, " Paganism Old and New " (or " Ancient and Modern," for I forget which wording I adopted), and accompanied it by some pieces of verse, on the chance that if the prose failed, some of the verse might meet acceptance. I enclosed a stamped envelope for a reply, since (as I said) I did not desire the return of the manuscript. Imprudently, perhaps, instead of forwarding the parcel through the post, I dropped it with my own hand into the letter-box of 43 Essex Street. There was consequently no stamp on it, since I did not think a stamp would be necessary under the circumstances. I asked you to address your answer to the Charing Cross Post Office. To be brief, from that day to this, no answer has ever come into my hands. And yet, more than a twelve-month since the forwarding of the manuscript, I am now informed that one of the copies of verse which I submitted to you (*i.e.* 'The Passion of Mary') is appearing in this month's issue of *Merry England*. Such an occurrence I can only explain to myself in one way, viz., that some untoward accident cut off your means of communicating with me. To suppose otherwise—to suppose it intentional—would be to wrong your known honour and courtesy. I have no doubt that your explanation, when I receive it, will be entirely satisfactory to me. I therefore enclose a stamped and addressed envelope for an answer, hoping that you will recompense me for my long delay by the favour of an early reply. In any case, however long circumstances may possibly delay your reply, it will be sure of reaching me at the address I have now given.— I remain, yours faithfully,

FRANCIS JOSEPH THOMPSON.

88

The Chemist's Capture

"*P.S.*—Doubtless, when I received no answer, I ought to have written again. My excuse must be that a flood-tide of misfortune rolled over me, leaving me no leisure to occupy myself with what I regarded as an attempt that had hopelessly failed. Hence my entire subsequent silence."

To this my father answered with an explanation and a repetition of his invitation to Francis to arrange for regular work, and despatched his answer by a special messenger to the address given, a chemist's shop in Drury Lane. The chemist's manner of accepting responsibility for the safe delivery of the letter was discouraging. He said that Thompson sometimes called for letters, but that he knew little of him. After a few days during which nothing was heard my father went himself in search. His obvious eagerness prompted a query from the man behind the counter : "Are you a relative ? he owes me three-and-ninepence." With that paid and a promise of ten-and-sixpence if he produced the poet, he agreed to do his best, and, many days after, my father, being in his workroom, was told that Mr. Thompson wished to see him. "Show him up," he said, and was left alone.

Then the door opened, and a strange hand was thrust in. The door closed, but Thompson had not entered. Again it opened, again it shut. At the third attempt a waif of a man came in. No such figure had been looked for ; more ragged and unkempt than the average beggar, with no shirt beneath his coat and bare feet in broken shoes, he found my father at a loss for words. "You must have had access to many books when you wrote that essay," was what he said. "That," said Thompson, his shyness at once replaced by an acerbity that afterwards became one of the most familiar of his never-to-be-resented mannerisms, "that is precisely where the essay fails. I had no books by me at the time save

The Discovery

Aeschylus and Blake." There was little to be done for him at that interview save the extraction of a promise to call again. He made none of the confidences characteristic of a man seeking sympathy and alms. He was secretive and with no eagerness for plans for his benefit, and refused the offer of a small weekly sum that would enable him to sleep in a bed and sit at a table. I know of no man, and can imagine none, to whom another can so easily unburden himself of uneasiness and formalities as to my father. To him the poor and the rich are, as the fishes and the flames to St. Francis, his brothers and his friends at sight, even if these are shy as fishes and sightless as flame. But the impression of the visit on my father was of a meeting that did not end in great usefulness—so much was indicated by a manner schooled in concealments. But Francis came again, and again, and then to my father's house in Kensington. Of the falsity of the impression given by his manner, his poetry in the address to his host's little girl is the proof :—

> Yet is there more, whereat none guesseth, love !
>   Upon the ending of my deadly night
> (Whereof thou hast not the surmise, and slight
>   Is all that any mortal knows thereof),
>   Thou wert to me that earnest of day's light,
> When, like the back of a gold-mailéd saurian
>   Heaving its slow length from Nilotic slime,
> The first long gleaming fissure runs Aurorian
>   Athwart the yet dun firmament of prime.
> Stretched on the margin of the cruel sea
>   Whence they had rescued me,
>   With faint and painful pulses was I lying ;
>   Not yet discerning well
> If I had 'scaped, or were an icicle,
>   Whose thawing is its dying.
> Like one who sweats before a despot's gate,
> Summoned by some presaging scroll of fate,
> And knows not whether kiss or dagger wait ;
> And all so sickened is his countenance

He Hesitates

The courtiers buzz, " Lo, doomed ! " and look at him askance :—
    At fate's dread portal then
    Even so stood I, I ken,
Even so stood I, between a joy and fear,
And said to mine own heart, " Now, if the end be here ! "

In the last four lines is probably an instance of his
habitual appropriation of things seen for his poetic
images. If the door of my father's room is here promoted to a part in *Sister Songs*, it takes its place with
the clock of Covent Garden, the arrowy minute-hand
of which Mr. Shane Leslie has remarked as suggesting
Thompson's description of himself when he

        Stood bound and helplessly
    For Time to shoot his barbéd minutes at me.

In the continuation of the same passage is found
another example :—

    Suffered the trampling hoof of every hour
        In night's slow-wheeléd car ;
    Until the tardy dawn dragged me at length
    From under those dread wheels ; and, bled of strength,
        I waited the inevitable last.

Even before he was knocked down by a cab, as
happened to him later, the heavy traffic of Covent
Garden, harassing the straggler in the gutter, may
well have been to him a type of danger and fears.

The idea of rescue came slowly and doubtfully to
Francis, who was far less ready than my father to
believe that he was fitted for the writing career.
Their first talks were of books ; of his history he said
nothing. He was willing to tell of the poets he had
read in the Guildhall Library, until the police, being,
as he said, against him, barred the entrance. He was
willing, too, that anything he had written should be
published, and bring temporary wealth ; but reluctant

to admit that he might become a worker and quit the streets—so fixedly reluctant that some strong reason was conjectured. He would visit my father, then living in Kensington, but it was long before he would accept substantial hospitalities ; coming in the evening or afternoon, he would leave to return to his calling—literally a calling—of cabs. That he was also during this time either parting with or searching for his Ann is not unlikely. He took his reprieve as he had taken his doom ; he went frightened and brave at once, at war with peace, at peace with war. With his hesitations, it was more than six months later that he wrote anew for *Merry England*, in the November issue of which appeared " Bunyan in the Light of Modern Criticism " ; his three previous appearances, in April, May, and June, with the " Passion of Mary," " Dream Tryst," and " Paganism Old and New," having exhausted the possible things among those first submitted. He was not an absentee because he could not write better than the oldest hand the articles exactly fitted for *Merry England*. The intention declared in an early number of my father's magazine was to give voice to a renascence of happiness ; " We shall try to revive in our own hearts, and in the hearts of others, the enthusiasm of the Christian Faith." This enthusiasm was to inform essays on social problems and essays in literary and artistic criticism, and an optimistic editor had told his contributors to recover the humour, and good humour, of the Saints and Fathers. " Paganism Old and New," in which it was sought to expose the fallacy of searching for love of beauty and sweetness in the pagan mythology, and to reveal the essential modernity, and even Christianity, of Keats' and Shelley's pagan beauties, was a triumph of journalistic obedience and appropriateness.

It ends : " Bring back even the best age of Paganism, and you smite beauty on the cheek. But you *cannot* bring back then, the best age of Paganism, the age when

Making of a Poet

Paganism was a faith. None will again behold Apollo in the forefront of the morning, or see Aphrodite in the upper air loose the long lustre of her golden locks. But *you may* bring back—*dii avertant omen*—the Paganism of the days of Pliny, and Statius, and Juvenal. . . . This is the Paganism which is formidable, and not the antique lamp whose feeding oil is spent, whose light has not outlasted the damps of its long sepulture." This he wrote, who might have been exercising his knowledge of ignominy in a *Ventre de Londres* or at least in such a book as the memorable *Rowton House Rhymes*.

The streets, somehow, had nurtured a poet and trained a journalist. He had gone down into poverty so absolute that he was often without pen and paper, and now emerged a pressman. Neither his happiness, nor his tenderness, nor his sensibility had been marred, like his constitution, by his experiences. To be the target of such pains as it is the habit of the world to deplore as the extreme of disaster, and yet to keep alive the young flame of his poetry; to be under compulsion to watch the ignominies of the town, and yet never to be nor to think himself ignominious; to establish the certitude of his virtue; to keep flourishing an infinite tenderness and capability for delicacies and *gentilezze* of love—these were the triumphs of his immunity. A mother not yet delivered of her child must be protected from all ills of mind and body lest they do injury to the delicate and susceptible life within her. Horrors must not be spoken in her presence; it has been held fit that she should have pictures about her bed of fair infants that her thoughts might instruct the features of the unborn child in good-favouredness. How otherwise was the poet dealt with, whose intellect was the womb of the word! The making of Viola, as he tells it, is a sweeter business than the making of a poet—of the maker of a " Making of Viola "—but not more natural and inevitable. Thompson's muse rose intact, but trailing bloody insignia of battle ; his spirit rose from the penal waters fresh as Botticelli's Venus. It had not been more marvellous if Sandro's lady, with cool cheeks, floating draperies, and dry curls, had risen from a real unplumbed, salt, estranging sea, instead of from the silly ripples of Florentine convention.

But physically he was battered ; and his condition led my father to prevail upon him, with much difficulty, to be examined by a doctor. "He will not live," was the first verdict, "and you hasten his death by denying his whims and opium." But the risk was taken, and Francis sent to a private hospital.

Thus he alludes to the change within himself :— "Please accept my warmest thanks for all your kindness and trouble on my behalf. I know this is a very perfunctory looking letter ; but until the first sharp struggle is over, it is difficult for me to write in any other way."

De Quincey thought that opium killed Coleridge as a poet, that it was the enemy of his authorship ; that the leaving off of opium creates a new heaven and a new earth. Thompson had now to experience such things by the denial of the drug. Of his links with Coleridge A. M. writes in the *Dublin Review*, January 1908 :—

"Of his alienation from ordinary life, laudanum was the sole cause, and, of laudanum, early and long disease. Coleridge's fault was Thompson's—an evasion of the daily dues of man to man. It was laudanum that dissolved Coleridge's bond to wife and child, and piled their unanswered letters by his bed of illusion and shattering dreams ; it was laudanum that held the hand bound to open them, turning it half callous and half timorous, as though insensibility should borrow of sensibility its flight, its cowardice, and its closed eyes ; or rather the sensitive and loving man was acting his own part, wearing a delusive likeness to himself, while laudanum cared nothing for wife or child. It was laudanum that sent Coleridge to take refuge on one alien hearth when no fire was kindled to welcome him in any home of his kindred. It was laudanum that was the unspoken thing, the un-

He Renounces Opium

named, in Coleridge's conscious talk ; other things he would confess, but not this, which was the daily desire, the daily possession, and the daily stealth. So it was also, in his own degree, with this later sufferer. Francis Thompson was not like Coleridge ; he had not Coleridge's bond and obligations ; but the laudanum was alike in the wronged veins, the altered blood, of both."

The renunciation of opium, not its indulgence, opened the doors of the intellect. Opium killed the poet in Coleridge ; the opium habit was stifled at the birth of the poet in Thompson. His images came toppling about his thoughts overflowingly during the pains of abstinence. This, too, was de Quincey's experience, told when he was unwinding " the accursed chain " : " I protest to you I have a greater influx of thoughts in one hour at present than in a whole year under the reign of opium. It seems as though all the thoughts which had been frozen up for a decade of years by opium had now, according to the old fable, been thawed at once."

" The Ode to the Setting Sun" was written at midsummer in 1889, and on receiving it, his editor, with my mother and a young friend, Mr. Vernon Blackburn, straightway took the train to congratulate him on this first conclusive sign of the splendour of his powers. For the poet had been placed with the monks at Storrington Priory, and it was the music of three wandering musicians heard in the village street that opened the ode [1] :—

> The wailful sweetness of the violin
> Floats down the hushéd waters of the wind,
> The heart-strings of the throbbing harp begin
> To long in aching music. . . .

Thus by accident were the words of Sir Thomas Browne, an author beloved of Francis—words quoted by

[1] He himself notes the circumstances of composition. " Mem.—' Ode to Setting Sun ' begun in the field of the Cross, and under shadow of the Cross, at sunset ; finished ascending and descending Jacob's Ladder (mid or late noon ?) " " The Song of the Hours" also was written at Storrington.

de Quincey—again made good : "And even that tavern music, which makes one merry, another mad, in me strikes a deep fit of devotion."

After requests for boots and writing-pads—walking and writing made up his days—he gives notice that with many misgivings he has fixed on Shelley for the theme of a first *Dublin Review* article :—

"I have done so principally because I remember more of him than any other poet (though that is saying little). Coleridge was always my favourite poet ; but I early recognised that to make him a model was like trying to run up a window-pane, or to make clotted cream out of moonlight, or to pack jelly-fish in hampers. So that until I was twenty-two Shelley was more studied by me than anyone else. At the same time I am exposed to the danger of talking platitudes, because so much has been written about Shelley of late years which I have never read. I may have one or two questions to ask you in relation to the subject as I go on. Thank you for the American paper. Only the poet feels complimented. Your criticisms on the *Merry England* article were (for once in a way) entirely anticipated by my own impressions. Happy are they that hear their detractions and can put them to mending. With regard to what you say about the advantage of my being in a more booky place than Storrington¹ I entirely agree. Nor need you fear the opium. I have learned the advantage of being without it for mental exercise ; and (still more important) I have learned to bear my fits of depression without it. Personally I no longer fear it."

In a later letter :—"Shelley was sent off yesterday. Herewith the few fugitive verses I spoke of. With re-gard to the article, please take no notice of any writing

¹ The Shelley Essay bears signs of the booklessness of Storrington. All the quotations were made from memory, and nearly all were inaccurate.

on the backs of the sheets, and disregard all pencilled writing, either front or back. The opening is carefully constructed so that, if you think advisable, you can detach it, and leave the article to commence on page 10."

His next runs :—

"Surprised about Shelley. Seemed to me dreadful trash when I read it over before sending it. Shut my eyes and ran to the post, or some demon might have set me to work on picking it again. Don't see but what we can easily draw the knife out of your heart by knocking out the praise of Swinburne. Won't grieve you if we leave in the disparaging part of the comparison, I hope? And I daresay you are perfectly right about it."

Of this Shelley article nearly the whole history is told in a long letter to his own and his family's friend, Dr. Carroll :—

"The article on Shelley which you asked about I finished at last, with quite agonising pain and elaboration. It might have been written in tears, and is proportionately dear to me. I fear, however, that it will not be accepted, or accepted only with such modifications as will go to my heart. It has not been inserted in the current issue of the *Dublin*—a fact which looks ominous. First, you see, I prefaced it by a fiery attack on Catholic Philistinism (exemplified in Canon T——, though I was not aware about him at the time I wrote the article), driven home with all the rhetoric which I could muster. That is pretty sure to be a stumbling-block. I consulted Mr. Meynell as to its suppression, but he said 'Leave it in.' I suspect that he thoroughly agrees with it. Secondly, it is written at an almost incessant level of poetic prose, and seethes with imagery like my poetry itself. Now the sober, ponderous, ecclesiastical *Dublin* confronted with poetic prose must be considerably scared. The editor probably cannot

The Discovery

make up his mind whether it is heavenly rhetoric or infernal nonsense. And in the midst of my vexation at feeling what a thankless waste of labour it is, I cannot help a sardonic grin at his conjectured perplexity. Mr. Meynell's opinion was ' " Shelley " is splendid.' . . .

"There can now be no doubt that the *Dublin Review* has rejected my article. Nothing has been heard of it since it was sent. I only hope that they have not lost the MS. That would be to lose the picked fruit of three painful months—a quite irreparable loss. I am not surprised, myself. What is an unlucky ecclesiastical editor to do when confronted with something so *sui generis* as this—my friend's favourite passage, and the only one which I can remember. I had been talking of the 'Cloud,' and remarking that it displayed ' the childish faculty of make-believe, raised to the nth power.' In fact, I said, Shelley was the child, still at play, though his play-things were larger. Then I burst into prose poetry. ' The universe is his box of toys. He dabbles his hands in the sunset. He is gold-dusty with tumbling amid the stars. He makes bright mischief with the moon. He teases into growling the kennelled thunder, and laughs at the shaking of its fiery chain. He dances in and out of the gates of heaven. He runs wild over the fields of ether. He chases the rolling world. He gets between the feet of the horses of the sun. He stands in the lap of patient Nature, and twines her loosened tresses after a hundred wilful fashions, to see how she will look nicest in his poetry.' The editor sees at once that here is something such as he has never encountered before. Personally, I recollect nothing like it in English prose. In French prose I could point to something not so dissimilar—in Victor Hugo. But not in English. De Quincey is as boldly poetical, and his strain far higher; but he is poetical after quite another style. The editor feels himself out of his latitude. He is probably a person of only average literary taste—that is, he can tell the literary

" Shelley " is Rejected

hawk from the literary handsaw when the wind is southerly. He feels that discretion is the better part of valour. The thing may be very good, may be very bad. But it is beyond or below comprehension. So he rejects it. Twelve years hence (if he live so long) he will feel uncomfortable should anyone allude to that rejection. Unless he has lost the MS. In that case the thing is gone for ever.

"I had a commission (through Mr. Meynell) to write an article for the jubilee number of the *Tablet;* but the editor would have nothing to do with it when it was written. I had said that Cardinal Wiseman too often wrote like a brilliant schoolboy (I *might* have said that, as regards his style, he seldom wrote like anyone else); and I had been guilty of other sins of omission and commission which were likely to bristle the hair of the Canon T——s."

And later, to the same correspondent :—

"*August.*—I have been re-reading what I said regarding my rejected Shelley article, and I see that you might possibly interpret my language as referring to its *merit*. This would make my words read arrogantly in the extreme. When I said that I knew nothing just like it in the language, I was speaking of its *kind*, its style. As to the *merit* of that style, I have ventured no opinion of my own, but simply given you my friends' opinion. I am so poor a judge of my own work, that they never pay any attention to what I think about it. Please always bear this in mind. You may be sure that in speaking about my own work I always follow the same rule, to tell you merely what my friends say as to its merit."

What little more remains to be told of the writing and the posthumous publication of the Shelley article comes from W. M. :—

"It happened that Bishop (afterwards Cardinal) Vaughan, who knew the poet's family well in Lancashire, and had known Francis

The Discovery

himself at Ushaw, met him in London at our house, and out of this meeting and the Bishop's wish to serve him, came the suggestion that he should contribute a paper to the *Dublin Review*. That venerable quarterly, founded by Cardinal Wiseman half a century before, Bishop Vaughan now owned but did not edit. It inherited ecclesiastical rather than literary traditions; and a due consideration for these dictated the opening passages of the Essay, since somewhat curtailed. Hence proceeded the plea that Theology and Literature might be reconciled—just such another reconciliation as Art had been adjured to seal with Nature at the end of the eighteenth century :

Go find her, kiss her, and be friends again !

And Thompson's plea had this added relevance—that the choice of a subject, left to himself, had fallen upon Shelley ; perhaps a dubious choice. At any rate the article was returned to him from the *Dublin*—one more of those memorable rejections that go into the treasury of all neglected writers' consolations, perhaps their illusions. Thrown aside by its discouraged author, the Essay [1] was found among his papers after his death. His literary executor thought it right that the Review for which it was originally designed should again have the offer of it, since a new generation of readers had arisen, and another editor, in days otherwise regenerate. Thus it happened that this orphan among Essays entered at last on a full inheritance of fame."

It appeared in the *Dublin* dated July 1908, and for the first time in a long life of seventy-two years the Review passed into a second edition. Its reissue in separate form has for preface Mr. George Wyndham's estimate of it as the most important contribution made to English literature for twenty years.

From F. T. to W. M :—

" The *Dublin* article having been sent, I write to ask you for more work, or directions as to work. I am afraid, however, that even if there is room for it the article will hardly be in time, and that through my own

---

[1] Also a Shelley " Selection," not published.

He Learns to Work

fault. I miscalculated the date from Father Driffield's letter, and seeing no newspapers, did not discover my error till I came to post it. This is something like a confession of failure, and I am naturally chagrined about it. But I have one comfort from the affair : I not only hope but think (though until I see how I proceed with my next book I will not speak decidedly) that it has broken me to harness. You ask me to write frankly, and so I will tell you just how I have found myself get on with my work. At first I could not get on at all. I tried regularly enough to settle myself to writing ; but my brain would not work. During the last four days I wrote at a pretty uniform rate, and wrote so continuously as I have never been able to write before—in fact, more continuously than I mean to write again, except in an emergency like this—I began to feel very shaken at the end of it. But the valuable thing is that I was able to make myself write when and for as long as I pleased. I want some more work now, but if left to myself I may lose a habit scarcely acquired. . . . The only two ideas in my head both require books. The one is for an article on Dryden, the other an old idea for an article on ' Idylls of the King.' Very likely my idea with regard to the latter has long been anticipated : so that to prevent any possible waste of labour let me briefly explain it. I have seen it objected to them that there are only the slightest and most arbitrary narrative links between them, and that they form no real sequence. My idea is to show that they have not a narrative, but a moral, sequence. (I have nothing to do with the allegory.) Tennyson's idea has been to show the gradual disruption of Arthur's court and realm through the ' little pitted speck in garnered fruit ' of Guinevere's sin, which ' rotting inward slowly moulders all.' This he does by a series of separate pictures each exhibiting in a progressive style the disintegrating process. Each exhibits some definite development of decaying virtue

The Discovery

in court or kingdom. Viewed in this light, they have a real relation to each other which is that of their common relation to the central idea. It is a *crescendo* of moral laxity; and throughout, by constant little side touches, he keeps before my mind how all this is sprung from the daily visible sin of the Queen's life. That is the idea: judge for yourself if it is worth anything. If you have any work ready for me, I should prefer to do that; I think I could now do work not originated by myself."

He continues :—

"I gather from her last poem that Miss Tynan is no longer with you, or I should have hardly sent you the longer verses (the 'Sere of the Leaf'), for I feel that I have taken a perhaps unwarrantable liberty in apostrophising her, even in her poetical and therefore public capacity. I can only plead that verse, like 'l'Amour' in Carmen's song—

> est enfant de Bohème,
> Qui n'a jamais, jamais connu de loi !

The thing would not write itself otherwise. She happened to set the current of my thought, and I could not quit the current."

Of this liberty Miss Tynan, one of the earliest of Francis's admiring and admired, wrote to her poet :—

"I must thank you very much for associating my name with your luxuriantly beautiful poem in the current number (January 1891) of *Merry England*, and for giving my words place on the golden and scarlet web and woof of poetry. No one could fail to be proud and grateful for such a distinction. I have been deeply interested in your poetry since the first day I saw your name to 'Dream Tryst.' I am sure I was one of the first to write and ask, 'Who is Francis Thompson ? ' "

And again in 1892 :—

" . . . You are too good to say you are indebted to me. If I thought you were, I should begin to feel proud of myself. I'd

The Confessional of Verse

like to think better of my own work than I do of some of my friends' work—Mr. Yeats is one, and you are another—but I can't. My faculty of admiration is too true and strong. . . . I hope you will write to me again, and I look forward to meeting and knowing you when I come to London. Your buying the 'Poppies' in the circumstances was indeed a tribute. I am very glad to know you are now lifted to a safer position, out of danger of such poverty. I am very glad for you to be the Meynells' friend." . . .

F. T. to W. M :—

"DEAR MR. MEYNELL,—How good and kind and patient you are with me ! far more than I am with myself, for I am often sick with the being that inhabits this villainous mud-hut of a body. . . . I beguiled the four ill nights I have spoken of, while the mental cloud was somewhat lifted, by writing the verses [one set of these was the 'Sere of the Leaf'] I herewith send you. If there be no saving grace of poetry in them they are damned ; for I am painfully conscious that they display me, in every respect, at my morally weakest. Indeed no one but yourself—or, to be more accurate, yourselves— would I have allowed to see them ; for often verse written as I write it is nothing less than a confessional far more intimate than the sacerdotal one. *That* touches only your sins, and leaves in merciful darkness your ignominious, if sinless, weaknesses. When the soul goes forth, like Andersen's Emperor, thinking herself clothed round with singing-robes, while in reality her naked weakness is given defenceless to the visiting wind, not every mother's son would you allow to gaze on you at such a time. And the shorter of the two pieces especially is such a self-revelation, I feel, as even you have hardly had from me before. Something in them may be explained to you, and perhaps a little excused, by the newspaper cutting I forward. For some inscrutable reason it has affected me as if I never expected it. I knew of it beforehand ; I thought I was familiarised

103

The Discovery

with the idea ; yet when the newspaper came as I sat at dinner, and I saw her name among so many familiar names, I pushed away the remainder of my dinner and —well, I will not say what I did. I have been miserable ever since. The fact is my nerves want taking up like an Atlantic cable, and recasing. I am sometimes like a dispossessed hermit-crab, looking about everywhere for a new shell, and quivering at every touch. Figuratively speaking, if I prick my finger I seem to feel it with my whole body." The shell he had cast, with lamentations, was the encrustation of disease, of opium, of street miseries.

In February 1890, having bidden good-bye at Storrington to Daisy "and Daisy's sister-blossom or blossom-sister, Violet (there are nine children in the family, the last four all flowers—Rose, Daisy, Lily, and Violet)," he returned to London. In town the poetry was continued. "Love in Dian's Lap" was written as he paced, in place of the Downs, the library floor at Palace Court ; and in Kensington Gardens, where I have seen him at prayer as well as at poetry, he composed "Sister Songs." Both were pencilled into penny exercise-books. His reiterated "It's a penny exercise-book" is remembered by every member of the household set to search for the mislaid first drafts of " Love in Dian's Lap "—he himself too dismayed to look.

In this form "Sister Songs" (written at about the time of "The Hound of Heaven," in 1891, but not published till 1895) was covertly handed as a Christmas offering to his friends, or rather left with a note where it would be seen by them :—

"DEAR MR. MEYNELL,—I leave with this on the mantel-piece (in an exercise-book) the poem of which I spoke. If intensity of labour could make it good, good it would be. One way or the other, it will be an effectual test of a theme on which I have never yet written ; if from it I

A Christmas Present

have failed to draw poetry, then I may as well take down my sign.—Always yours,   FRANCIS THOMPSON."

Later, having recovered the manuscript to add to it the " Inscription " he returned it with :—

" Before I talk of anything else, let me thank you *ab imis medullis* for the one happy Christmas I have had for many a year. Herewith I send you my laggard poem. I have been delayed partly through making some minor corrections, but chiefly through having to transcribe the ' Inscription ' at the close of it."

He had watched the piling up of family presents before making his own, and in the " Inscription " he tells :—

> But one I marked who lingered still behind,
> As for such souls no seemly gift had he :
>   He was not of their strain,
> Nor worthy so bright beings to entertain,
> Nor fit compeer for such high company ;
> Yet was he surely born to them in mind,
> Their youngest nursling of the spirit's kind.
>   Last stole this one,
> With timid glance, of watching eyes adread,
> And dropped his frightened flower when all were gone ;
> And where the frail flower fell, it witheréd.
> But yet methought those high souls smiled thereon ;
> As when a child, upstraining at your knees
> Some fond and fancied nothings, says, " I give you these."

Of the first notion for this poem's title, " Amphicypellon," he wrote :—

" It refers to the ἀμφικυπελλον which Hephaestus, in Homer, bears round to the gods when he acts as cup-bearer by way of joke. When Schliemann's things from Troy were first exhibited at South Kensington, I remember seeing among them a drinking-cup labelled ' Perhaps the *amphicypellon* of Homer.' It was a boat-shaped cup of plain gold, open at the top and with a crescentic aperture at either extremity of the rim, through which the wine could either be poured or drunk. So that you could pour from either end, and (if the cup were *brimmed* with wine) two people could have drunk from it at the same time, one at either extremity. In a certain sense, therefore, it was a double cup. And it had also two handles, one at either of its boat-shaped sides, so that it was a two-handled cup. You will see at once why I have applied the name to my double poem."

Later this title was abandoned :—

" Let it be 'Sister Songs' as you suggest. But keep ' an offering to two sisters' where it now is—on the title page. 'Sister Songs' was my own first alteration of the title, but was dropped I hardly know why."

One of his first articles after he left his always beloved Storrington was the notice of General Booth's *In Darkest England*. Called "Catholics in Darkest England," and signed "Francis Tancred," it appeared in *Merry England* for January 1891. Mr. Stead, in the *Review of Reviews*, wrote :—

" Tancred sounds a bugle-blast which, it is hoped, will ring through the Catholic ranks not only in England, but in all Catholic Christendom. After speaking highly of General Booth and his large, daring, and comprehensive scheme, he points out that it will of necessity lead to the proselytising of neglected Catholics. He, therefore, cries aloud for the creation of a Catholic Salvation Army, or rather, for the utilisation of the Franciscans, Regulars and Tertiaries, for the purpose of social salvation."

" Mr. Francis Tancred " received from Mr. Stead the following letter :—

" *January* 12, 1891.

" DEAR SIR,—I beg to forward you herewith a copy of the *Review of Reviews*, in which you will find your admirable article quoted and briefly commented upon. Permit me to say that I read your article with sincere admiration and heartfelt sympathy, and that it delighted the Salvation Army people at headquarters more than anything that has appeared for a long time. 'That man can write,' said Bramwell Booth to me, and I think he sincerely grudges your pen to the Catholic Church.—I am, yours truly,   W. T. STEAD." [1]

Cardinal Manning [2] thereupon summoned Francis through my father, who was the Cardinal's friend, and to this single meeting Francis alludes in "To the Dead Cardinal of Westminster," a poem written, when, a year later, 1892, Manning died. Of this, A. M. has written :—

" In 1892 his editor asked him for a poem on Cardinal Manning, just dead, whom the poet had once visited; surely never was a poem 'to order' so greatly and originally inspired. I have alluded to days of deep depression in Francis Thompson's life, and they occurred now and then, with fairly cheerful intervals, at this time. It was in the grief and terror of such a day that he wrote 'To the dead Cardinal of Westminster,' which is a poem rather on himself than on the dead, an all but despairing presage of his own decease, which, when sixteen years later it came, brought no despair."

Claiming the ear of the dead, because the Cardinal asked the poet to go often to him, he writes in a first version of the poem :—

> I saw thee only once,
> Although thy gentle tones
> Said soft :—
> " Come hither oft."

---

[1] There perished with Mr. Stead in the *Titanic* disaster in 1912 a Catholic priest, who had, shortly before sailing, recommended "The Hound of Heaven " (with the strangely significant line " Adown Titanic glooms of chasméd fears ") to a friend, as an antidote to decadent poetry.

[2] At this time he met another Cardinal, then without his Hat, who knew his people in Manchester. There were many pauses when the talk turned to his home. Francis, untamable in shabbiness, even to the point of rags, explained afterwards: " I did not like to dwell on the subject, lest he should discover that I was in poor circumstances. You see he corresponds with my father." But his father did, of course, already know of his need. A letter, dated April 1892, from Bishop Carroll, runs :—

" MY DEAR MR. MEYNELL,—Francis Thompson's father has agreed to give me a small sum weekly (3s. 6d.) for his son. I have consented to forward it, and will do so monthly, adding a little myself. I now enclose a cheque for 24s. It is not much, but it will help.—Ever yours sincerely,
                                           J. CARROLL."

The Discovery

Therefore my spirit clings
Heaven's porter by the wings,
    And holds
    Its gated golds

Apart, with thee to press
A private business ;
    Whence
    Deign me audience.

Your singer did not come
Back to that stern, bare home : [1]
    He knew
    Himself and you.

I saw, as seers do,
That you were even you ;
    And—why,
    I too was I.

In that, as in " The Fallen Yew "—

> " I take you to my inmost heart, my true ! "
> Ah fool ! but there is one heart you
> Shall never take him to !—

his theme is one that often pressed home upon him :—

" There is such goodwill to impart, and such goodwill to receive, that each threatens to become the other, but the law of individuality collects its secret strength ; you are you and I am I, and so we remain."

These concluding words are transcribed with a suppressed verse of " To the Dead Cardinal of Westminster " —a verse suppressed, I imagine, because its poetry was not approved rather than because it committed its author to a too definite theory of Individualism. While he marks the impenetrability of mind and mind, he writes

---

[1] The old Archbishop's House in Carlisle Place.

hotly nevertheless of the Political Economist's Individualism :—

"For diabolical this doctrine of Individualism is ; it
is the outcome of the proud teaching which declares it
despicable for men to bow before their fellow-men.
It has meant, not that a man should be individual, but
that he should be independent. Now this I take to be
an altogether deadly lie. A man *should* be individual,
but not independent. The very laws of Nature forbid
independence. . . . Independent, he puts forth no
influence ; he is sterile as the sands of the desert.
For it is little less than an immutable ordinance
throughout the universe that without intercommunion
nothing is generated. The plant may reproduce on
itself, but if you would rise above mere vegetation, or
the lowest forms of animal life, there can be no true
hermaphroditism ; aye, even in the realm of Mind,
'male and female created He them.' There is but one
thing you can do for yourself ; you can kill yourself.
Though you may try to live for yourself, you cannot,
in any permanence, live by yourself. You may rot by
yourself, if you will ; but that is not doing, it is ceasing."

Afterwards he was to learn even more strictly from
Patmore that the unit of the world has two persons.

As in the realm of Mind, so in the Spiritual. What
might seem the culmination of secret Individualism, the
Communion between Christ and the Soul, is made
universal in the Open Court of Catholicism. However
strict the segregation of Francis's spiritual experiences,
they were, save in some rare and awful moments of
estrangement, offered to Christ, through Christ to the
Church, through the Church to the men from whose
intercourse he found himself debarred. Tolstoy's "every
man in the depths of his soul has something he alone
comprehends, namely, his attitude towards God " is a
thought divinely expressed in the " Fallen Yew," but it is

The Discovery

only one aspect of the truth, as the single reflection in a looking-glass is but a single aspect of the thing before it. Second thoughts, like second mirrors, encircle and multiply the first impression.[1]

[1] At this time he wrote to W. M. of an article in *Merry England :*—
"The Franciscan article is decidedly good. But I am getting a little sick of this talk of 'individualism,' which only darkens counsel. The writer seems to mean by it not at all what it means to me—and, I think, to the Cardinal. What *he* calls regulated individualism many people would call Socialism. In fact, some Socialists claim the Franciscans as a Catholic and religious experiment in the direction of Socialism. It seems to me that you can juggle with words like 'individualism' to suit your own whims."

CHAPTER VI: LITERARY BEGINNINGS

THE discovery that a man cannot, with any permanence, live by himself was made after his experience in London and at Storrington. He had returned to my father's neighbourhood resolved, not only to be a poet, but to meet the social labours of journalism. This, the elbowing with other workers at a close-packed table in the private room where, every Thursday, my father produced with superhuman effort a fresh number of his *Weekly Register*, meant, much more than a visit to a Cardinal, a return to the humanities. He fell, with much talk, right into the thick of it. He was put to small tasks as much that he might be put out of train for talk as for the use he was. But no device was good enough to do that; set him to write and there would be endless conversation on nibs and paper, of what was advisable to write, what to ignore, of his readers' alleged susceptibilities, and his care for the paper's circulation. In the end after a hard day there might, or might not, be a "par" to show, or some doggerel not to show. To this last order belongs a later attempt to describe the frenzied atmosphere of work :—

> In short, with a papal
> Election for staple,
>   Were our inkpot a tun
> And our pen like a Maypole,
>   We'd never be done
> With leader, leaderette, pad, comment, and citing,
>   Nor I with this blighting
> Frenzy for jingles and jangles in-*iting*,

III

Literary Beginnings

And writing
And inditing
And exciting
And biting
My pencil, inviting
Inspiration and plighting
My hair into elf-locks most wild, and affrighting,
And *Registering*, and daying and nighting ;
Our readers
Delighting
With leaders
That Whiteing
Might envy before he found work more requiting.

The instant demands of the "busy day" he never learnt to supply, nor was he put at all seriously to the task of learning. He was too tedious a pupil for hurried masters. On one busy day, when his platitudes had been so long chanted that they had got written into the manuscripts of his distracted audience, he was put in charge of a visitor who could match all commonplaces with tumultuously brilliant talk. But it was Thompson's day. With numbers on his side—his repetitions came in hordes fit to annihilate opposition—he plodded through a long afternoon in another room with the silent saviour of the workers. To the dinner table he came with the bright eye of enthusiasm ; "I have never known G—— more brilliant," he explained in all honesty.

At times he would be sent for short visits to Crawley, whence he writes :—

"I began a letter to you last Wednesday, but it never got finished in consequence of the devotion with which I have since been working at a short article. Now that I feel on my feet again, I am longing to be back amongst you all. Touchstone, with the slightest alteration, voices my feelings about country life : ' Truly, shepherd, in respect of itself, it is a good life ; but in respect that

it is a shepherd's life, it is naught. In respect that it
is solitary, I like it very well ; but in respect that it is
private, it is a very vile life. Now in respect it is in the
fields, it pleaseth me well ; but in respect it is not in the
city, it is tedious.' I hope, nevertheless, that I shall not
see you long after I return. For I hope that before the
season gets too late you will yourself make your escape
from that infectious web of sewer rats called London.
I know how ill you were before I left ; and it is disgust-
ing to think that here am I, like the fat reed that rots
itself in ease on Lethe wharf, while you are hung up
body and soul for the benefit of the villainous blubber-
brained public. . . . The *Register* gave me a 'turn,' by
the way, last week. My eyes strayed carelessly across
the announcements of deaths, and suddenly saw—
' Monica Mary.' My heart stood still, I think. Of course
the next second I knew it must be some other Monica
Mary, not she who walks among the poppies—and the
restaurants. How, unwell as you must be, you have
managed to make such good work of the *Register* and
of *Merry England* I don't understand. *M. E.*, in particular, is an excellent number. There is not a poor article
in it—except my own, which is dull enough to please a
bishop. B.'s article I think the best of his that I have
seen. It is really very good, allowing for the fact that
it is essentially imitative writing. B., in fact, has
made to himself a pair of breeches from Mrs. Meynell's
cast-off petticoats. But it is cleverly done, and I did
not think B. had been tailor enough to do it. There
are really felicitous things in the article, though the art
of them *has* been caught from her. For instance, the
bit about the crops ' bearing their sheaves of spires,' the
transformation of the sheep-bells, the weeds putting on
' the solistic immortality of sculpture,' &c. At bottom,
doubtless, he has not much to say. But he has said it
so well—that it is a pity someone else could have said
it so much better.'

Literary Beginnings

Or, like as not, instead of to the country, he would be sent forth on some expedition with the children to whom he bore himself as a sweet and eager, though not from their point of view an exciting, companion. He would concentrate on companionable things, and we have him writing like the gravest sportsman and intentest child of skating in Kensington Gardens in the winter of 1891 :—

"DEAR MR. MEYNELL,—The discovery of what I have done to my own skates leads me to ask you to warn Monica next time she goes skating. If she wishes to preserve her skates, do not let her climb in them the bank of the Round Pond, where it is set with stones. Indeed, she ought not to go on the bank in her skates at all ; it is most destructive to them. For which reason, doubtless, I invariably do it myself. But you must make her understand I am like certain saints—that man of exalted piety, St. Simeon Stylites, for instance—to be admired for my sublime virtues, but not recommended for imitation. I forget how many feet of sublime virtue St. Simeon had ; mine defies arithmetic. Monica can already skate backwards a little—I can't. She can do the outside edge a little—I can't. It is true that her mode of terminating the latter stroke is to sit down rapidly on the ice ; but this is a mere individualism of technique. It is a mannerism which, as she advances in her art, she will doubtless prune in favour of a severer style ; but all youthful artists have their little luxuriances. Let me thank you for your kindness in trusting the children to me. Or shall I say trusting me to them? For on reflection, I have a haunting suspicion that Monica managed the party with the same energy she devotes to her skating. Do not infer hence that she tyrannised over me. On the contrary, both she and Cuckoo were most solicitously anxious lest I should mar my own pleasure in attending to theirs. A needless anxiety, since I desired nothing better than to play with them."

In Kensington Gardens

Thus the fellowships he was learning at the work table were supplemented by younger friendships. There was no angel to pluck them from him by the hair; no printer's boy to pluck his sleeve when he would attend elsewhere, save when he carried his work to Kensington Gardens and admonitory nurse-maids doubted him :—

"The notice of Mr. Yeats is my absolute opinion : indeed I have reined in a little of the warmth of language to which I was disposed, lest my pleasure and surprise should betray me into extreme praise. If the reviews are not very brilliant, you must excuse me if you can, for I myself am not very brilliant just now. Fact is, the dearest child has made friends with me in the park; and we have fallen in love with each other with an instantaneous rapidity not unusual on my side, but a good deal more unusual on the child's. I rather fancy she thinks me one of the most admirable of mortals ; and I firmly believe her to be one of the most daintily supernatural of fairies. And now I am in a fever lest (after the usual manner of fairies) her kinsfolk should steal her from me. Result—I haven't slept for two nights, and I fear I shall not recover myself until I am resolved whether my glimpses of her are to be interdicted or not. Of course in some way she is sure to vanish—elves always do, and my elves in particular."

For the New Year, 1890, he offered his compliments in the letter and little fairy-tale that follow. They will be understood by everyone who knew how my father tended the needs of others :—

"DEAR MR. MEYNELL,—I have imagined at times that in certain moments you may be inclined to have certain thoughts, just as I myself have fits in which I see the black side of everything. Will you pardon if I have not surmised them truly, and pardon me also for what is perhaps, I fear, the impertinence of sending you the enclosed little bit ? As a matter of fact it was just an attempt to put into a sentence or two what I was thinking this New Year's Eve ; when I pondered on the great work I discern you to have done, and still to be doing. I hope that many a New Year to come will see you~spreading it ; and wish I could be your right hand in it ; not the clog I am. On account of your services to the Angelic Art in particular, I am sure the angels must be rehearsing a special chorus for you in Paradise. I thought so when I read Miss Probyn's poem. May they sprinkle every stone in your house.—Ever most truly your   FRANCIS THOMPSON."

The " enclosed little bit " was :—

" Within the mid girth of banyan was the banyan-spirit, all an-ache with heavy heaving through the years ; and he was saddened, because he doubted to what end his weary pain of them had been. For beyond his trunk the banyan spirit looked not. While without, the great grove hailed him sire ; and from every bird nestling among its thousand branches, Heaven's ear heard *his* voice."

In 1891, at the birth of my brother Francis, he wrote to W. M. :—

" I hardly, I fear, gave you even commonplace thanks for the favour you conferred on me in choosing me for your little son's godfather. Even now I am utterly unable to express to you what I feel regarding it ; I can only hope that you may comprehend without words. As for the quietness with which I took it on Saturday—for the premeditated of emotion in speech I have an instinctive horror which, I think, you share sufficiently to understand and excuse in me. Besides, the words which one might use have been desiccated, fossilised, by those amiable persons who not only use

A Wandering Contributor

the heart as a sleeve-ornament, but conspicuously label it—'This is a Heart.' One can only, like Cordelia, speak by silence.

"Give my love to Monicella, and Cuckoo, and all the children. As for F. M. M., I doubt the primitive egoism is still too new in him for him to care a baby-rattle about my love."

That he carried in his "copy" a day late mattered little; that he then further delayed it by some accident seemed serious only to himself, and he would write thus to W. M. :—

"I called at Palace Court on Friday, and, finding you were gone, started to follow you. Unfortunately I fell into composition on the way, and when I next became conscious of matters sublunary, found myself wandering about somewhere in the region of Smithfield Market, and the time late in the afternoon. I am heartily sorry for my failure to keep my appointment, and hope you will forgive me. I thought I had disciplined myself out of these aberrations, which makes me feel all the more vexed about the matter.—Always your   F. T."

Or, still more distressed :—

"I don't know what I shall do, or what you shall do. I haven't been able to write a line, through sheer nervousness and fright. Confound Canon Carroll! It is he who has put me into this state. I wish you had never incumbered yourself with me. I am more in a condition to sit down and go into hysterics like a girl than to write anything. I know how vexed and impatient you must feel to hear this from me, when you had expected to have the thing from me this morning. Indeed I feel that you have already done too much for me ; and that it would be better you should have nothing more to do with me. You have already displayed a patience and tenderness with me that my kindred would never have displayed ; and it is most unjust that I should any longer be a burden to you. I think I am fit for nothing : certainly not fit to be any longer the object of your too great kindness. Please understand that I entirely feel, and am perfectly resigned to the ending of an experiment which even your sweetness would never have burdened yourself with, if you could have foreseen the consequences. F. T."

With such fits my father made it his business to deal, and this he did with a persuasiveness and love that I think no other man could have summoned. But for his peculiar power F. T. would have returned to the streets.[1]

At Friston, in Suffolk,

> Summer set lip to earth's bosom bare,
> And left the flushed print in a poppy there.

At Friston he was given the poppy and wrote the poem. I remember him as measuring himself, on the borders of a marsh, against a thistle, the fellow to that which stands six foot out of Sussex turf in "Daisy"; I see him with the poplars on the marshes, and associate him with a picnic on the Broads among pine-cones and herons. I think it is he I see coming in at the farmgate dusty from a road still bright in the dusk. But the recollections are elusive. His place in childish memories is not defined, like that of Brin, the friend who hit a ball over the farm roof, of the chicken pecking at the dining-room floor, a sister's first steps, the boy who twisted the cows' tails as he drove the cattle up from the pastures at night; and better remembered is the hard old man who, stooping over his work in the vegetable garden, suddenly rose up and threw a stone as big as a potato at a truant boy. The boy and man,

[1] In after years Francis wrote letters that seemed to supply no possible opening for the comforter. Read to-day, their desperation offers no outlet but a return to the streets. But no sooner did F. T. come into my father's presence, than he was consoled, often without the exchange of a word.

In the Land of Flag-lilies

the cry of the one and the grunted curses of the other, and their remorseless manner of settling again to work, were things for a London child to marvel at. But the poet, himself as gentle as children, is remembered, and remembered vaguely, as part of the general gentle world. Others are remembered for competence, for large authority, the freedom of their coming and going, their businesses, affluence, dreariness, or laughter ; they are the substantial people, more substantial than the people of to-day.

There was a certain mightiness about them, like that of a mighty actor ; but Francis Thompson is not in the cast. Moreover, he is not among the insufferable "supers" who held one's hand too long or whose aspect was abhorrent to the fastidious eye of youth. In my earlier memories he is as unsubstantial as the angel I knew to be at my shoulder. Looking back I cannot see either clearly, but am not incredulous on that account.

But however insignificant he may have been in the injudicious view of a boy, he was of consequence to the farm housewife, who could never bring herself to call him anything but " Sir Francis."

There is more of Friston and the Monica of "The Poppy " in later verses :—

> In the land of flag-lilies,
> Where burst in golden clangours
> The joy-bells of the broom,
> You were full of willy-nillies,
> Pets, and bee-like angers :
> Flaming like a dusky poppy,
> In a wrathful bloom.
>
> .   .   .   .   .   .
>
> Yellow were the wheat-ways,
> The poppies were most red ;
> And all your meet and feat ways,
> Your sudden bee-like snarlings,
> Ah, do you remember,
> Darling of the darlings ?
>
> .   .   .   .   .

Literary Beginnings

Now at one, and now at two,
Swift to pout and swift to woo,
The maid I knew :
Still I see the duskèd tresses—
But the old angers, old caresses ?
Still your eyes are autumn thunders,
But where are *you*, child, you ?   ⌡

My father, before the idea of a published volume had taken shape, sewed up into booklets a few copies of the poems already printed in *Merry England*. One copy was sent by a common friend to Tennyson, who gave thanks, through his son, thus briefly :—

" DEAR MR. SNEAD-COX,—Thanks for letting us see the vigorous poems.—Yours truly,   HALLAM TENNYSON."

Browning, on the other hand, who was a visitor at Palace Court and on whose ready sympathy for personal details my father would rely, wrote at generous length :—

" ASOLO, VENETO, ITALIA, *Oct.* 7, '89.

" DEAR MR. MEYNELL,—I hardly know how to apologise to you, or explain to myself how there has occurred such a delay in doing what I had an impulse to do as soon as I read the very interesting papers written by Mr. Thompson, and so kindly brought under my notice by yourself. Both the Verse and Prose are indeed remarkable—even without the particulars concerning their author, for which I am indebted to your goodness. It is altogether extraordinary that a young man so naturally gifted should need incitement to do justice to his own conspicuous ability by endeavouring to emerge from so uncongenial a course of life as that which you describe. Surely the least remunerating sort of ' literary life ' would offer advantages incompatible with the hardest of all struggles for existence, such as I take Mr. Thompson's to be. Pray assure him, if he cares to know it, that I have a confident expectation of his success, if he will but extricate himself—as by a strenuous effort he may—from all that must now embarrass him terribly. He can have no better friend and adviser than yourself—except *himself*, if he listens to the inner voice. " Pray offer my best thanks to Mrs. Meynell for her remem-

Browning's Letter

brance of me—who am, as she desires, profiting by the quiet and beauty of this place—whence, however, I shall soon depart for Venice, on my way homeward.[1] I gather, from the absence of anything to the contrary in your letter, that all is well with you— and so may it continue! I do not forget your old kindliness, though we are so much apart in London ; and you must account me always, dear Mr. Meynell, as yours cordially,

ROBERT BROWNING."

F. T. to W. M. :—

"I have received Mr. Sharp's new *Life of Browning*, which reminds me to do what I have been intending to do for a long time past; but whenever I wrote to you, my mind was always occupied with something else which put the subject out of my head. I had better do it now, for even my unready pen will say better what I wish to say than would my still more unready tongue. It is simply that I wanted to tell you how deeply I was moved by the reading of Browning's letter in *Merry England*. When you first mentioned it to me you quoted loosely a single sentence ; and I answered, I think, something to the effect that I was very pleased by what he had said. So I was ; pleased by what I thought his kindliness, for (misled by the form in which you had quoted the sentence from memory) I did not take it more seriously than that. When I saw *Merry England* I perceived that the original sentence was insusceptible of the interpretation which I had placed upon your quotation of it. And the idea that in the closing days of his life my writings should have been under his eye, and he should have sent me praise and encouragement, is one that I shall treasure to the closing days of *my* life. To say that I owe this to you is to say little. I have already told you that long before I had seen you, you exercised, unknown to myself, the most decisive influence over my mental development when without such

---

[1] Browning left Asolo at the end of October, and died in Venice early in December.

an influence my mental development was like to have
utterly failed. And so to you I owe not merely
Browning's notice, but also that ever I should have been
worth his notice. The little flowers you sent him were
sprung from your own seed. I only hope that the time
may not be far distant when better and less scanty
flowers may repay the pains, and patience, and tenderness of your gardening."

The poems as they appeared in *Merry England* or in
journals quoting *Merry England* found notable adherents.
"The Making of Viola" was re-printed by Miss
Katharine Tynan in 1892 in a Dublin paper, to which
she contributed a London letter, and it was in that
form that Mr. Garvin, to be later the poet's inspiring
critic and friend, first chanced upon Thompson. A
leader-writer on the *Newcastle Daily Chronicle*, he found
that "up in the north here, if one has a passion for the
finer letters, one must possess his insulated soul in
silence." After reading "The Making of Viola" ("I
cannot tell you," he wrote to W. M. from Newcastle,
"what I think of the angelic ingenuousness of that
poem ; it exercised over me an instant fascination from
which I never shall escape") he heard nothing more of
Thompson till the publication of *Poems*. His welcome
of that volume is quoted in another page. *Poems*
came to him while he was writing "leaders," and his
brother, already Thompson-mad, declaimed "The Hound
of Heaven" beside a desk where politics and poetry have
fought hotly for the field, and where they have been
known to embrace as unexpectedly as Botticelli's angels
and shepherds. "I was obdurate and a little irritated
when these 'snatches of Uranian antiphon' broke
grandly through my comments on the Russo-German
commercial treaty, or Professor Garner's theories about
the garrulous gorilla." One marvels that the garrulous gorilla leader was perfectly intelligible in next

Enter Mr. Garvin

morning's *Chronicle.* Mr. Garvin's readers could not guess that Thompson's poems were already beginning "to swarm in his head like bees." He contrives to write about treaties, or make them, so that half the world knows nothing of the winged muse at his elbow. She herself may have sometimes thought him obdurate, for she has never yet succeeded in marring a "leader." Letters from Mr. Garvin, written ten years later, were kept among Francis's few valued possessions. The two were to meet at Palace Court in 1894 and at many other dates.

My father had also the satisfaction of printing several of the poems ("Daisy, A Song of Youth and Age" and "To my Godchild") in his anthology, *The Child set in the Midst, by Modern Poets*, the first book in which anything of F. T.'s had appeared. Thus to W. M. in his preface fell the task of writing of him as one "who has eluded fame as long as Shelley did, but cannot elude it longer. To most readers the poems will come as the revelation of a new personality in poetry, the last discovered of the Immortals."

Francis's own chronicle of the period is found in a letter to Canon Carroll, a middle-man to whom he could write with somewhat less difficulty than to his family :—

"A.D. 1890. Finished *August* 12. Begun, Heaven knows when.
[May 1890.]

"DEAR CANON,—I must beg your and everybody's pardon for my long silence. The fact is that I have been for months in a condition of acute mental misery, frequently almost akin to mania, stifling the production of everything except poetry, and rendering me quite incapable of sane letter-writing. It has ended in my return to London, and I am immensely relieved; for the removal of the opium had quite destroyed my power of bearing the almost unbroken solitude in which I found myself. As for my prospects, unfortunately the

123

Literary Beginnings

walls of the Protestant periodical press remain still unshaken and to shake. I have done recently a review of Lilly's *Century of Revolution* for the *Register*, which has, I fancy, appeared, but in some number which I have not seen. Poor work, and I don't want to see it. Also a review of Mr. Sharp's recent *Life of Browning*, which may or may not appear in the *Register*—it is only just finished. No doubt you saw in the famous January *Merry England* Browning's letter about me. It is, I see, alluded to in Mr. Sharp's *Life*. Sharp's book has been remarkably successful, no doubt because it has come out just during the Browning boom, and has no rival. But it is badly written, and therefore very difficult to review. As for the verses published in this month's *Merry England*, don't know why they were published at all. Mr. Meynell told me himself that he did not care particularly for them, because they were too like a poem of Mrs. Browning's. (You will find the poem—a poem on Pan making a pipe out of a reed—where it first appeared, namely, in one of your two old volumes of the *Cornhill Magazine*. There I read it; and it is a great favourite of mine. The last two stanzas, with their sudden deeply pathetic turn of thought are most felicitous, I think.) The verses on Father Perry in last month's *Merry England* were the first verses of mine that attracted any praise from Catholic outsiders. An old priest wrote from Norwich expressing his admiration ; and Father Philip Fletcher also praised them to Mr. Meynell.

"This must have been grateful to Mr. Meynell, for his previous experience had been very different. Good Uncle Edward (whom I shall write to after you, now that I am taking up my arrears of correspondence) writing about my first two little poems, liked 'The Passion of Mary,' but used words about 'Dream Tryst' that usually bear a not very pleasant signification. Who do you think chose to put himself in a ferment about the 'Ode'? Canon T——! When the editor of the *Tablet* was in Manchester, Canon T—— attacked him about the article on me which appeared in that paper. What, he asked, was the 'Ode' all about? He couldn't in the least understand what it was all about. But even if he had understood it, he was quite sure that it was not a thing which ought to have appeared in a Catholic magazine! And Mr. Meynell subsequently received an anonymous letter, in which he was warned against publishing anything more of mine, since it would be found in the end that paganism was at the bottom of it. This with regard to me, who began my literary career with an elaborate indictment of the ruin which the re-introduction of the pagan spirit must bring upon poetry! As for the 'Song of the Hours,' to which you referred, Mr. Meynell was greatly pleased with it; but considered that while it avoided the violence of diction which deformed the 'Ode,' it was not equal to that in range of power.

.   .   .   .

"Since I wrote the foregoing pages a considerable time has elapsed. How long, I do not know, for they were written at intervals, and so were not dated. My health has been consistently bad; though I have had, and have, nothing definite the matter with me, except dyspepsia and constant colds. My writing powers have deserted me, and I have suffered failure after failure, till I have been too despondent to have any heart for writing to you. Much, no doubt, is due to this infernal weather. Confined to the house and deprived of sunlight, I droop like a moulting canary. It was not so when you knew me; but my vital power has been terribly sapped since then. Only air and exercise keep me going now. As to the literary enterprises alluded to in the early part of this letter, they have successively failed.

Literary Beginnings

"The lines on Father Perry have taken hold of *Merry England* readers as nothing of mine has done. Mr. Meynell had several letters from ecclesiastics (including one from the head of a monastery—I forget where or in what Order) expressing admiration of the poem; and the sub-editor of the *Tablet* had one from some priest in Liverpool. I meant the thing merely for a pretty, gracefully turned fancy; what the Elizabethans would have called an excellent conceit. That it is nothing more, I quite agree with Mr. Blackburn, whose judgment I much value. In the first place he generally represents Mrs. Meynell's judgment, who is his guide and friend in everything—and such a guide and friend no other young man in England has. In the second place he has an excellent judgment of his own. Of Mr. Meynell's opinion, I know merely that he dropped me a post-card saying the poem was 'very fine.'

"Another very small poem on Shelley, Mrs. Meynell has pronounced 'a little masterpiece.' The expression, however, may have been hastily and inaccurately reported by Mrs. Blackburn; I prefer to take it with caution. Another poem, a sonnet, I have heard nothing about; but I have never yet really succeeded with a sonnet. I did a little minor work on the *Tablet* during the editor's absence—part of the Chronicle of the Week, and two or three of the Notes, including a paragraph on Rudyard Kipling and a ferocious little onslaught on the trashy abomination which Swinburne has contributed to the *Fortnightly*. In last week's *Scots Observer* appeared an exquisite little poem by Mrs. Meynell—the first she has written since her marriage. A long silence, disastrous for literature! The poem is a perfect miniature example of her most lovelily tender work; and is, like all her best, of a signal originality in its central idea no less than in its development.

126

Prose in Embryo

"Most women of genius—George Eliot, Charlotte Brontë, and Mrs. Browning, who, indeed, alludes to her husband's penetration in seeing beyond 'this mask of me' —have been decidedly plain. That Mrs. Meynell is not like them you may judge from 'Her Portrait.' Nor will she attain any rapid notice like them. Her work is of that subtly delicate order which—as with Coleridge, for instance—needs to soak into men for a generation or two before it gets adequate recognition. Nevertheless it is something to have won the admiration of men like Rossetti, Ruskin, and, shall I add, the immortal Oscar Wilde ? (A witty, paradoxical writer, who, nevertheless, *meo judicio*, will do nothing permanent because he is in earnest about nothing.) Known or unknown, she cares as little as St. Francis de Sales would have cared what might become of his writings.

"At present my prose article is like a lady about whom Mr. Blackburn told me—renowned for her malapropisms. A friend met her in Paris, and was about to address her when the lady put up her hand : 'Hush, don't recognise me ! I am travelling in embryo.' So is my prose article. And now I think this letter should be big enough to cover a multitude of sins of omission in my correspondence. I see that you and a number of our friends were at Ushaw for the Exhibition week. The death of my old master, Mr. Formby, to which you referred in your postcard, I saw in the *Register*. I was deeply sorry. Wishing not to bring myself under anyone's notice until I felt my position more assured, I had abstained from following my first impulse, which was to send him a copy of the magazine containing my 'Ode,' and accompanying it by a letter. Now I wish I had pocketed pride, and done so. Not knowing my circumstances, he may have thought I had forgotten him. But I had not forgotten him, as I will venture to think he had not forgotten me.

"With best love to my father, and to Polly when you

next may see her (Maggie, I suppose, will by this time be beyond the reach of messages), I remain, yours affectionately,   FRANCIS THOMPSON.

" *P.S.*—My address is still that given at the beginning of this letter, which is so enormous that I shall have to send it in two envelopes. I am afraid that you will have to read it by easy stages, unless you subdivide labour by calling in your curate. By the way, I spoke of my lines on Shelley as being risky for a Catholic audience. Let me explain the reason, lest you should suppose something worse. They are founded on a letter given in Trelawny's *Recollections*—a letter from Jane Williams to Shelley two days before his death. The poem is put into the mouth of the dead Shelley, and is supposed to be addressed by the poet's spirit to Jane while his body is tossing on the waters of Spezzia. Now Jane Williams was a married woman. I have carefully avoided anything which might not be addressed by one warm friend to another ; but Catholic readers (witness Canon T——) are apt to shy sometimes at shadows. . . . When a poet writes love-verses to a lady, and gives them to her husband for her, it is surely evident that neither pistols nor the divorce court are necessary. Now that is what Shelley did."

To Pantasaph in Wales, where he lodged at the gates of the Capuchin Monastery, he went early in 1892. His first business was the passing of *Poems* for the press. Busy over the proof sheets, he writes in answer to some suggestions of my father's as to the dedication :—

" I cannot consent to the withdrawal of *your* name. You have of course the right to refuse to accept the dedication to yourself. But in that case I have the right to withdraw the dedication altogether, as I should certainly do. I should belie the truth and my own feelings if I represented Mrs. Meynell as the sole person to

The Clogged Wheels Move

whom I owe what it has been given to me to accomplish in poetry. Suffer this—the sole thing, as unfortunate necessities of exclusion would have it, which links this first, possibly this only volume, with your name—suffer this to stand. I will feel deeply hurt if you refuse me this gratification."

A slight difficulty in sight, he writes on the impulse:—

"I find Lane has already announced the poems in his book-list, so I am bound to go through with them; else I would let them go to the devil. I made myself ill with over-study, and have been obliged to give my head three weeks' entire rest. But I am much better again now. Inwardly I suffer like old Nick; but the blessed mountain air keeps up my body, and for the rest—my Lady Pain and I are *au mieux*. I send you two or three odd bits of verse; but I hardly think you will find anything in them. . . . The country here is just beginning to get beautiful, and I am feeling the first quickening pulse of spring. Lord, it is good for me to be here—very good. The clogged wheels in me are slowly beginning to move."

The proofs reached him by way of Palace Court:—

"47 PALACE COURT, *July* 19, 1893.

"MY DEAR FRANCIS,—I am very glad that Mr. Lane asked me to send you the first pages of the book—your poems, to which Wilfrid and I have so long looked forward. It is a great happiness to me to do so. . . . I cannot express to you how beautiful your poems are.—Always, my dear child, your affectionate

ALICE MEYNELL."

And again, in August, my mother writes:—

"Here are your wonderful poems—most wonderful and beautiful. It is a great event to me to send you these proofs. You will, I trust, change the title, 'The Dead of Westminster.' People will think of nothing but Westminster Abbey. Please send me the revises, sixteen pages at a time."

Literary Beginnings

F. T. to A. M. concerning final suggestions made in proof by Coventry Patmore and my parents :—

" DEAR MRS. MEYNELL,—I have received the finding of the Court Martial over which you presided ; to which the undersigned begs to make answer, in form and manner following—

" 1. To the first indictment he pleadeth guilty, and knows not how he omitted to alter the word, as had been his own intention. He begs, therefore, that for ' soilured ' may be substituted ' stealthwon.'

" 2. In answer to the third indictment he submits himself to the judgment of the court, and desires that *Domus Tua* shall be omitted, and the requisite alteration made in the numbering of the poems.

" 3. In regard to the second indictment, having already considered the matter, he refuseth to submit himself to the court, remaineth *en contumace*, and is prepared, in token of his unalterable resolution, to suffer the utmost rigours of the critics."

And he continues, all on account of a misprinted comma in a magazine :—

" Now I carry the war into the enemy's country.

" I do claim to wit that a foul and malicious alteration has been committed on the body of our King Phœbus' lieges, in a magazine bearing the style and denomination of *Merry England*. And I hereby warn you, that if the same outrage is extended to the same unoffending poem in my volume, I shall hold you all and severally responsible. Hereunder follow the details of my accusation. There should be no fresh stanza and no stop after ' fertilise.' The pause should come after ' impregnating ' in the previous line ; and then the next lines run on (as in the corrected pages I returned on Thursday) :

> For flowers that night-wings fertilise
> Mock down the stars' unsteady eyes, &c.

A Boast of Intimacy

"The meaning (which I must have perfectly clear) is that flowers which are fertilised by night-insects confront the moon and stars with a glance more sleepless and steady than their own. Surely anyone who knows a forest from a flower-pot is aware that flowers which are fertilised by night-insects necessarily open at night, and emit at night their odours by which those insects are attracted. The lines unfortunately altered are, in fact, explanatory of the image which has gone before.

"But I sometimes wonder whether the best of you Londoners do not regard nature as a fine piece of the Newlyn School, kindly lent by the Almighty for public exhibition. Few seem to realise that she is alive, has almost as many ways as a woman, and is to be lived with, not merely looked at. People are just as bad here for that matter. I am sick of being told to go here and to go there, because I shall have 'a splendid view.' I protest against nature being regarded as on view. If a man told me to take a three-quarter view of the woman I loved because I should find her a fine composition, I fear I should incline to kick him extremely, and ask whether he thought her five feet odd of canvas. Having companioned nature in her bed-chamber no less than her presence room, what I write of her is not lightly to be altered."[1]

He is a Gascon for boasting his knowledge of Nature's bed-chamber; but he had some reason. In Wales he slept a night in the woods. Daring, he entered. One night means much for such as hold eternity in an hour. For Francis, any single sunrise opened a Day of Creation, and any sunset awoke in him a comprehension of finality and death, of rebirth and infinity. The increase and decrease of darkness, the lights of diminishing and

---

[1] For all that, Mr. Wilfrid Blunt, who walked over his own acres with Thompson as his guest, wrote :—" He could not distinguish the oak from the elm, nor did he know the name of the commonest flowers of the field."

approaching day, were crowded into that single performance.

" What you say of your night in the woods," writes Mrs. Hamilton King, " is interesting. But it needed courage. I should never expect to sleep in a wood at night. The wood sleeps by day and wakes by night, and this grows more and more terrible and true as you approach the tropical forest, where no man alone can survive the night. ' At night all the beasts of the forest do move,' as the Psalmist says."

" In regard to the alterations I now enclose to you in the 'Fallen Yew,' by the correction of two words I hope that I have removed the obscurity, grammatical and otherwise. In 'Monica Thought Dying' I have simply substituted ' eleven ' for 'thirteen.' The word ' eleven ' fits the metre perfectly well without altering the rest of the line ; since the final ' e ' is a natural elision. Most elisions are artificial and conscious. Such is the elision of the ' a ' in ' seraph,' whereby the line in the ' Fallen Yew ' *does* scan, and so needs no alteration on that score. But there are a few words wherein we make unconscious elision, even in daily conversation. The final ' en ' after a ' v ' we always so elide ; and consequently it is the exception for a poet to count the final ' en ' in such words as ' heaven,' ' seven,' or ' eleven.' "

It is almost the rule that the author on the point of publishing should flout his public :—

" As for ' immeditatably ' it is in all respects the one and only right word for the line ; as regards the exact shade of meaning and feeling, and as regards the rhythmical movement it gives to the line. So it must absolutely and without any question stand—woe's me for the public ! But indeed, what is the public doing *dans cette galère ?* I believe, it is true, the public has an odd kind of prejudice that poems are written for its benefit. It might as well suppose that when a woman loves, she bears children for its benefit ; or (in the case of the poem in question) that when a man is hurt, he bleeds for its benefit."

The Flouted Public

But whether he will or not, he bleeds and writes for mankind. If he stands by his "immeditatably," it is only because he knows that the public will come to stand by it too. He chooses to be obstinate on behalf of someone who waits for the word. In flouting his public, the poet is like a man who, scattering sweets for children, tosses them away only that they shall be recovered; or, hiding them, is distressed if they are not found. Thompson put his sweets in difficult places; but only that he and the others might have the keener recreation.

After more sheets had been corrected and returned to Palace Court, he writes :—

"It seems to me that they read better than I had expected—particularly the large additions to 'To a Poet Breaking Silence,'[1] which were written at a time when I was by no means very fit for poetry. Your interest in the volume is very dear to me. I cannot say I myself feel any elation about it. I am past the time when such things brought me any elation.

"I have not either of your books,[2] and of course should most greatly value them. I need not say how deeply I rejoice at your success."

[1] The poem by which my mother broke silence was " Veni Creator."
[2] Among the things he wrote when A. M.'s book came to hand is this of "Domus Angusta," an essay they had discussed before. " Never again meditate the suppression of your gloomy passages. It is a most false epithet for anything you could ever write. You might as well impeach of gloominess my favourite bit in ' Timon,' with the majestic melancholy of its cadence—

> ' My long sickness
> Of wealth and living now begins to mend,
> And nothing brings me all things.'

Both that passage and yours are poignant; both are deeply sad; while yours has an added searchingness which makes it (in De Quincey's phrase) veritably 'heart-shattering'; but how can you call 'gloomy' what so nobly and resignedly faces the terror it evokes?"

47 PALACE COURT

CHAPTER VII: "POEMS"

IN 1893 Messrs. Elkin Mathews and John Lane published *Poems*, a square book in brown boards with gold circles and a frontispiece by Laurence Housman. The poet viewed it with pleasure, and elsewhere the praise and blame it received were both wholehearted :—

"Many thanks for the copies. The book is indeed beautifully got up," he writes. "I have to thank you for the *Chronicle* and to thank Mr. Le Gallienne for his article. Such unselfish enthusiasm in a young poet for the work of a brother poet is as rare as it is graceful in these times, when most *littérateurs* have adopted the French author's maxim : 'There are no writers of genius except myself and a few friends—and I am not certain about my friends.'"

And later :—

"I have read in the *Register* with great surprise that the first edition is exhausted. I am even more glad for my publisher's sake than for my own. The *St. James's* article, as unusually appreciative as that of the *Chronicle*, I am very pleased with."

Recurring, in another letter to W. M., to Mr. Le Gallienne's *Chronicle* article, he writes :—

"When the first whirl of language is over (was it not a sin of my own former prose when I waxed enthusiastic?) he settles down to appreciation which is at the

same time criticism. Will it be believed, however, that
after deprecating superlatives I am actually disposed to
rank myself higher than Mr. Le Gallienne's final sentence
might seem to imply. I absolutely think that my poetry
is 'greater' than any work by a new poet which has
appeared *since Rossetti*. Unless, indeed, the greater work
to which the critic referred was Mrs. Meynell's. I
frankly admit that her poetry has exquisite unclamorous
qualities beside which all the fireworks of my own are
much less enduring things. Otherwise, I will not vail
my crest to Henley, or Robert Bridges, or even William
Watson. For the rest I have nothing but warm and
surprised gratitude for your untiring efforts on my
behalf. I am very pleased with all the letters you have
sent me, particularly Vincent O'Sullivan's from Oxford.
Am I going to found a school there?

" The minor versifier has at any rate the asterisks in
a 'Judgment in Heaven' which he can catch on to.
There he can have the latest device in poetry, the whole
apparatus procurable at my printer's. I have not forgotten that it was Le Gallienne's admiration for the
specimen sent to Lane which finally decided the publication of my book; and I should indeed be sorry to
know that I had repaid him by wounding his feelings.

F. T."

In part his was but a share in the general welcome
then accorded to the poets. Davidson was being hailed
with intense zest; Norman Gale himself, singing amid
applause, offered congratulations and a review to F. T.
Only with the appearance of *Sister Songs* and *New
Poems* was he roundly and viciously abused. But
already round the standard of " An Old Fogey " (Andrew
Lang), raised in the *Contemporary Review*, February 1894,
à propos of " The Young Men," there was a considerable
gathering. From the press cuttings of the year a good
crop may be got of such sentences as :—

He Reads the Reviews

" I must agree with Mr. L.'s judgment of Mr. Francis Thompson. His faults are fundamental. Though he uses the treasure of the Temple, he is not a religious poet. The note of a true spiritual passion never once sounds in his book. . . . He owes much to the perseverance of Mr. and Mrs. Meynell and the Catholics whom they influence." [1]

It fell to a critic on the *Westminster Gazette* to do the out and out "slating." Leading off with quotations from "A Judgment in Heaven," he asks "Is it poetry? is it sense? is it English?" His case, with such phrases as "Supportlessly congest" well to the fore, was good. Quoting "To My God-child" as a happier example, he concluded, "This, too, is somewhat wild, but it means something."

"The poet of a small Catholic clique" was a description given by one of the two or three writers who constituted the opposition to his claims to a great place in English literature. They all made a common discovery—Francis Thompson was a Catholic.

" We had," said the *Weekly Register*, " Mr. de Vere, Mr. Wilfrid Blunt, Mrs. Hamilton King, Mr. Coventry Patmore, to name no others. We need not then have awaited Mr. Thompson's arrival to undermine the Press of England in the interests of ' Sectarianism ' ! "

It came to pass that this poet of fewest friends was

---

[1] His work having appeared in a Catholic magazine, it was known to the Catholic papers. Apart from the *Weekly Register*, where notices of his periodical writings were printed, priority belongs to *The Tablet*, which printed, September, 1889, and 19th July, 1890, serious notices of the issues of *Merry England* containing the " Ode to the Setting Sun " and " The Hound of Heaven "; and to Miss Katharine Tynan, who quoted the whole of " The Making of Viola " from *Merry England*, May, 1892, in the *Irish Independent* in the course of the same month. The Catholic papers made no particular sign of welcome when the books themselves were published, but it may be noted that the *Ave Maria*, Notre Dame, Indiana, had praise for the much-abused extravagance of the opening of the " Corymbus for Autumn." To the *Catholic World*, February, 1895, Mr. Walter Lecky contributed many compliments and several biographical inaccuracies. In the secular press of America F. T. fared less well. *The New York Post*, 19th of January, 1898, found his work ". . . not altogether hopeful, since his impulses are wayward, like his life." *The Critic*, July, 1894, would by no means allow Browning's phrase, " conspicuous abilities," to pass unchallenged.

charged not only with log-rolling, but with belonging
to a "clique" that had its headquarters at Palace Court.
The fact was that his few friends were even shyer than
his friends' friends of praising him publicly. One young
reviewer (the "Vernon" already mentioned) came at the
stroke of morning's eight to shout through their bedroom doors his new discovered joy—a poem in *Merry
England* by F. T. "I know at last," was his loud confidence, "that there is a poet who may worthily take a
place as Shakespeare's second." But in the papers this
critic's notices were very halting : his praises did not
call through the press as they did through the key-
hole. The "clique" is proved in his notice the most
unprofitable and unfriendly of companies. In Henley's
National Observer he writes :—

"Mr. Francis Thompson is a young poet of considerable parts,
whose present danger lies in the possibility of his spoiling. Having
recently put forth to the world a book of poems, modest enough in
bulk, he was presently attacked by a most formidable conspiracy
of adulation. . . . Few writers of really distinguished quality
have been introduced to the world under the shelter of such a
farrago of nonsense."

This writer, almost the only personal friend of
Thompson's on the literary press, does not confine his
strictures to the alleged "promoters" of *Poems*. He
points to passages, ungainly and ugly, which explain
why the book as a whole "proves repellent to the
majority of readers" ; but

"Let him take heart, then, and sedulously pursue a path of most
ascetic improvement. A word, too, in his ear ; let him not use
the universe quite so irresponsibly for a playground. To toss
the stars about, ' to swing the earth,' &c., is just a little cheap."

The same friend had his say in the *Pall Mall Gazette*
and the *Tablet*, so that there was indeed one "con-
spirator" among his reviewers. With all such things
Francis was well pleased ; he enjoyed the smart of

The Clever Donkey

them, and cut them out and pasted them in a scrap-book along with the panegyrics :—

"In regard to Vernon," he wrote, "I am quite satisfied with his articles. You must consider that he and I have in the past exhorted each other to a Spartan virtue of criticism when one deals with a friend—if one thinks a friend can stand it. In taking placidly such unflinching candours there is a glow of self-approving delight akin to that afforded by taking the discipline, or breaking the ice to wash, or getting up in the morning, or any other unnatural act which makes one feel blessedly above one's neighbours."

Another of his friends thought such treatment salutary : Coventry Patmore to A. M., February 3, 1894 :—

"Lang is a clever donkey. It will do F. T. nothing but good to be a little attacked."

Coventry Patmore's own article in the *Fortnightly*, July, 1894, was written before he and Thompson had met. It was easy for even frequent callers at Palace Court to miss F. T., since he never kept appointments. At this time A. M. wrote to F. T. :—

"I have been much disappointed at not having the opportunity of introducing you to Coventry Patmore. He wished so much to see you. If you knew the splendid praises he crowned you with !

"He wants to review your book. He would have done so in the paper he calls the 'Twopenny Damn'[1] (don't be shocked), if it had not died. As it is, he will do it somewhere."

As a matter of fact the critics knew neither the poet nor his address. Even his occasional editors, among whom was Mr. Henry Newbolt, were for their convenience saved direct communication with him. He knew

[1] The *Anti-Jacobin*, edited by Mr. Frederick Greenwood

nobody ; and those who knew everybody did not know him.   Mr. Yeats wrote at his death to W. M. :—

" Now I regret that I never met him, except once for a few minutes.   There seems to be some strange power in the forms of excess that dissolves, as it were, the external will, to make the character malleable to the internal will.   An extreme idealism of the imagination seems to be incompatible in almost all with a perfectly harmonious relation to the mechanics of life."

Another of the circle of his unacquaintance, Mr. Norman Gale, writing as an anthologist, for permission to quote, says to the poet :—

" Let me take this opportunity of congratulating you from my heart on the success of your book.   I have said what I thought of it in print.   I was candid."

That, at least, does not betoken the log-roller.   If Thompson was one of " a group "—it was a day of groups —it was composed of cowled friars and the deaf Welsh hills.   When from Mr. Hugh Chisholm, then the assistant editor of the *St. James's Gazette*, and the writer of an appreciative notice in that paper, came a request, rein-forcing his printed admiration, for an autograph copy of the " Daisy " the compliment was made through a third person, and such personalities as his review contained were not based on an acquaintance with the poet. Another stranger, Mr. John Davidson, wrote, I believe, the *Speaker's* praises, but disclaimed any responsibilities for his reviews when asked, in later years, if a passage from his article might be quoted—he never meant any-thing said in reviews, was his afterthought about them.   Nevertheless, since his were the words of a fellow-poet, I give them :—

" Here are dominion—domination over language, and a sin-cerity as of Robert Burns. . . . We must turn from Mr. Thompson, the latest, and perhaps the greatest, of English Roman Catholic poets of post-Reformation times, to the exalted Puritan voice that

Log-rolling

sang ' At a Solemn Music ' for a strain combining in like manner intensity and magnificence." . . . (*Of* "*Her Portrait.*") " A description, masterful and overmastering, in which a constant interchange of symbol between earthly and heavenly beauty pulses like day and night."

With the publication of *Sister Songs* in 1895 the same charge was renewed ; the *Realm* felt

" sorry for Mr. Thompson to think that he had been spoiled by indiscreet flatterers. He ought not to run away with the idea that anything he chooses to write is poetry."

"The frenzied pæans of his admirers by profession" were the words of a leading critic, and might well have stirred a desire in Francis to explain that he neither knew nor could profit his reviewers. When one journal became more explicit in its charges he went so far as to compose, but not to despatch, a reply made principally on somebody else's behalf :—

" My business is," he wrote, "as one of the—I suppose I should say shameful—seven pilloried by your critic, to give my private witness for Mr. Le Gallienne. The *gravamen* of the charge against him is not that he praised too effusively ; it is the far more heinous accusation of log-rolling—in other words, of praising in return for favours received, or favours which it was understood were to come. Here, then, are the facts in my own case. When my book appeared it was reviewed by Mr. Le Gallienne in terms no less generous than those used by him recently in the *Weekly Sun*. When his first review appeared Mr. Le Gallienne and myself were totally unacquainted and unconnected. Before the second, printed in the *Weekly Sun*, we had met once casually. And this is the whole extent of my personal acquaintance or communication with one who is accused of praising me because he is my friend. Nor does the meanness anonymously attributed to Mr.

Le Gallienne end here.   He is accused of praising me
not only as a friend but as one whom I praise in return.
Allow me then to say that I have never before or since
his review of my poems written a line about him in any
quarter."

His reserve in public did not mean that he was so
little contentious that he never smote his foes in private.
He was full of unspoken arguments, like the man you
see talking to himself, or smiling as he walks, and of
whom you may be sure that he is confounding or dis-
missing an opponent.   The solitary man is full of good
answers, but they belong to an interview from which,
over soon, he is speeding; for his triumph, generally, is
the sad one of putting together a repartee or clinching
an argument—too late.   So it was with Thompson.   He
thought out his brisk repartees purely for his own satisfaction and at leisure, and would have blushed to answer
his belittlers in the open.   But in the mental "ring," in
the note-book, he occasionally triumphed :—

" I need hardly say I have not escaped the accusation
of belonging to a ' Mutual Admiration Society.'   There
are few writers, I fancy, but have at one time or another
been surprised by the experience.   For it is often an
odd surprise.   I myself, for example, am a recluse ; with
one or two intimate friends whom I see and one or
two whom I don't.   If in the latter case you deny the
intimacy you fail to grasp that I am a recluse.   I saw
them ten years ago—there's intimacy.   I might see them
again next week, or year—why then, there's more
intimacy.   And I don't need to see them at all—go to,
would you desire better intimacy ?   The chapter of my
intimate friends is as of the snakes in Ireland.   My intimate friends I do, past question, encounter of odd
times—if that constitute the acquaintance, it is the limit
of mine.   But speculative assumption, as it is without

knowledge, so cannot have knowledge of its own incongruity.

" Nor is the reciprocal admiration of small men necessarily foolish : it is foolish only when it admires what each wishes to be, not what he is. For my part I have known in true literary men generosity united with unflinching plainness of speech. They love literature too much, that they should bring into her presence less than severe truth, within the scope and compass of their conception."

If Thompson had been scolded for his Catholic friends, his Catholic friends were to be scolded for their Thompson, but on a different score. In the *American Ecclesiastical Review*, for June 1898, Canon Sheehan, author of *The Triumph of Failure*, wrote :—

" For the present he will write no more poetry. Why ? I should hardly like to intrude upon the privacy of another's thoughts ; but Francis Thompson, who, with all his incongruities, ranks in English poetry with Shelley, and *only* beneath Shakespeare, has hardly had any recognition in Catholic circles. If Francis Thompson had been an Anglican or a Unitarian, his praises would have been sung unto the ends of the earth. He would have been the creator of a new school of poetry. Disciples would have knelt at his feet. But, being only a Catholic, he is allowed to retire, and bury in silence one of the noblest imaginations that have ever been given to Nature's select ones—her poets. Only two Catholics—literary Catholics—have noticed this surprising genius—Coventry Patmore and Wilfrid Meynell. The vast bulk of our co-religionists have not even heard his name, although it is already bruited amongst the Immortals ; and *the* great Catholic poet, for whose advent we have been straining our vision, has passed beneath our eyes, sung his immortal songs, and vanished."

Another view of the poet's attitude towards his reception comes from Mrs. Blackburn at Pantasaph, 1894 :—

" As for Francis, I hardly know what to say. I wish he would show some kind of human elation at his unprecedented success, but he seems to take it all in a dull, mechanical way, which is distressing. It is two months now since there has been any change in him. He stays away for days together, and, although he has promised to come to tea with me this afternoon, ten to one I shan't see him. Bishop Carroll was here last week, and saw Francis a good deal at the Monastery. He told me he would ask him to come and stay a short time with him at Stalybridge, and take him to see his father. Francis seems so much to want to see his own people again. It is odd to read all the well-merited praise, and then realise how outside the pale of humanity this great genius is, more irresponsible than any child, with a child's fits of temper and want of foresight and control. He isn't doing a stroke of work, and stays in bed the best part of the day, and lately he falls asleep when he comes to see me. No one can do anything with him."

It was this man who, nevertheless, was as near his public as it is possible for a writer to be ; he made his public. Nobody thought Mr. H. D. Traill misjudged the chances of popularity when, on the publication of *Poems*, he wrote to W. M. :—

" I quite agree with you in thinking him a remarkable poet, but, if he is ever to become other than a ' poet's poet ' or ' critic's poet '—if indeed it is worth anyone's ambition to be other than that—it will only be by working in a different manner. A ' public ' to appreciate ' The Hound of Heaven ' is to me inconceivable."

Mr. William Archer, a splendid appreciator, expressed much the same view. Yet in the three years after Thompson's death the separate edition of " The Hound of Heaven " sold fifty thousand copies ; and, apart from anthologies, many more thousands were sold of the books containing it.

The *Athenæum* notice fell to Mr. Arthur Symons (3 Feb. 1894), moved to note the worst, that " inchoate poem, ' A Judgment in Heaven,' " and to remark the closeness of imitation of Mr. Patmore and Crashaw—" Can a man serve two such masters ? "—and other influences sharing " the somewhat external quality of Mr. Thompson's

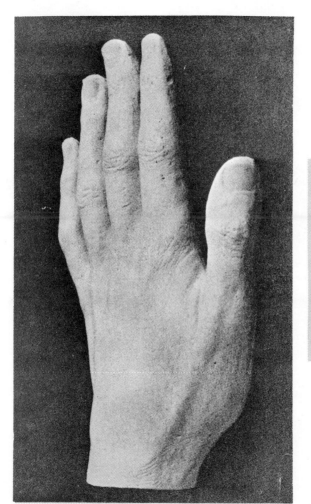

Cast of Francis Thompson's Hand

inspiration." Mr. Symons was equally careful to establish, coldly enough, his appreciation of such importance
as might be safely allowed the new poet. No doubt that
review, though W. M. labelled it favourable, made the
generosity of Mr. Le Gallienne and the splendid
appreciation of Mr. Garvin doubly valuable to send
to Pantasaph.

F. T. to W. M. :—

" I think Traill's article excellent and kind. But the
Athenæum!— Call you this dealing favourably with
a man ? Heaven save me, then, from the unfavourable
dealers ! Of course, he is right about the "To
Monica Thought Dying"; but that and one or two
other poems are not sufficient on which to base a charge
of making Mr. Patmore a model. It would have been
well, indeed, for the restraint and sanity of the poems
if I *had* submitted somewhat to the influence of Mr.
Patmore's example. As for what Watson says, it is not,
like Symons', unfair. The sale of the book is indeed
astonishing. Let us hope that the league of the weeklies
will not materially damp it."

When, with *Sister Songs* in 1895, came a second
batch of reviews, F. T. wrote :—

" I should much like to see further notices of my
book, if you would not find it too much trouble. Lane
has sent me only Le Gallienne's in the *Star*.[1] From
another source I have had the *Daily Chronicle, St. James's*
and *Manchester Guardian.* Lane speaks of reviews in

[1] Of *Sister Songs* Mr. Le Gallienne wrote:—

"Critics are continually asking a writer to be someone else than himself, but
happily Mr. Thompson seems to be one of those poets who go their own way,
oblivious of the cackle of Grub Street. . . . Passion, in its ideal sense, has
seldom found such an ecstatic, such a magnificently prodigal expression.
For the love that Mr. Thompson sings is that love which never finds, nor
can hope to find, ' its earthly close.' It is the poet's love of love in the
abstract, revealed to him symbolically in the tender youth of two little girls,
and taking the form of a splendid fantastic gallantry of the spirit."

" Poems "

the *Realm, Saturday,* and *Athenæum.* If the two latter
are by Symons, as he says, I do not want to see them.
He is the only critic of mine that I think downright
unfair. . . . Coventry has sent me a poem of Mrs.
Meynell's from the *P. M. G.*—' Why Wilt Thou Chide ? '
No woman ever wrote a thing like that : and but one
man—Coventry himself."

From Patmore's article on *Poems* in the *Fortnightly
Review,* July 1894, which stands as the most important
page in the history of the new poet's reception :—

" Mr. Francis Thompson is a writer whom it is impossible that
any qualified judge should deny to be a ' new poet,' one altogether
distinct in character from that of the several high-class mediocrities
who, during the past twenty years or so, have blazed into immense
circulation, and have deceived for a while many who have seemed
to be of the elect among critics. And, unlike most poets of his
quality, who have usually had to wait a quarter of a century or
more for adequate recognition, this poet is pretty sure of a wide
and immediate acknowledgment. ׀ A singular and very interesting
history will convince thousands whom the rumour of it may reach,
that he is an ' extraordinary person ' ; the heroic faith in and
devotion to the interests of his genius which, through long years,
has been shown by at least two friends, one of them a lady not
inferior in genius to his own ; his recognition of her helpfulness
by a series of poems which St. John of the Cross might have addressed to St. Theresa, and which, had she not established by her
own writings a firm and original hold on fame, would have carried
her name to posterity in company with that of 'Mrs. Ann Killigrew";
the very defects of his writing, which will render manifest, by contrast, its beauties, thereby ingratiating ' the crowd, incapable of
perfectness ' ; his abundant and often unnecessary obscurities,
which will help his popularity, as Browning's did his, by ministering to the vanity of such as profess to be able to see through mill-
stones, are all circumstances which will probably do more for his
immediate acceptance by the literary public than qualities which
ought to place him, even should he do no more than he has done,
in the permanent ranks of fame, with Cowley and with Crashaw.
" Considering that these eighty-one pages of verse are all that
Mr. Thompson has done, there would seem room for almost any

Taste

hope of what he may do, but for one circumstance which seems to limit expectancy. He is, I believe, about thirty-five years old—an age at which most poets have written as well as they have ever written, and at which the faculty of 'taste,' which is to a poet what chastity is to a woman, is usually as perfect as it is likely ever to be. It was Cowley's incorrigible defect of taste, rather than any fault of the time, that was responsible for the cold conglomerate of grit which constitutes the mass of his writing, though he was occasionally capable of ardent flights of pure and fluent verse; and it is by the same shortcoming in Crashaw that we are continually reminded that what he would have us accept for concrete poetic passion is mainly an *intellectual* ardour. The phraseology of a perfectly poetic ardour is always 'simple, sensuous, and passionate,' and has a seemingly unconscious *finish from within*, which no 'polish' can produce. Mr. Thompson, as some critic has remarked, is a 'greater Crashaw.' He has never, in the present book of verses, done anything which approaches, in technical beauty, to Crashaw's 'Music's Duel'; but then Crashaw himself never did anything else approaching it; and, for the rest of his work, it has all been equalled, if not excelled, in its peculiar beauties, as well as its peculiar defects, by this new poet. . . . Mr. Thompson's poetry is 'spiritual' almost to a fault. He is always, even in love, upon mountain heights of perception, where it is difficult for even disciplined mortality to breathe for long together. The lady whom he delights to honour he would have to be too seraphic even for a seraph. He rebukes her for wearing diamonds, as if she would be a true woman if she did not delight in diamonds, if she could get them; and as if she could be truly seraphic were she not a woman. The crown of stars of the *Regina Cœli* is not more naturally gratifying and becoming to her who, as St. Augustine says, had no sin, 'except, perhaps, a little vanity,' than the tiara of brilliants is to the *Regina Mundi*. Mr. Thompson is a Titan among recent poets; but he should not forget that a Titan may require and obtain renovation of his strength by occasional acquaintance with the earth, without which the heavens themselves are weak and unstable. The tree Igdrasil, which has its head in heaven and its roots in hell (the 'lower parts of the earth '), is the image of the true man, and eminently so of the poet, who is eminently man. In proportion to the bright and divine heights to which it ascends must be the obscure depths in which the tree is rooted, and from which it draws the mystic sap of its spiritual life. Since, however, Mr. Thompson's spirituality is a real ardour of life, and not the mere negation of life, which passes, with most people, for spirituality, it seems somewhat ungracious to complain of its predominance. It is the greatest and noblest of defects, and shines rather as an eminent virtue in a time when most other Igdrasils are hiding their heads in hell and affronting heaven with their indecorous roots."

In talk with F. T. he said :—

" I look to you to crush all this false mysticism. Crush it ; you can do it if you like ; you are the man to do it."

Although C. P. had seen the proofs he had not met F. T. before the publication of *Poems* or his criticism of it in the *Fortnightly*. The proofs bear the marks of a critic intolerant of everything in which he detected excess of diction or imagery. One short poem he struck clean out, with the comment " It will do harm." He was the elder with a system, the master who knew "the end and aim of poetry," but later, speaking as with words fully weighed, he said in talk with F. T., "I am not sure you may not be a greater poet than I am."
Sister Songs, published two years later, belongs to the same period of composition as *Poems*. In all the poetry there is personal revelation, his own experience being the invisible wind that moves the cloudy pageant of his verse. But in *Sister Songs* we see the experience itself ; he alludes to his nights in the streets, and can here say with Donne : ". . . my verse, the strict map of my misery . . ." But not in the first place is it a poem of sad experience, an unfit offering for little girls. It is what it would be—beautiful, elaborate, innocent. The second part is addressed to Monica Meynell ; the first is a dance of words in honour of a younger sister—" For homage unto Sylvia, her sweet, feat ways."

F. T. to W. M. :—

" I have been wondering what criticisms had appeared on Mrs. Meynell. I have seen none, except the *Fort-*

" I Told You So "

nightly and the *Chronicle.* Coventry all abroad about her poetry, Le Gallienne all abroad about her prose. But the latter's notice of her poetry showed real perception. Coventry was excellent with regard to the side of her prose which he had seized ; but rather provoking for seizing it, since he has sent the *Chronicle* off after him on what is a false trail. The side is there ; but it is not the prominent side, and certainly not the side most markedly characteristic of her."

C. P. to F. T. :—

"LYMINGTON, *July* 29, 1895.

" MY DEAR THOMPSON,—I am glad you think as I do about those ' wonderful verses ' (A. M.'s). I have quoted your words in a letter I have written to our Friend. They will delight her greatly. . . .

" It is good news that you are writing prose. You know how perfectly great I think what I have read of your prose. After all, the greatest things must be said in prose. Music is too weak to follow the highest thought. I will try and go to Pantasaph as soon as I have arranged some engagements which have come into the foreground since I wrote to you.

" I hear that Traill and Henley (who abused your first Book) are in raptures (should they not be written *ruptures ?*) with the last !

" When will the ' critics ' understand the difference between an ounce of diamond dust and a diamond that weighs an ounce ! These gentlemen have written almost nothing about *Rod, Root, and Flower.* I suppose they can make nothing of it. But Bell tells me it sells fairly.—Yours ever,

COVENTRY PATMORE."

Thompson himself adopted the view that *Sister Songs* lacked a proper sequence of idea and incident, or rather that, to the unready reader, it apparently lacked such sequence.

Mr. Arnold Bennett's "Don't say I didn't tell you," saved fortunately from the flimsy pages of *Woman,* July 3, 1895, reads proudly now :—

" I declare that for three days after this book appeared I read nothing else. I went about repeating snatches of it—snatches such as—

> The innocent moon, that nothing does but shine,
> Moves all the labouring surges of the world.

My belief is that Francis Thompson has a richer natural genius, a finer poetical equipment, than any poet save Shakespeare. Show me the divinest glories of Shelley and Keats, even of Tennyson, who wrote the 'Lotus Eaters' and the songs in 'The Princess,' and I think I can match them all out of this one book, this little book that can be bought at an ordinary bookseller's shop for an ordinary, prosaic crown. I fear that in thus extolling Francis Thompson's work, I am grossly outraging the canons of criticism. For the man is alive, he gets up of a morning like common mortals, not improbably he eats bacon for breakfast; and every critic with an atom of discretion knows that a poet must not be called great until he is either dead or very old. Well, please yourself what you think. But, in time to come, don't say I didn't tell you."

Mr. Arnold Bennett was to discover for himself the secret of large sales : he did not negotiate them for his poet, who complained of " my ill-starred volume— which has sold only 349 copies in twelve months." Bad enough, of course ; but poets of distinction have since then been contented, or discontented, with the sale of thirty in the same interval. *New Poems* did much worse.

F. T. to W. M. :—

" Many thanks for the *Edinburgh*, which has indeed pleased me. I did not expect such an enthusiastic review of my work, and particularly of my last book, from a periodical so conservative and slow-moving. I am very gratified by what you say about Meredith. You know, I think, that I hold him the most unquestionable genius among living novelists. I have read five of his novels : *Harry Richmond, Evan Harrington, Richard Feverel, Diana of the Crossways, One of our Conquerors*. Nothing beyond this."

The " Edinburgh " Reviewer

In another letter he again mentions the *Edinburgh* reviewer :—

" The writer shows not only taste, but what is nowadays as rare, that acquaintance with the range of English poetry, which ought to be a natural essential in the equipment of any poetical critic. Even where he is mistaken, he is intelligently mistaken. One remark goes curiously home—that on the higher poetic rank of metaphor as compared to simile. It has always been a principle of my own ; so much so, that I never use a simile if I can use a metaphor. The observation on the burden of the poem to Sylvia shows a metrical sense unfortunately very unusual in our day."

CHAPTER VIII: OF WORDS; OF ORIGINS; OF METRE

THE *Morning Post* reviewer dwelt on his "incomprehensible sentiments and unknown words," and even his friends had before publication warned him that his meanings were lost in the "foam and roar of his phraseology."

Lionel Johnson was hardly more candid than some others when he said of Francis Thompson that he had done more to harm the English language than the worst American newspapers: *corruptio optimi pessima.* And Mr. Gosse saw him as the defiler of the purity of the English language.

But he was no very hardened coiner of words to be thus taken aback by objections :—

"By the way, I see Blackburn has queried (on MS. of *Sister Songs*) 'lovesome.' Is there no such word? I never made a doubt that there was. It is at any rate according to analogy. If it is an error, then 'lovely' must be substituted throughout, which differs somewhat in *nuance* of meaning."

He meets Mr. Archer's complaint by quoting Campion's "Cold age deafs not there our ears," and Shakespeare's "Beastly dumbed by him," and Keats' "Nighing to that mournful place" :—

"In all this I am a born rebel, founding myself on observed fact before I start to learn theory of theorisers, systems of system-mongers. I doubt me but English

The Born Rebel

verbs are, or were, commonly suggested and derived from adjectives ; and had I time and a British Museum ticket would resolve the matter for myself. Anyway I have coined nought to the like ; I mistrust not but your same 'dumbed' is all Archer has against me in this quarrel, and all he shall advance against me whereon to build such charge, nor shall he find another like verb in ought of verse I have written, search he like a lantern of Diogenes. The word lay to my hand and was a right lusty and well-pithed word, close grained and forcible as a cudgel, wherefore I used it ; and surely I would have used a dozen such had they served my turn."

In another case his defence is ready ; thus did he consider the weight, rarity, and character of a word or phrase :—

"Of 'nervure'; I should not, in a like passage, use *cuticle* of the skin of a flower or leaf : because it is a *streaky* word—its two *K* sounds and mouse-shrewd *u* make it like a wire tweaked by a plectrum. The *u* of nervure is not only unaccented, therefore unprominent in sound, but the soft *v* and *n* quite alter its effect from that it has when combined with k's and parchment-tight t's."

" ' In nescientness, in nescientness,' " complained A. T. Q. C. in the *Speaker*, June 5 and May 29, 1897, " puts me at once into a frame of mind unfavourable to thorough enjoyment of what follows. . . . Undoubtedly the eulogies of his friends have been at once so precipitate and defiant as to lead us to suspect that he is being shielded from frank criticism ; that his are not the rare and most desirable friends, who love none the less for their courage to detect faults and point them out ; and that, by consequence, he is not being given a fair chance of correcting his excesses. . . . ' *Monstrance*,' ' *vaultages*,' ' *arcane*,' ' *sciential*,' ' *coerule*,' ' *intemperably*,' ' *englut*' (past participle), '*most strainedest*' (double superlative)—these and the like are not easily allowed by anyone possessing a sense of the history of the language."

Of Words; Of Origins; Of Metre

"Monstrance" is not the only word in that list that shows how hastily the critics fell foul of him, and those who think that Shakespeare bears some part in "the history of the language" may take "Most stillest" for a fair precedent of a double superlative.

Mr. E. K. Chambers, reviewing *Sister Songs* in 1895, wrote:—

"He showers out obsolete words, or at will coins new ones, with a profusion that at times becomes extravagant and grotesque. . . . His freaks of speech rarely prove anything but ugly linguistic monstrosities."

"The obsolete 'riped,'" "the rare 'heavened,'" "impitiable," "saddenedly," "anticipatedly," "immeditatably"—with these the critics were wroth. Parodies appeared in the *Saturday Review*—"Latinate Vocabules"—and in the *Westminster Gazette*. While "monstrance" was found to have the suspect ring of a coined word, many of the words he did coin (according to Mr. Beacock's Concordance they number 130 odd) passed unnoticed. They include plain-going utilitarian feminine forms such as *auxiliatrix, consortress;* plurals such as *innocences, translucencies;* adjectives with the prefix *un,* such as *undelirious;* verbs with the suffix *less,* such as *rebukeless* and *delimitless;* a number of substantives called into use as verbs, *e.g. mænadize, empillared, chaplet;* and a less comfortable group of adverbs, such as *supportlessly, predilectedly,* and the unsustainable *tamelessly,* meaning untamably. (Browning's "abashless" is of the same class.)

He did not, like Rossetti, go to the glossaries; but "Nares," of which he never possessed a copy, contains his credentials. Thus *shard* is Shakespearian. Drayton has *shawm.* "*Soilure*" is in "Troilus and Cressida"; "with drunken *spilth* of wine" in "Timon of Athens." "*Swart*," "*swink*," "*targe*," "*amerce*," "*avouch*," "*assoile*" are all of common acceptance; "*bruit*," "*eld*," "*empery*,"

The Latinisms

"*immediacy*," "*ostent*," "*threne*," "*incarnadine*," and
"*troublous*" are all Shakespearian, and more. "*To
gloom*," according to precedent, is a verb, and so are
"*to englut*," and "*to fantasy*"; "*lustyhed*" is Drayton's
and Spenser's. "*Rondure*" is common; "*rampire*" is
in Dryden even; "*to port*" and "*ported*," and, of course,
"*natheless*" are accepted. "*Crystalline*," being Cowley's
if for no other reason, would be ready to his tongue;
"*devirginate*," which has the sound of one of his own
prolongations, is Donne's; "*adamantean*" he would
probably have coined, if Milton had not done so before
him. "*Temerarious*" came to him as naturally as to
Sir Thomas Browne. "*Femineity*" is Browning's, and
"*devisal*" Patmore's, in their modern usage. "*Immures*"
as a substantive still annoys his readers, but only before
they find it in "Troilus and Cressida."

His Latinisms were frequent. Of these the only test
to the point is Dryden's : "If too many foreign words
are poured in, it looks as if they were designed, not
to assist the natives, but to conquer them." From a
mature opinion of Sir Thomas Browne, a constant
favourite, that his "prose suffered neither from excess
of Latinities nor from insufficiency in the vulgar
tongue," we learn that Thompson was careful to observe the balance.

In answer to the common rebuke against F. T., A. M.
in the *Nation*, November 23, 1907, says :—

"Obviously there are Latinisms and Latinisms! Those of
Gibbon and Johnson, and of their time generally, serve to hold
passion well at arm's length ; they are the mediate and not the
immediate utterance of human feeling. But in F. T. the majestic
Latin word is forged hot on the anvil of the artificer. No Old
English in the making could be readier or closer."

His own rule of writing was, "That it is the infantries
of language, so to speak, which must make up the mass
of a poet's forces; *i.e.* common diction of the many in

Of Words ; Of Origins ; Of Metre

every age; the numerous terms of prose, apart from special poetic diction."

In an early review Thompson writes :—

"We have spoken somewhat contemptuously of 'fine language.' Let no one suppose from this that we have any antipathy to literary splendour in itself, apart from the subject on which it is exercised. Quite the contrary. To write plainly on a fine subject is to set a jewel in wood. Did our givers of literary advice only realise this, we should hear less of the preposterous maxim 'aim always at writing simply.' Conceive merely Raleigh, Sir Thomas Browne, Jeremy Taylor, Milton, and de Quincey rendered into 'simple English.' Their only fit place would be the fire. The true abuse of 'fine language' is rich diction applied to a plain subject, or lofty words to weak ideas ; like most devices in writing this one also is excellent when employed as a means, evil when sought as an end."

This is in an early essay : it is doubtful if later he would have so precisely matched fine writing and good matter. In his own work the finer meanings are not seldom put into the humbler words.

For his words he had no need to seek far ; they were more naturally remembered for use in the poetry of splendid artifice than the language of the street. His search was not deliberate. In the offices of the Church he found words to his hand, but he did not go to the offices on their account. It is doubtful if he borrowed even a monosyllable from a poet he did not love. Very rarely he made notes : "*Pleached*—an invaluable word," is the only memorandum I have come across. He had no list, like Rossetti's, of "stunning words for poetry," among them "gonfalon," "virelay," "citole," and "shent." He was at no pains to coin or collect, nor even to possess a theory. Bulwer Lytton's wholesale

Rough Drafts of Creation

condemnation of Latinisms, and professed preference for such forms as *scatterling* and *doomsman* for "vagabond" and "executioner," were not the ways of a liberal master :—

"The labour, the art, the studious vocabulary," says the writer in the *Nation*, November 23, 1907, "are locked together within the strenuous grasp of the man's sincerity. There is no dissociating, no disintegrating, such poems as these ; and Francis Thompson's heart beats in the words ' *roseal*,' ' *cymars*,' ' *frore*,' ' *amiced*,' ' *lamped*,' and so forth."

Being led on in certain studies he became attached to the terms specially connected with those studies. The process may be traced in the case of his use of the names of extinct animals. Their discovery he calls pure romance ; "but the romance which lies in the new and unimagined forms, hidden from the poets and tale-tellers of all previous ages, and given up to eyes almost satiate with wonders, has yet to find its writers. . . . Tennyson has seen its uses for large and impressive allusion—

Nature brings not back the Mastodon, —

but Tennyson is almost alone even in the use of the theme. In an occasional later and younger poet you may find mention of the plesiosaure or other typical monster." Again, still reviewing Mr. Seeley's *Dragons of the Air*, Thompson writes :—

"We have strayed, it seems, into the ancient forge and workshop of Nature, where she is busy with her first experiments. . . . We behold, cast off from her anvil, in bewildering succession, shapes so fantastical, grotesque, and terrible, as never peopled the most lawless dreams of an Eastern haschish-eater ; apparitions of intertwisted types and composite phantasms, more and more strange than all the brute gods of Egypt. We are among the rough drafts of a creation."

Of Words ; Of Origins ; Of Metre

The " occasional later and younger poet" was himself.
Of his partial acceptance of the criticism of the Press
he makes sign in a note he had intended printing in
New Poems:—

" Of words I have coined or revived I have judged
fit to retain but few; and not more than two or three
will be found in this book. I shall also be found, I
hope, to have modified much the excessive loading both
of diction and imagery which disfigured my former work."

That the note was not printed must not strictly be
taken to mean that he repented of his repentance. But
he was not easily brought to correct or discard—the
initial process of composition had been too careful to
be lightly tampered with. In A. M. he had a very stern
critic for such words as " tameless," but he was found
less amenable than George Meredith, who, accepting
correction, altered two uses of words so formed. This
letter was written during the making of *Poems:*—

"Palace Court House, *Friday*.

" My dear Francis,—The Bible has ' unquenchable,' and I
don't think it could have ' quenchless.' Lowell has ' exhaustless '
somewhere. I think one can strictly hold ' less ' to equal ' minus '
or ' without,' and with these the verb is impossible. I remember
refusing to be taught a setting of some words of Praed's that had
' tameless ' for ' untamable,' so you see it is an old objection
with me.

" I must confess that ' dauntless ' has taken a very firm place
in the language.

" Never has there been such a dance of words as in ' The Making
of Viola.' All other writers make their words dance on the ground
with a certain weight, but these go in the blue sky. I have to
unsay everything I said in criticism of that lovely poem. I think
the long syllables make themselves valued in every case. But I
do not like three syllables in the course of the poem—the three
that give the iambic movement. I have not made up my mind
as to the alternative endings. They are all so beautiful.—Ever
most sincerely yours, Alice Meynell."

The Habit of Words

The suggestions as to metrical modifications he accepted. I print here a letter of which, however, the interest for me is not etymological : its interest is that he troubled to write at all to an inattentive Yahoo of a friend :—

" Dear Ev., as to the note you asked the Latin *simplex* is from *plecto* (or rather its root) 'I entwine,' and some root allied to the Greek 'together.' The root-meaning is therefore 'twined together,' and it primarily means that which has synthesis or unity as opposed to that which is confused or perplexed by lack of oneness. When Wordsworth (is it not ?) somewhere speaks of a being 'simple and unperplexed,' consciously or unconsciously, he uses the word mainly in this original sense, though few even thoughtful folk explicitly so grasp it. It is degenerated in the common mouth to the meaning almost of 'elementary.' Milton, saying poetry should be simple, sensuous, and passionate (is that the third word ?), by *simple* means synthetic—opposed to prose (especially, doubtless, he had in mind philosophic prose), which is analytic.—Yours, F. T."

He never dropped the habit of words. One of the last letters he wrote, dated from Rascals' Corner, Southwater, September 14, 1907, was written when he had detected a random paragraph of A. M.'s in the *Daily Chronicle :*—

" DEAR MRS. MEYNELL,—You might have added to the *willow* par. the Latin *salex* and the Eng. *sallow :*

> Among the river sallows borne aloft
> Or sinking, as the light wind lives or dies !

The English, I should guess, may be from one of the Romance tongues ; if so all these modern forms are, mediately or immediately, from the Latin. But it is interesting to find the Latin and the Irish really identical (if you neglect the inflectional endings in the former)— salic and salagh. 'Tis but the difference 'twixt a plain

Of Words ; Of Origins ; Of Metre

and a guttural hard consonant—for connective vowels are unstable endlessly. As for k and g, you see, *e.g.*, *reg*-o evolve *rec*-tum.

" Excuse this offhand note, but your paragraph interested me.

" With warm love to yourself, Wilfrid, and all the *quondam* kids who are fast engaging themselves off the face of my earth.—Yours ever, dear Mrs. Meynell,

FRANCIS THOMPSON."

He watched with much interest his words creep into currency. *Roseal*—"most beloved of my revivals"— which he had known only in Lodge's *Glaucus and Scylla*, he saw reappear in Dowson and other writers, and realised it was probably from Thompson and not from Lodge that it had been learnt. In this he saw the sign—the only one, he said—of his influence. He could hardly have expected that two years after his death " labyrinthine " would be a word used not only in poetry books, but on political platforms—by Mr. George Wyndham and his less-versed opponents. Words that ten years earlier irked the reader in poetry became, with a change of mood, acceptable in public speaking, so that Mr. Asquith's use of " fuliginous " irked nobody.

The objection to a poet's range of phrase finds no support in the dictionaries, whose abundance is a reproach to the restricted scope of the modern tongue. Johnson is three parts made up of terms neglected or discarded, for the reason, chiefly, that we are lazy and unlearned. The coster-monger whose speech comprises fewer words each year, thinks the parson a fop for the extent of his vocabulary, and the parson in his turn is impatient with his poets. The curtailment of our speech goes on apace, and if we love the poet—the Wordsworth of " Daffodils " or the Thompson of " Daisy "—as a man of few words, we should admire him for being at times a man of many.

*   *   *   *   *   *   *

At Rossetti's Death

By 1889 Rossetti had become an absorbing interest, but Coleridge, in what F. T. calls his Pre-Rossettian days, "had been my favourite poet." Before Coleridge, Shelley.

An early poem not elsewhere printed, written on the anniversary of Rossetti's death, illustrates the closeness of his affection—

> This was the day that great, sad heart,
>   That great, sad heart did beat no more,
> Which nursed so long its Southern flame
>   Amid our vapours dull and frore.
>
> .   .   .   ı   ı   .
>
> Through voice of art and voice of song
>   He uttered one same truth abroad,—
> Through voice of art and voice of song—
>   That Love below a pilgrim trod :
> He said, through women's eyes, " How long !
>   Love's other half's with God ! "
>
> ?   .   .   .   .   ı
>
> He taught our English art to gaze
>   On Nature with a learner's eyes :
> That hills which look into the heaven
>   Have their fair bases on the earth ;
> God paints His most angelic hues
>   On vapours of a terrene birth.
>
> May God his locks with glories twine,
>   Be kind to all he wrought amiss !
> May God his locks with glories twine,
>   And give him back his Beatrice.
> This day the sad heart ceased to pine,
>   ¡I trust his lady's beats at his,
> And two beat in a single bliss.

Of all Thompson's lines the second of the sunset-image—

> Day's dying dragon lies drooping his crest,
> Panting red pants into the West,

has been found the most ludicrous. No critic hesitated in condemning it, and your reader most often splits

the line with a laugh, thinking the while of Hope
Brothers. But the poet thought upon his own thought
and upheld his line in face of the query marks confidently balanced on the margin of his proofs ; he remembered Coleridge's—

> As if this earth in fast, thick pants were breathing.

"Red" or "thick," there is little for the parodist to choose
between them. Much closer borrowing from Coleridge,
in which he pronounces the words and rhymes of his
master but keeps his voice ringing high with personality,
is found at the close of "To my Godchild." It is easy
to know with what keen recognition he must have read
Coleridge's "Ne Plus Ultra." He borrowed its weakest
lines because he dared not borrow the strongest ; they
would not have become more famous on his hands.
Coleridge's poem ends :—

> Reveal'd to none of all the Angelic State,
> Save to the Lampads Seven [1]
> That watched the Throne of Heaven !

Thompson's ending is

> Pass the crystalline sea, the Lampads seven :—
> Look for me in the nurseries of Heaven.

We have seen an ending ; here is a borrowed opening :—

> Like a lone Arab, old and blind,
> Some caravan had left behind,
> Who sits beside a ruin'd well,
> Where the shy sand-asps bask and swell ;
> And now he hangs his aged head aslant
> And listens for a human sound—in vain, &c.

It develops into an allegory of illusion : the poet sits

[1] Revelation iv, 5, ". . . there were seven lamps burning before the
Throne, which are the seven spirits of God."

desolate, and, thinking Love visits him, is deceived. Just thus is Thompson's passage beginning—

> As an Arab journeyeth
> Through a sand of Ayaman,
> Lean Thirst, lolling its cracked tongue, &c. . . .

The staging, the characters, are the same. Perhaps curiosity in opium-eating led him early and impressionably to the study of Coleridge. "The Pains of Sleep" brings their experiences cheek to cheek—haggard cheek to haggard cheek. Thompson wrote a prose tale embodying the same terror of dreams and dream-existence. Both used humorous verse and conversation for a means of escape. They laughed to forget, and punned, not so much to laugh, as to be distracted in the exercise. One of them did the talking much better than the other; but their tongues moved to the same command, their voices ran on from the same fear. Even "Love dies, Love dies, Love dies—Ah! Love is dead" is the reflection of a page of Coleridge's commonplaces.

These are casual likenesses, found on the penetrable levels of resemblance, comparable to the coincidence of the after-collegiate enlisting of the two men, the Bowles connexion, or the Strand experience. But Francis Thompson, as it happens, has been explicit on the subject of the unreachable quality of Coleridge :—

"No other poet, perhaps, except Spenser has been an initial influence, a generative influence, on so many poets. Having with that mild Elizabethan much affinity, it is natural that he should be a 'poets' poet' in the rarer sense—the sense of fecundating other poets. As with Spenser, it is not that other poets have made him their model, have reproduced essentials of his style (accidents no great poet will consciously perpetuate). The progeny are sufficiently unlike the parent. It is that he has incited the very sprouting in them of the laurel-bough, has been to them a fostering sun of song. Such a primary influence he was to Rossetti—Rossetti, whose model was far more Keats than Coleridge. Such he was to Coventry Patmore, in whose work one might trace many masters rather than Coleridge." ("Such he was to me," F. T., a reviewer in a public print, refrained from adding.) "'I did not try to imitate his style,' said that great singer. 'I can hardly explain *how* he influenced me : he was rather an ideal of perfect style than a model to imitate ; but in some indescribable way he did influence my development more than any other poet.' No poet, indeed, has been senseless enough to imitate the inimitable. One might as well try to paint air as to catch a style so void of all manner that it is visible, like air, only in its results. . . . Imitation has no foothold ; it would tread on glass." [1]

F. T. noted in the *Academy*, November 20, 1897, the direct coincidence of Browning's

> Its sad in sweet, its sweet in sad,

and Crashaw's

> Sweetness so sad, sadness so sweet.

It did not come within his scope as a reviewer to mention the doubly direct coincidence (or something nearer) of his own :

> At all the sadness in the sweet,
> The sweetness in the sad.

Coleridge and the other poets to whom Coleridge had guided him ; Shelley and, in prose, de Quincey, are prominent in his early reading. To go to de Quincey's " Daughter of Lebanon " for the pedigree of " The Hound

---

[1] F. T. in the *Academy*, February 6, 1897.

of Heaven " is like going to the grocer's for the seeds, in coloured packets, of the passion flower. But the Victorian tassels of the earlier piece do not hide its lessons— "to suffer that God should give by seeming to refuse " —and pursuit is the theme common to both, and common to writers of most ages. De Quincey did no more than hand it on. From St. Augustine's " Thou wast driving me on with Thy good, so that I could not be at rest until Thou wast manifest to the eye of my soul "; to Meister Eckhart's " He who will escape Him only runs to His bosom ; for all corners are open to him," and so on, the idea is the same, though less elaborated and dramatic than in " The Hound."

In the "Mistress of Vision" the scenery and the lady are Shelleyan ; one marvels that Thompson's teaching comes from those illusive lips. Thus would it have been written had such thoughts gained desired expression through Shelley. The thoughts are Francis Thompson's ; the mode the other's. Mr. Beacock refers one to passages of the " Witch of Atlas," but the likeness is too elusively general to be caught in particular verses, and such things as the borrowing of " blosmy " are nothing more than clues, like the fragmentary débris of a paper-chase, to the whereabouts of an influence.

An early book of transcription contains a deal of Donne and Stevenson (including *Father Damien* and poems), a touch of Andrew Lang, more of Blunt, a little Meredith ; much Rossetti and Cowley, some Suckling, the inevitable Browne, and a Theodore Watts. Drayton, too, is met in the Thompsonian verses: " Hear, my Muses, I demand," &c., so that when Mr. Chesterton says that the shortest way of describing the Victorian age is to say that Francis Thompson stood outside it, he might have gone on, with a little access of wilfulness, to say that the seventeenth century was best described by saying that in it was Francis Thompson.

Marvell he had not read till after his first books—" Just

Of Words ; Of Origins ; Of Metre

Crashaw and a little Cowley—and I had formed my style before I knew Cowley, whom I really did curiously resemble ; though none perceived it, because none had read Cowley."

The Crashaw descent may be traced by way of Coleridge, who said of certain lines of the " Hymn to St. Teresa " that " They were ever present in my mind whilst writing the second part of 'Christabel' ; if, indeed, by some process of the mind, they did not suggest the first thought of the whole poem." Crashaw's Romanism did not interfere with Coleridge's pleasure, though in reading Herbert, whom he found " delicious," and at a time when he could note " that he was comparatively but little known," he paused over inquiries as to the exactness of that author's conformity to Protestantism. Coleridge was much taken with Herbert's " The Flower," a poem " especially affecting "—and naturally, to a poet. It is easy to suppose that Francis gave it particular attention on S. T. C.'s recommendation, and that he had in his mind the lines

> I once more smell the dew and rain
> And relish versing

when, conscious of the wings " Of coming songs that lift my hair and stir it," he praises the

> Giver of spring, and song, and every young new thing !

Herbert, welcoming a return of grace in his heart, writes :—

> How fresh, O Lord, how sweet and clean
> Are Thy returns ! ev'n as the flowers in spring.

Thompson, in " From the Night of Forebeing," writes :—
> From sky to sod,
> The world's unfolded blossom smells of God.

Crashaw and a little Cowley

Closer still is the resemblance, noted by Mr. Beacock, between Herbert's

> Only thy grace, which with these elements comes,
>> Knoweth the ready way,
>> And hath the privie key
> Op'ning the soul's most subtile rooms ;
>> While those to spirits refin'd, at doore attend
>> Despatches from their friend,

and Thompson's

> Its keys are at the cincture hung of God.

Mr. Beacock has also pointed out the resemblance between Southwell's

> Did Christ manure thy heart to breed him briers ?
> Or doth it need this unaccustom'd soyle
> With hellish dung to fertile heaven's desires ?

and Thompson's

> Whether man's heart or life it be which yields
>> Thee harvest, must Thy harvest-fields
>> Be dunged with rotten death ?

Remembering his own acknowledgment—"just Crashaw and a little Cowley"—one may turn to Mr. Garvin's equally accurate summing up in the *Bookman*, March 1897 :—

"He is an argonaut of literature, far travelled in the realm of gold, and he has in a strange degree the assimilative mind that takes suggestions as a cat takes milk. . . . 'The Daisy' was strangely Wordsworthian. But 'Dream-Tryst' was like Shelley, and had that strange ethereal poignancy. There was the 'Dead Cardinal of Westminster,' with its stanzas of shuddering beauty upon the prescience of death. There was the resplendent 'Judgment in Heaven,' with the trenchant Elizabethan apothegm of its epilogue. The 'Corymbus for Autumn' was an overwhelming improvisation of wild and exorbitant fantasy. To be familiar with it is to repent of having ever reproached it for a splendid

167

pedantry and a monstrous ambition. On the whole, if Mr. Thompson had stopped at his first volume we should have judged him more akin in stature and temperament to Marlowe than to any other great figure in English poetry. It seemed to reveal the same 'high astounding terms,' the same vast imagery ; the same *amour de l'impossible ;* the soul striking the sublime stars, the intolerable passion for beauty. But Mr. Thompson did not stop there. After the publication of his second volume, when it became clear that the 'Hound of Heaven' and 'Sister Songs' should be read together as a strict lyrical sequence, there was no longer any comparison possible except the highest, the inevitable comparison with even Shakespeare's Sonnets. The Sonnets are the greatest soliloquy in literature. The 'Hound of Heaven' and 'Sister Songs' together are the second greatest ; and there is no third. In each case it is rather consciousness imaged in the magic mirror of poetry than explicit autobiography. As to Mr. Francis Thompson, what strange indentures bound him to the Muse we cannot tell. We are permitted to guess some strict and sad apprenticeship paid with bitter bread and unimaginable dreams, some ultimate deliverance of song. It is only possible to realise all the beauty of Mr. Thompson's work when it is read as a lyrical sequence related to Shakespeare's Sonnets on the side of poetry, and to de Quincey's *Opium Eater* on the side of prose."

To a certain extent Thompson states his own case in treating of Mangan's liberties with his Irish originals :—

"They are outrageous, or would be outrageous were the success not so complete. But poetry is a rootedly immoral art, in which success excuses well-nigh everything. That in the soldier is flat blasphemy which in the captain, the master of his craft, is but commendable daring. Exactly as a great poet may plagiarise to his heart's content, because he plagiarises well, so the truly poetical translator may reindite a foreign poem and call it a translation."

And in reviewing Henley's *Burns* he writes, again with the braggart touch of one who may have gone the same rascally road :—

"Spartan law holds good in literature, where to steal

To Steal is Honourable

is honourable, provided it be done with skill and dexterity: wherefore Mercury was the patron both of thieves and poets."

Touching a more serious aspect of the case, he writes with Patmore in his mind :—

"There are some truths so true, that upon everyone who sees them clearly they force almost the same mode of expression ; they create their own formulas."

It might not have been guessed that the author of "Horatius" had the means wherewith to lend to the wealthy ; but Macaulay's lines "On the Battle of Naseby"—

Oh ! wherefore come ye forth, in triumph from the North,
   With your hands, and your feet, and your raiment all red ?
And wherefore doth your rout send forth a joyous shout ?
   And whence be the grapes of the wine-press which ye tread ?

Oh ! evil was the root, and bitter was the fruit,
   And crimson was the juice of the vintage that we trod ;
For we trampled on the throng of the haughty and the strong,
   Who sate in the high places, and slew the saints of God !—

supply the model for the ecclesiastical ballad "The Veteran of Heaven" which begins —

O Captain of the wars, whence won Ye so great scars ?
   In what fight did Ye smite, and what manner was the foe ?
Was it on a day of rout they compassed Thee about,
   Or gat Ye these adornings when Ye wrought their overthrow ?

"I am disposed to put in a good word for Macaulay's ballads," F. T. has said.

A fair thought, a keen observation, a neat phrase are seldom strictly preserved. If accident does not take two or more writers to the same hill, show them the same sunset, and charge their minds with the same words, plagiarism will serve the purpose. Even

169

Of Words ; Of Origins ; Of Metre

if Cowley's rare wit had remained in manuscript **unseen**, its turns would not have been for **many** centuries entirely his own. Literature will out. To one or the other, to plagiarism or accident, is due a likeness between Thompson's

> So fearfully the sun doth sound,
>   Clanging up beyond Cathay ;
> For the great earthquaking sunrise rolling up beyond **Cathay,**

and Mr. Kipling's " And the sun came up like **thunder** out of China, 'cross the Bay."

> A wind got up frae off the sea.
> It blew the stars as clear could be.
> It blew in the een of a' the three,
>   And the mune was shining clearly !

sang Stevenson's Highlander years before Thompson wrote

> And a great wind blew all the stars to flare.

But in neither case is Thompson, though the dates are against him, proved a thief.

Of a review of his *Poems* in the *St. James's Gazette :*—

" I only deprecate in it the implied comparison to Dante, and the to-me-bewildering comparison to Matthew Arnold. 'Tis not merely that I have studied no poet less ; it is that I should have thought we were in the sharpest contrast. His characteristic fineness lies in that very form and restraint to which I so seldom attain : his characteristic drawback in the lack of that full stream which I am seldom without. The one needs and becomes strict banks—for he could not fill wider ones ; the other too readily overflows all banks. But these are casual specks on an appreciative article—an article as unusually appreciative as that in the *Chronicle.*"

The Vulgate

"French poetry—all modern European poetry—may in the ultimate analysis be found derivable from the Latin hymn," says an *Edinburgh* reviewer (January 1911). Francis Thompson in that case was familiar with the remote ancestry of his house. He helped himself from the hymns.

Of the prose of the Vulgate he wrote in a review of a paper by Dr. Barry on St. Jerome's revision :—

"No tongue can say so much in so little. And literary diffuseness is tamed in our Vulgate not only by the terser influence of the rustic Latin, but by the needs begotten of Hebrew brevity. Nor to any un-prejudiced ear can this Vulgate Latin be unmusical. For such an ear the authority of John Addington Symonds (though Dr. Barry adduces that authority) is not needed to certify its fine variety of new move-ment. ' *Surge, propera, amica mea, columba mea, formosa mea, et veni;*' that and the whole passage which follows, or that preceding strain closing in—' *Fulcite me floribus, stipate me malis, quia amore langueo*' : could prose have more impassioned loveliness of melody? Compare it even with the beautiful corresponding English of the Authorised (Protestant) Version ; the advantage in music is not to the English, but to the soft and wooing fall of these deliciously lapsing syllables. Classic prose, could it even have forgotten its self-conscious living-up to foreign models, had never the heart of passion for movement such as this, or as the queenly wail of the *Lamentations* — ' *Quomodo sedet sola civitas plena populo! facta est quasi vidua domina gentium!*'

"If the Vulgate be the fountain-source, the rivers are numerous—and neglected. How many outside the ranks of ecclesiastics ever open the Breviary, with its Scriptural collocations over which has presided a won-derful symbolic insight, illuminating them by passages from the Fathers and significant prayers? The offices of the Church are suggested poetry—that of the Assumption, for example, the 'Little Office,' and almost all those of Our Lady. The very arrangement of the liturgical year is a suggested epic, based as it is on a deep parallel between the evolution of the seasons and that of the Christian soul of the human race."

And further on :—

"It is a pedant who cannot see in St. Augustine one of the great minds of the world, master of a great style. Some flights in the *Confessions* are almost lyric, such as the beautiful '*Sero te amavi*,' or the magnificent discourse on memory. The last books especially of the *City of God* would sometimes be no wise incongruous beside the *Paradiso* of Dante. St. Bernard's prose rises at times into a beauty which is essentially that of penetratingly ethereal poetry : not for nothing has Dante exalted him in the *Paradiso* ; not for nothing does such a man exalt such men. In them is the meat and milk and honey of religion ; and did we read them our souls would be larger-boned."

Of his early acquaintance with the Bible he writes :—

"The Bible as an influence from the literary standpoint has a late but important date in my life. As a child I read it, but for its historical interest. Nevertheless, even then I was greatly, though vaguely, impressed by the mysterious imagery, the cloudy grandeurs, of the Apocalypse. Deeply uncomprehended, it was, of course, the pageantry of an appalling dream ; insurgent darkness, with wild lights flashing through it ; terrible phantasms, insupportably revealed against profound light, and in a moment no more ; on the earth hurryings to and fro, like insects of the earth at a sudden candle ; unknown voices uttering out of darkness darkened and disastrous speech; and all this in motion and turmoil, like the sands of a fretted pool. Such is the Apocalypse as it inscribes itself on the verges of my childish memories. In early youth it again drew me to itself, giving to my mind a permanent and shaping direction. In maturer years Ecclesiastes (casually opened during a week of solitude in the Fens) masterfully affected a temperament in key with its basic melancholy. But not till quite later years did the Bible as a whole become an influence. Then, however, it came with decisive power. But not as it had influenced most writers. My style, being already formed, could receive no evident impress from it: its vocabulary had come to me through the great writers of our language. In the first place its influence was mystical; it revealed to me a whole scheme of existence, and lit up life like a lantern."

"Assumpta Maria" is "vamped" from the office of Our Lady; he had no notion of concealing its origin, but rather sought to point it out. The prayer to the Virgin is itself a confession—

Remember me, poor Thief of Song!

He wrote in 1893, with an enclosure of poems, including the "Assumpta Maria":—

"They are almost entirely taken from the Office of the Assumption, some from the Canticle, a few images from the heathen mythology. Some very beautiful images are from a hymn by St. Nerses the Armenian, rendered in *Carmina Mariana*. You will perceive therefore the reason of the motto from Cowley: 'Thou needst not make new songs, but say the old.'"

It is at the close of the poem that Francis calls himself "poor Thief of Song." The theme put honesty out of reach. It has been treated too often. Even Donne's

Of Words ; Of Origins ; Of Metre

"Immensity cloistered in the dear womb" is part of "the great conspiracy" of Marian Song.

The lines most in question in St. Nerses's hymn, thus rendered in English by W. H. Kent, are—

> Dwelling-place of light, be gladsome ;
> Temple, where the true Sun dwelleth ;
> Throne of God, rejoice, thou bearest
> Him, the Word of the Almighty . . .
> Home of him whom none may compass ;
> Hostel, where the sun finds resting . . .
> Daniel's great Stone-bearing Mountain ;
> Solomon's fair Hill of Incense ;
> Fountain sealed for him that keeps it ;
> Garden closed for him that plants."

"I remember," Francis writes, "Father Anselm's expression of comical surprise at a passage in ' Her Portrait,' where I had employed the terms of Canon Law relating to ecclesiastical property. Why, he said, here's a whole page of *De Contractibus* in poetry. His surprise was increased when I remarked that I had never read any work on the subject. . . . I said I got the terms where any one else could get them—from English history.

"Equal was the surprise of another person at finding a whole passage of Anna Kingsford in my poetry. It was a passage describing the earth's *aura*, really remarkably like a passage in a book I had not at the time read."

In all these cases he is an imitator by choice—independent in taking only what suits him and depending only where he will. In one case he was an imitator not by choice but by compulsion, a slavish follower. There was no more choice for him in following Patmore than for a son born like his father. Such a poem as "By Reason of Thy Law" was born of the *Unknown Eros* odes.

*   *   *   *   *   *   *

Poets do not Err

Here are quoted various sentences from F. T.'s note-books, letters, and published prose bearing on metre, or allied subjects.

Of the learning of poets :—

"I have studied and practised metre with arduous love since I was sixteen; reviewed poets and poetasters this twenty years or more, and never yet impeached one of such a matter as infraction or ignorance of academic metrical rule. For I know they don't *do* it—either poet or poetaster. Poetasters least of all men, because they are your metrical Tybalts and fight by the book—one, two, and the third in your bosom; poets because they have the law in their members, assimilated by eager obedience from their practised youth; their liberty is such liberty won by absorption of law, and is kept in its orbit by their sensitive feodality to the invisible—the hidden—sun of inspiration. 'They do not wrong but with just cause': such faults as they may commit in metre belong not to this elementary class. I have criticised poets' metre, but ever in the broader and larger things where blemish accused them not of ignorance or the carelessness that comes of inattention to rule. I repeat, they don't do those things, and my study of metre, poetry, and poets early taught me that."

And he cites an unjustified attack on Stephen Phillips as a case in point.

Of "Heard on the Mountain," a translation from Hugo in *New Poems*—a metrical experiment :—

"That splendid fourteen-syllable metre of Chapman, to which Mr. Kipling has given a new vitality, I have here treated after the manner of Drydenian rhyming heroics; not only with the occasional triplet, but also the occasional Alexandrine, represented by a line of eight accents. Students of metre will see the analogy to be strict, the

175

line of eight being merely the carrying to completion of the catalectic line of seven, as the Alexandrine is merely the filling out of the catalectic line of five accents."

Of "The Ode to the Setting Sun" :—

"An ode I have thought not unworthy of preservation, though it was my first published poem of any importance. In view of the considerable resemblance between the final stanza and a well-known stanza in Mr. Davidson's 'Ballad of a Nun,' it is right to state that 'The Ode to the Setting Sun' was published as long ago as 1889. The poem has some interest to me in view of the frequent statement that I modelled the metre of 'The Hound of Heaven' on the ode metre of Mr. Patmore. 'The Ode to the Setting Sun' was published before I had seen any of Mr. Patmore's work ; and a comparison of the two poems will therefore show exactly the extent to which the later poem was affected by that great poet's practice. The ode metre of *New Poems* is, with this exception, completely based on the principles which Mr. Patmore may virtually be said to have discovered."

Of accent and quantity :—

"The classic poets are careful to keep up an interchange between accent and quantity, an approach and recession, just as is the case with the great English poets. Yet with all the lover-like coquetry between the two elements, they are careful that they shall never wed—again as with the great English poets. But (and here lies the difference) the position of the two elements is *exactly reversed*. It is quantity which gives the law—is the masculine element—in classic verse ; it is accent in English. In English, quantity takes the feminine or subordinate place, as accent does in classic verse. In both it is bad metre definitely to unite the two."

Blank Verse

Sending poetry from Pantasaph, October 1894, he writes to A. M. :—

" My dear lady, . . . the long poem, ('The Anthem of Earth') was written only as an exercise in blank verse ; indeed, as you will see, I have transferred to it whole passages from my prose articles.   So it is solely for your judgment on the metre that I send it.   It is my first serious attempt to handle that form, and it is not likely that I have succeeded all at once ; especially as I have not confined myself to the strict limits of the metre, but have laid my hand at one clash among all the licences with which the Elizabethans build up their harmonies. The question is whether individual passages succeed sufficiently to justify the belief that I might reach mastery with practice, or whether I fail in such a fashion as to suggest native inaptitude for the metre.   M—— thinks the poem a failure.   Being a mistress of numerous metre, she counts all her feet ; though her chosen method is the dactylic, since she uses her fingers for the purpose.   It is well known that by this profound and exhaustive method of practical study, you may qualify yourself to sit in judgment on Shakespeare's metre, if he should submit his MS. to you from the Shades.   I confess my practice is so slovenly that if anyone should assure me that my lines had eleven syllables apiece, I should be obliged to allow I had never counted them. We poor devils who write by ear have a long way to go before we attain to the scientific company of poets like M——, who has her verses at her fingers' ends.—F. T."

To the same purpose are notes on Henley's " Voluntaries " :—

" They are in so-called 'irregular' lyric metre, ebbing and flowing with the motion itself.   Irregular it is not, though the law is concealed.   Only a most delicate response to the behests of inspiration can make such

Of Words ; Of Origins ; Of Metre

verse successful. As some persons have an instinctive sense of orientation by which they know the quarter of the East, so the poet with this gift has a subtle sense of hidden metrical law, and in his most seeming-vagrant metres revolves always (so to speak) round a felt though invisible centre of obedience."

The immethodical exactitude of his method is further suggested in his note-book :—

"Temporal variations of metre responsive to the emotions, like the fluctuations of human respiration, which also varies indefinitely, under the passage of changeful emotions, and yet keeps an approximate temporal uniformity."

Here he evidently alludes particularly to the ode metre of "The Unknown Eros," for which Patmore claimed that the length of line was controlled by its emotional significance. On this subject another note must directly bear. It is to the effect that the matter forces the metre; that the poet is the servant, not master, of his theme, and that he must write in such metre as it dictates.

Again he writes :—

"Every great poet makes accepted metre a quite new metre, imparts to it a totally new movement, impresses his own individuality upon it."

And again :—

"All verse is rhythmic; but in the graver and more subtle forms the rhythm is veiled and claustral; it not only avoids obtruding itself, but seeks to withdraw itself from notice."

And again :—

"Metrically Poe is the lineal projector of Swinburne,

Numerous Versification

and hence of modern metre at large—an influence most disastrous and decadent, like nearly all his influence on letters."[1]

His own choice among his metrical exercises was "The Making of Viola," of which a critic has said (the *Nation*, November 23, 1907) "that the words seem never to alight, they so bound and rebound, and are so agile with life."

In an early *Merry England* article he writes of Crashaw :—

"His employment (in the 'Hymn to St. Teresa' and its companion 'The Bleeding Heart') of those mixed four-foot Iambics and Trochaics so often favoured by modern poets, marks an era in the metre. Coleridge (in the *Biographia Literaria*) adopts an excellent expression to distinguish measures which follow the changes of the sense from those which are regulated by a pendulum-like beat or tune—however *new* the tune—overpowering all intrinsic variety. The former he styles *numerous* versification. Crashaw is beautifully numerous, attaining the most delicate music by veering pause and modulation—

> Miser of sound and syllable, no less
> Than Midas of his coinage.

We have said advisedly that the 'St. Teresa' marks an era in metre. For Coleridge was largely indebted to it and acknowledged his debt."

---

[1] To this he recurs in a note on Tennyson :—"Tennyson too pictorial. Picture verges on marches of sister-art, painting. Feminine ; only not so entirely so as Swinburne ;—still has remnants of statelier mood and time. Metre—beginning of degeneration completed in and by Swinburne."

CHAPTER IX : AT MONASTERY GATES

In 1892 F. T. had gone to Pantasaph. He was quartered, at first, in Bishop's House, at the monastery gates,[1] and the sandalled friars looked after all his wants—from boots to dogma.

"Thompson is ever so much better," writes Fr. Marianus soon after the poet's arrival. " He looks it too. He is less melancholy, in fact at times quite lively." And they cared for him delicately :—

" There is only one little thing about which I have some difficulty. I know Thompson must need now and again some little things, but I don't like to ask him does he need anything (though I have supplied him with paper, ink, &c.), and I should feel grateful if you would kindly write to Thompson and tell him to ask me for anything he may want—that I am his procurator."

His own first letter from Wales :—

" *C'en est fait,* as regards the opium. . . . I am very comfortable, thanks to your kindness and forethought. Father Anselm seems to have taken a fancy to me—also he is afraid of my being lonely—and comes to see me every other day. He took me all over the Monastery on Monday, and has just left me after a prolonged discussion of the things which ' none of us know anything about,' as Marianus says when he is getting the worst of an argument."

Father Anselm, now Archbishop of Simla, was the one of the friars of whom the poet spoke as his philosophical

[1] Afterwards he lodged at the post-office, and finally in a cottage on the hill behind the monastery.

schoolmaster, and to whom he was indebted for the awakening of new intellectual interests. Coventry Patmore, too, as his correspondence testifies, knew how to appreciate the hospitality and good talk of the friars. Both the poets contributed to the *Annals* of Father Anselm's editorship. Between the younger poet and Father Anselm there sprang up a close friendship, which was not without its influence upon Thompson's later work. During his Guardianship at Crawley Father Anselm was responsible for the inception of the Roger Bacon Society, whose meetings F. T. sometimes attended.

Father Alphonsus, whose death in 1911 deprived English Franciscans of their Provincial, also had much intercourse with Francis Thompson. For this priest, as he himself alleged, the odes of Coventry Patmore made a new earth and a new Heaven.

It is not, perhaps, impertinent here and now to attribute to the younger poet's association with the friars an allusion in one of the most famous of his lines. "The bearded counsellors of God" has the local colour if not of Paradise, at least of Pantasaph.[1]

"Poetry clung about the cowls of his Order," wrote Francis, in dealing with the works of St. Francis and of Thomas of Celano. He had the right companions, as far as any were admitted, for the new periods of composition.

They, as he, had sacred commerce *cum Domina Paupertate*. These, his companions, were once named by her "my Brothers and most dear Friends"; they, entertaining her on bread and water, had given her a couch upon earth and the grass.

"When she asked for a pillow, they straightway brought her a stone, and laid it under her Head. So, after she had slept for a brief space in peace, she arose and asked the Brothers to show

---

[1] The Capuchins (Franciscans), are peculiar in aspect among Religious Orders as bearded friars.

her their Cloister. And they, leading her to the Summit of a Hill, showed her the wide World, saying : This is our Cloister, O Lady Poverty. Thereupon she bade them all sit down together, and opening her mouth she began to speak unto them Words of Life."

Francis her poet heard, though at that time he was not come to the hills about Pantasaph. He had himself found stones for pillows in the market-place, and had written of one to whom he had half-likened himself—

> Anchorite, who didst dwell
> With all the world for cell ! [1]

St. Francis himself had other words for the same thought :—" Meditate as much while on this journey as if you were shut up in a hermitage or in your cell, for wherever we are, wherever we go, we carry our cell with us ; Brother Body is our cell."

Of the grounds for a good understanding between the priests and the poet there are hints in Richard de Bary's *Franciscan Days of Vigil* :—

" Francis Thompson was just then [1894] a favourite with the Order, and there were keen discussions about his mystical intuitions. In the spirit of the Franciscan *Laudes Domini*, the Breviary Offices of the Seasons, Thompson recalled them, and expounded the phases of asceticism that ran with them in his poem, ' From the Night of Forebeing.'

* * * * * * *

" The centre of interest in the household was the poet, Francis Thompson, who spent the summer of that year in a neighbouring cottage. Walks in the late evening did not result in much conversation ; but at evening gatherings in my room the poet used often to join the party, and argued with vigour and persuasiveness on favourite topics. The Franciscans had learnt a kind of

---

[1] This was written long before Mr. Montgomery Carmichael's translation of *The Lady Poverty* brought the thirteenth-century writer's claim to the world as the Franciscan cloister to Thompson's notice.

More Poetry

art of drawing their mystical guest into conversation. The way was to introduce a subtle contradiction to his pet theories, which would in a moment produce a storm of protesting eloquence."

They drew him also on one only occasion into more formal speech. Fr. Anselm prevailed upon him to enter into the discussion that followed a paper read by the Hon. W. Gibson, now Lord Ashbourne, at a meeting of the Roger Bacon Society, held at the Monastery, Crawley, in January 1898.

In April, 1894, an observer writes to W. M. :—

"You will be glad to hear that Francis has written an Ode which I hear is longer than anything he has done yet. Also that the 'frenzy' being on him he has begun another poem yesterday. No one sees him but Fr. Anselm, to whom he comes every evening and whom he tells of his work. He told him last night that since you had left he seemed to have a return of all the old poetic power. Of course he is flying over hill and dale and never to be seen, but I am sure you will be as glad as I am at this fresh development—especially as your and Alice's visit has evidently called it forth." [1]

To the departed visitors the poet himself wrote :—

"BISHOP'S HOUSE, PANTASAPH.

"DEAREST WILFRID AND ALICE,—As you are together in my thoughts, so let me join you together in this note. I cannot express to you what deep happiness your visit gave me; how dear it was to see your faces again. I think 'the leaves fell from the day' indeed when your train went out of the station ; and I never heard the birds with such sad voices.

"I send you herewith the poem I have been at work on. It is very long, as you will see—as long, I think, as Wordsworth's great ode. That would not matter—'so I were equal with him in renown.' But as it is—— !

"My fear is that thought in it has strangled poetic impulse. However of all that you are better judges than I.

[1] "After Her Going" was written in these days.

183

At Monastery Gates

"Does the dear Singer still refuse me her songs? My health is better again, though unfortunately more fluctuant than I could wish. Love to all the chicks. With very best love to yourselves, dear ones,—Yours ever,

FRANCIS THOMPSON."

In another letter F. T. tells of his recurring powers of composition.

"Am overflowing with a sudden access of literary impulse. I think I could write a book in three months, if thoughts came down in such an endless avalanche as they are doing at present. But the collecting and recasting of my later poems for Lane blocks the way for the next month, so that I can only write an essay in an odd hour or two when I lie awake in bed."

He heralds the coming of his sacred poetry in "From the Night of Forebeing"—

> . . . The wings
> Hear I not in prævenient winnowings
> Of coming songs, that lift my hair and stir it?
>
> .   .   .   .
>
> That—but low breathe it, lest the Nemesis
> Unchild me, vaunting this—
> Is bliss, the hid, hugged, swaddled bliss!
> O youngling Joy caressed,
> That on my now first-mothered breast
> Pliest the strange wonder of thine infant lip.

From the highlands of his poetry, from the glory of height in which he wrote "The Dread of Height" and other poems of "Sight and Insight," he looked down upon his former poetry :—

> Therefore I do repent
> That with religion vain,
> And misconceivèd pain,
> I have my music bent
> To waste on bootless things its skiey-gendered rain.

Depression

The writing done, he is again cast down :—

"I should be very glad if you will send me the *Edinburgh*. It would do me good; I never since I knew you felt so low-hearted and empty of all belief in myself. I could find it in my heart to pitch my book into the fire; and I shall be thoroughly glad to get it off to you, for my heart sinks at the sight or thought of it. The one remaining poem which had stuck in my gizzard at the last I succeeded in polishing off last night, sitting up all night to do it; and I must start on the preface as soon as this letter is off."

A neighbour's reminiscence is that given by Fr. David Bearne, S. J., in *The Irish Monthly*, November 1908, who

"recalls two occasions on which I had the privilege of chatting with the poet—once *tête-à-tête* in the delightful seclusion of the gardens at St. Beuno's College, within sight of Snowdon and of the sea ; once in the thick of the pious crowd that throng each year to Pantasaph for the Portiuncula. Of each occasion I retain the happiest memories, though I cannot recall the exact words of any single sentence that he uttered. He knew me only as a Jesuit student of theology, and though I longed to tell him how much I loved his work, I failed to do so, partly from a sort of reverential shyness, and partly because, though he was no chatterer, he led the conversation. On one occasion I know he had just been making a pilgrimage to St. Winefride's Well. He spoke of it at length and with great enthusiasm. But my own mind was occupied with the man, rather than with what he said. . . . As men commonly understand the word there was no ' fascination ' about Thompson. There was something better. There was the *sancta simplicitas* of the true poet and the real child."

In 1893 his father was at Rhyl, and Francis sought him there, but without invitation. He writes :—

"I went over on Monday—only to find that he had left the previous Wednesday, after having been there for a month, which things are strange."

To Dr. Thompson the strangeness would be in Francis's
185

unwontedly active desire to see him. It is probable
that each exaggerated the other's feeling of estrangement. When, in April 1896, Francis heard that his father
was dying, he went to Ashton, but too late. After the
funeral he writes :—

"I never saw my father again, I cannot speak
about it at present. ——— ——— made it very bitter
for me. It has been nothing but ill-health and sorrow
lately, but I must not trouble you with these things.
I saw my sister looking the merest girl still, and
sweeter than ever. She did not look a day older than
ten years ago. She said I looked very changed and
worn." [1]

At Downing he had neighbours in the Feilding family,
and it was to the monastery church that Lady Denbigh
came to "make her soul" at the penitential seasons of
the year. This church her husband began to build
when he was an Anglican ; then, changing his religion,
he had changed the dedication of his bricks and mortar.
From a letter of the Hon. Everard Feilding to W. M.
after F. T.'s death :—

"Your letter reached me at a time when my mind, like that,
I think, of many others, was full of Francis Thompson ; and during
the preceding three nights I had been reading and re-reading aloud
to two or three friends certain of his poems which had specially
touched me, including the *Nocturn*, infinitely pathetic from my
knowledge, however slight, of the man.

"Need I say that I am truly touched to hear that Thompson
should have thought my modest appreciation of his work as anything more than the most natural thing in the world ? I only
met him three times, each time in the company of my friend
Head,[2] who shared my admiration. Our meeting came about in
an absurd enough wise. A ghost (possibly you have heard, or

---

[1] The mortuary card, preserved in F. T.'s prayer-book, runs .—
"Of your charity pray for the soul of Charles Thompson, M.R.C.S., L.S.A.,
who departed this life April 9th, 1896, aged 72, fortified by the rites of
Holy Church"—with the motto "The silent and wise man shall be
honoured."
[2] Dr. Henry Head, F.R.S.

Charles Thompson

Mary Turner Thompson

Francis Thompson's Parents

The Pantasaph Ghost

not heard, of my taste for these creatures) was reported active in the neighbourhood of Pantasaph, on my brother's place in Wales. My own inclination supplied the motive, and an idle week of Head's the occasion, of a visit there, and we camped a few nights in a derelict mansion, rejoicing in the appropriately ominous name of Pickpocket Hall, in hopes of interviewing the spectre. Needless to say, we failed. But we got the story of the Irish monk; also the story of the practical nun, who scented buried treasure which she hoped to unearth to the profit of her community; and of the oldest inhabitant; and, finally, of the Poet. The people at the monastery had told us that Thompson had been a witness, and we decided on a call; and at about five one evening made our way to the tiny cottage where he lodged, and asked for him. He was still in bed. We returned at 6.30. He was *still* in bed. So we concocted a letter, suitable, as we imagined, to the person who had written Thompson's poems, not quite English, somewhat elided, and as inverted as we could manage, ending with an invitation to breakfast at 9.30 that night and a conference with our hobgoblin. And somewhat pleased with our effort, we retired to our haunted mansion and awaited events. At 9.30 he came and breakfasted while we supped. We said at once to one another: ' This is not the man to whom we wrote that letter.' For, instead of parables in polysyllables and a riot of imagery, we found simplicity and modesty and a manner which would have been almost commonplace if it had not been so sincere. But the charm and interest of his talk grew with the night, and it was already dawn when, the ghost long since forgotten, we escorted him back across the snow to his untimely lunch. He told us, I remember, of his poetical development, and of how, until recently, he had fancied that the end of poetry was reached in the stringing together of ingenious images, an art in which, he somewhat naïvely confessed, he knew himself to excel; but that now he knew it should reach further, and he hoped for an improvement in his future work. *New Poems* was subsequent to this meeting. It was only in his account of the ghost, which had ' charged his body like a battery so that he felt thunderstorms in his hair,' that the imaginary individual to whom we had addressed our letter revealed himself.

" He dined with us twice afterwards, the second time appearing an hour late, with his head tied up in an appalling bandage, the result of having been knocked down by a hansom, so that I took his arrival under the circumstances as a compliment second only to your own kind letter. For years I haven't seen him. A letter,

At Monastery Gates

to ask him if he would renew acquaintance, has several times trembled on the tip of my pen; but I was told he had become inaccessible, and it never went, and now I am very sorry."

Something of the Pantasaph ghost got into verse, which I take from a note-book:—

> More creatures lackey man
> Than he has note of : through the ways of air
> Angels go here and there
> About his businesses : we tread the floor
> Of a whole sea of spirits : evermore
> Oozy with spirits ebbs the air and flows
> Round us, and no man knows.
> Spirits drift upon the populous breeze
> And throng the twinkling leaves that twirl on summer trees.

In notes headed "Varia on Magic" he quotes the *Anatomy of Melancholy :*—

"The air is not so full of flies in summer, as it is at all times of invisible devils: this Paracelsus stiffly maintains."

F. T. wrote to A. M. after the meeting:—

"Is it true that you are going to collect your contributions to the papers during the last few years? I sincerely hope so. . . . There was a Dr. Head, a member of the Savile Club, over here last autumn with Everard Feilding, who spoke with great enthusiasm of your "Autolycus." He quoted a bit relating, I think, to Angelica Kaufmann,[1] who spent a large number of years in 'taking the plainness off paper.' The phrase delighted him, as it did me who had not seen it. . . . I passed a pleasant night with the two. We were sleeping in a haunted house to interview the ghost; but as he was a racing-man, he probably found our conversation too literary to put off his incognito."

[1] It was not Angelica, but Mrs. Delany.

He is in Difficulties

The friars helped him to another companion, Coventry Patmore, who as a member of the Third Order, went in 1894 to stay at Pantasaph. There Father Anselm, a bachelor of St. Francis, with the Lady Poverty first among his feminine acquaintance, could meet the greatest of English love-poets upon equal terms. It was to Fr. Anselm that Francis had lent Patmore's *Religio Poetæ* before trusting himself to review it, and it was by the same friar that he was helped to appreciate Patmore's trustworthiness as a witness to divine truths. By none save by a priest of the Church would the poet of the Church have been satisfied that he might lawfully accept, or attempt to accept, teaching that had once seemed to him inimical to orthodoxy. *Religio Poetæ*, at first a stumbling-block, was to become the corner-stone of his later poetry. Two years before (in August 1892) he had said there were two points in C. P.'s teaching—as to the nature of the union between God and man in this world and the next, and the definition of the constitution of Heaven—that he refused absolutely to accept. He went specially to Crawley in 1892 to consult Fr. Cuthbert on these points. And he had at first only unwillingly admitted Patmore's power over him. To a passage of St. John (chap. xxi.) he adds a note that reveals his mood :—

" Amen, Amen, I say to thee ; when thou wert younger, thou didst gird thyself, and didst walk where thou wouldst. But when thou shalt be old, thou shalt stretch forth thy hands and another shall gird thee, and lead thee where thou wouldst not."

To this he adds : " Apply to spiritual maturity."

The barriers down, they quickly recognised cause for intimacy. It was during Patmore's first visit that Francis made the discovery. He seems at first hardly to have known it. Writing of it to A. M. :—

" Dear Lady, I thank you for your kind letter, though

it observed an impenitent silence on the subject of your songs unsent. (That last phrase has a ring of the only Lewis.)[1] I have had a charming visit from Mr. Patmore. He bore himself towards me with a dignity and magnanimity which are not of this age's stature. By the way, he repeated to me two or three short poems addressed to yourself. I hope there may be a series of such songs. You would then have a triple tiara indeed—crowned by yourself, by me, and highest crowned by him."

But afterwards in the more vivid light of memory, he said :—

"Though never a word on either side directly touched or explained the exceptional nature of the proposal, it was well understood between us—by me no less than by him—that it was no common or conventional friendship he asked of me. Not therefore has he sought out my Welsh hermitage ; and scalpelled the fibres of me."

As a rule Francis found as much solitude among the Welsh mountains as in the desolation of the Harrow Road, but now Patmore walked with him.

F. T. notes their common pleasure in the landscape, "particularly beautiful—something to do with the light, Patmore thinks." To be in common light is even better preparation for the communion of poets than to be on common ground. Friar and seer between them enclosed him at evening in the monastic parlour. Patmore writes :—

"Francis Thompson and all the Fathers spent two hours last night in my room, and we had excellent talk. Father Anselm, the Superior, and a profound contemplative, said he had never read anything so fine as the ' Precursor.' He and I had a long talk about nuptial love, and he went all lengths with me in honour of the marriage embrace. The Fathers help me to get through my cigarettes, of which I should like to have another consignment as soon as possible."

---

[1] An allusion to Lewis Morris's *Songs Unsung.*

Sanctity Essential Song

And again:—

" I spend part of my day with Francis Thompson, who is a delightful companion, full of the best talk."

With the reading of *Religio Poetæ* and the little book of St. Bernard translations, Francis discovers their author to be "deeply perceptive of the Scriptures' symbolic meanings, scouted by moderns ; and his instant intuitional use of the symbolic imagery gives his work the quality of substantial poetry. In proportion to the height of their sanctity the Saints are inevitable poets. Sanctity is essential song." These essays moved Francis to the rare point of letter-writing :—

" THE MONASTERY, PANTASAPH, *June* 15, '93.

" DEAR SIR,—The esoteric essays—which I naturally turned to first—could only have come from the writer of *The Unknown Eros.* One alone I have gracelessness— not to dispute—but to wish to extend. It is that on the ' Precursor,' where I quite admit the interpretation, but am inclined to stickle for an interpretation which would cover and include your own. Against one reprehensible habit of yours, however, revealed in this book, I feel forced to utter a protest. In a fragment of a projected article, which has remained a fragment, I had written of ' poets born with an instinctive sense of veritable correspondences hidden from the multitude.' Then I went on thus : ' In this, too, lies real distinction and fancy. Leigh Hunt, interpreting Coleridge as shallowly as Charmian interpreted the Soothsayer, said that fancy detected outward analogies, but imagination inward ones. The truth is that inward resemblance may be as superficial as outward resemblance ; and it is then the product of fancy, or fantasy. When the resemblance is more than a resemblance, when it is rooted in the hidden nature of things, its discernment is the product of imagination. This is the real distinction : fancy detects resemblances, imagination identities.' Now if

191

you will return to your own *Religio Poetæ*, you will
see of what I accuse you. Masters have privileges, I
admit, but I draw the line at looking over their pupils'
shoulders various odd leagues away.

"To be serious; your little book stands by a stream of
current literature like Cleopatra's Needle by the dirt-
eating Thames.

"I fear, alas! it will not receive the mysterious hiero-
glyph of the British Artisan. I remain, yours sincerely,
FRANCIS THOMPSON."

And a little later, of his own "Orient Ode":—

"DEAR MR. PATMORE,—I shall either send you with
this, or later, a small poem of my own; not for its
literary merit, but because, without such a disclaimer,
I fear you would think I had been the first to find your
book 'd——d good to steal from.' As a matter of fact,
it was written soon after Easter, and was suggested
by passages in the liturgies of Holy Saturday, some
of which—at rather appalling length—I have quoted
at the head of its two parts. That was done for the
sake of those who might cavil at its doctrines. Indeed
—with superfluous caution—I intended much of it to be
sealed; but your book has mainly broken the seals I
had put upon it. There is quite enough in it of yours,
without the additional presumption that I had hastened
to make immediate use of your last book. As far as
others are concerned, it must rest under that imputation
to which the frequent coincidence in the selection of
symbolism — as an example, the basing of a whole
passage on the symbolic meaning of the *West*—very
naturally leads. To yourself such coincidence is ex-
plicable, it will not be to 'outsiders.'—Yours always,
FRANCIS THOMPSON."

And later:—

"What I put forth as a bud he blew out and it
blossomed. The contact of our ideas was dynamic;

Egyptian Worship

he reverberated my idea with such and so many echoes that it returned to me greater than I gave it forth. He opened it as you would open an oyster, or placed it under a microscope, and showed me what it contained."

"CRECCAS COTTAGE, PANTASAPH, *Tuesday.*

"DEAR MR. PATMORE,—The poem, even if I am to take your high and valued praises quite literally, has a defect of which you must be conscious, though you have courteously refrained from noticing it. It echoes your own manner largely, in the metre, and even in some of the diction—the latter a thing of which, I think, I have seldom before rendered myself guilty.

"Now it is possible in rare cases — *e.g.* Keats' 'Hyperion'—for an echo to take on body enough to survive as literature. But even should my poem so survive it must rest under the drawback of being no more distinctive Thompson than 'Hyperion' is distinctive Keats.

"With regard to the other poem, I want to allude particularly to your invaluable correction of my misuse of the Western symbolism. On re-examination, the whole passage discloses a confusion of thought naturally causing a confusing of symbolism. My attention was called to the point about Egyptian worship by a footnote in Dr. Robert Clarke's 'Story of a Conversion,' in *Merry England.*[1] I at once perceived its symbolic significance,

---

[1] On this subject, and the derivation of portions of Ecclesiastes, he corresponded with Fr. Clarke. The contents of commonplace-books of a somewhat early period suggest a taste for many kindred themes. In one he has entered random "Varia on Magic," accounts of and comments on many heresies, suspicions of the Masons, and fears of a Divine Visitation upon the general wickedness in the shape of general war; with these are important notes on Creation Myths, the Chaldean Genesis, the Egyptian Crocodile, the Kabbalist Doctrine of the Pre-existence of Souls; some symbols connected with the Incarnation, the Lotus, the ritual of the funeral sacrifice, with transcriptions from the *Book of Respirations*, the *Prayer to Ammon Ra, &c.;* and *The meaning of Easter*, a cutting scored with his own excursions into the etymology of the word—from Ishtar, the Chaldæan goddess—"And Ishtar I take to be Ashak Tar (or Tur) the Lady of the Light of the Way." But at the turn of a few pages he is found enlarging and correcting. Still nearer his real concern are the notes on varieties of the Cross symbol.

and asked myself how it came that we reckoned our points of the compass facing to the North. The only explanation I could surmise was that it was a relic of Set-worship among our Saxon ancestors. Do you mean that *historically* men have prayed in three distinct periods to W., E., and N. ?

Always yours,
FRANCIS THOMPSON."

C. P. to F. T. :—

"LYMINGTON, HANTS, *September* 10, '95.

"MY DEAR THOMPSON,—I hope I have not kept your Poem too long. I have read it several times, and found it quite intelligible enough for song which is also prophecy. We are upon very much the same lines, but you, I think, are more advanced than I am. 'Dieu et ma Dame' is the legend of both of us, but at present Ma Dame is too much for the balance, peace, and purity of my religion. There is too much of heart-ache in it.

"I have ventured to affix a few notes of interrogation to unusual modes of expression.

"I hear, from Mrs. Meynell, that Mr. Meynell is with you. Please remember me very kindly to him.—Yours ever truly,
COVENTRY PATMORE.

"*P.S.*—The world has worshipped turning to the West, to the East, and to the North. The 'New Eve' is the South, and, when we turn thither, all things will be renewed, and God will 'turn our captivity as Rivers in the South,' and we shall know Him in the flesh 'from sea to sea.'"

He later explains that the "South" is the symbol of Divine Womanhood. The next letter from Patmore, dated a month later, is also of symbolism :—

"I wish I could see and talk to you on the subject of the symbolism you speak of. The Bible and all the theologies are full of it, but it is too deep and significant to get itself uttered in writing. The Psalms especially are full of it. On the matter of the 'North' note that verse : 'Promotion cometh not from the South, nor the East, nor the West.' That is, it cometh from the North. The North seems always to signify the original Godhead, the 'Father'

The North

—or the Devil. For the same symbol is used in the Bible and in the mythologies for either extreme.[1] 'Water,' for example, is constantly used for the sensible nature in its extreme purity, as in the Blessed Virgin, or in its extreme corruption. This honouring of the 'North' may very likely have been at the bottom of the seeking of the points of the compass from that quarter.

"I hope, some day, to see and have speech with you on this and other matters. Meantime I will only hint that the North represents the simple Divine virility, the South the Divine womanhood,[2] the East their synthesis in the Holy Spirit, and the West the pure *natural* womanhood 'full of grace.' I could give you no end of proofs, but it would take me months to collect them, from all I have read and forgotten."

This spacious correspondence, on things that will not "get themselves uttered in writing," was, nevertheless, continued. F. T. writes:—

"You rather overlook the purport of my inquiry in regard to the symbolic question. I wanted to know if there had been any actual progressive development among the nations with regard to the quarters in which they worshipped—as an historic fact, apart from symbolic meaning. But this is such a minor matter, and the concluding hint of your letter contains so much of value to me, that I am not sorry you misapprehended me. Of course I am quite aware that it is impossible to answer openly—indeed impossible to ask openly—deeper matters in a letter. But that is not requisite in my case. It is enough that my gaze should be set in the necessary direction ; the rest may be safely left to the practised fixity of my looking. Indicative longings such as you

---

[1] In a poem " The Schoolmaster for God," which Francis thought just not good enough to put into a volume, he represents Satan as scaling the walls of God's garth, stealing the seed, and giving it a clandestine growth, which grew to fruit that made men who ate it an-hungered for God. And in this poem Satan is named "that Robber from the North." Again, in one of the " Ecclesiastical Ballads," the Veteran of Heaven declares, " The Prince I drave forth held the Mount of the North."

[2] See F. T.'s poem " The Newer Eve," or " After Woman," with whom the world should rise instead of fall.

employed in your letter, you may safely trust me to understand. With regard to what you say about the symbolism of the North, I had substantially discerned for myself. Indeed it formed part of a little essay already written. It will be none the worse for the corroboration of your remarks; there is always something in your way of stating even what is already to me a *res visa*, which adds sight to my seeing. The quotation from the Psalms is new and grateful to me. But I was aware of the thing to which it points. Shakespeare speaks of 'The lordly monarch of the North' (I was confusing it with a passage in *Comus*), and Butler remarks—

> Cardan believed great states depend
> Upon the tip o' the Bear's tail's end.

" Set was given by the Egyptians the lordship of temporal powers; and of course I am aware of the esoteric meaning of this and of Cardan's saying—indeed this was what I intended by my observation that I surmised our Northern aspect in reckoning the compass to be a relic of Set-worship among our Teuton ancestors; though of course I was aware that Set, by that name, was an Egyptian deity.

" Also I am familiar with the principle and significance in this and mythological imagery generally. Indeed, without the knowledge of this principle both Scripture and the mythologies are full of baffling contradictions. When I began seriously to consider mythologies comparatively, I cut myself with the broken reed on which all the 'scientific' students fall back—this significance belongs to an earlier, that to a later, development. But having eyes which 'scientific' students have not, I soon saw that fact gave me the lie in all directions. And when I came to make a comprehensive study of the Hebrew prophets, with the Eastern mythologies in mind, I speedily discovered the systematic use of the dual significance, and the difficulty vanished."

Perfection beyond Hope

From Coventry Patmore :—

" Thank you for your very interesting letter, which shows me how extraordinarily alike are our methods of and experience in contemplation. . . .

" God bless and help you to bear your crown of thorns, and to prosper in the great, though possibly obscure, career He seems to have marked out for you ! My work, such as it is, is done, and I am now only waiting, somewhat impatiently, for death, and the fulfilment of the promises of God, which include all that we have ever desired here, in perfection beyond all hope.— Yours,   .   C. P."

CHAPTER X: MYSTICISM AND IMAGINATION

I saw Eternity the other night,
Like a great ring of pure and endless light.
—VAUGHAN.

I look to you to crush all this false mysticism.
—C. P. to F. T.

POEMS of "Sight and Insight," the first section of the new book, were to have been called "Mystical Poems." But the word mystical was, in the event, abandoned. As Catholic and thinker, he feared association with a label which means anything from mystification to "refined and luxurious indolence"—Mr. Edward Thomas's phrase for Maeterlinck's "Serres Chaudes." Unlike Thompson, the modern mystic shirks the rigid necessities of mental deportment. Like the swimmer who discards half his nimble faculties with his tweeds and lies, without swiftness or horizon, beating the water with heels shaped for boots and the road, the modern mystic fancies himself a better man out of his element than in it.

Even while the false mystic hopes to keep vacuity at arm's length, shadows press closely. His school is of shadows as the other of Light. Maeterlinck, on Mr. Arthur Symons's page of approval, is bidden take his place in the gloomy company. "He has realised how immeasurable is the darkness out of which he has just stepped, and the darkness into which we are about to pass. And he has realised how the thought and sense of that two-

198

Morality to the Nth Power

fold darkness invades the little space of light, in which, for a moment, we move ; the depth in which they shadow our steps, even in that moment's partial escape." The difference is not of words only ; or if of words only, loose thinking or slack experience is abroad. The whole school of Catholic mystics insists, in opposition, upon the exterior radiance trailing clouds of glory as they come into a world that is in the shadow, whether of God's or of a sinister hand.

Apart altogether from Maeterlinck's merits, his commentator's insistence illustrates the temper of the 'nineties. It is mainly the artistic value of his mystic's sense of mystery that appeals to Mr. Symons. The void, like the sheet-iron which makes stage thunder, has specific uses ; chunks out of the abyss make his scenery ; for his most effective dialogue he borrows largely from silence. Did he fight his way into the midst of mystery ; did he cleave it with revelation, or morality, its artistic uses would be gone. Darkness is the stronghold of such interesting emotions as terror — "fear shivers through these plays." " The mystic, let it be remembered, has nothing in common with the moralist," asserts Mr. Symons ; on the contrary, Francis Thompson's nearest exponent used the definition, " Mysticism is morality carried to the nth power."

Thompson's wariness about the word marks his respect for it. Joan, the hearer of voices, required a clear head when she stood her trial among the Theologians. Nor was the poet beguiled into the unorthodox. Compared with Meredith's philosophy—an illumination, it is true, but such illumination as candles give in his own draughty woods of Westermain— Thompson's authority is steady as the sheltered lamp of the sanctuary.

The mysticism that Thompson sought to avoid was obscuration, a thickening of the mental atmosphere by

Mysticism and Imagination

stray gleams, like the thickening of the air in a dusty room into which a sun-ray slants obliquely. The mysteries offer an excuse for confused thinking; the men and women who discover the doctrine of unity are lost in the jungle of its simplicity. The name of God, and the titles of His attributes must set the generations groping somewhat blindly if they carry no lantern of authority, or if the names of God and His attributes are too often taken into the babelling languages of empirics, or too anxiously conned.

"It is easy for a man to know God if he does not force himself to define Him" is a saying that covers much of a poet's reticence. For Thompson religion was never confusion; his mysteries blurred none of the common issues; they were packed as carefully as another man's title deeds; they were, he would have claimed, tied with red tape, cut from the cloth of the College of Cardinals.

"He is," said Patmore, "of all men I have known most naturally a Catholic. My Catholicism was acquired, his inherent."

Thompson carried his demand for clarity of thought and intention, if not always of diction, to great lengths :—

"A little common-sense," he once wrote at a time of slight misunderstanding, "is the best remedy—and I at least mean to have it"—a brave vaunt for a poet, but one which he made over and over again in regard to various aspects of the poetic character. "There is something wanting in genius when it does not show a clear and strong vein of common-sense. . . . Dante, indeed, is a perfect rebuke to those who suppose that mystical genius, at any rate, must be dissociated from common-sense. Every such poet should be able to give a clear and logical prose résumé of his teaching, as terse as a page of scholastic philosophy."

A Recantation

If portions of *New Poems* prove difficult and mysterious, we must go to Patmore for the defence: "A systematic philosopher, should he condescend to read the
following notes (*Rod, Root and Flower*), will probably
say, with a little girl of mine to whom I showed the stars
for the first time, ' How untidy the sky is ! ' "

Mysticism, as F T. knew it, " is morality carried to
the nth power." Mysticism — "rational mysticism "—
has been defined as "an endeavour to find God at first
hand, experimentally, in the soul herself independently
of all historical and philosophical presuppositions."
But at the same time Von Hügel condemns the
mysticism that is self-sufficient ; the constitutional and
traditional factors are essential to the Church. And
the religion of the Church is not, firstly, an affair
between the God and the man, but an affair between
God and Man ; is not an affair of the heart, but an
affair of Love ; not an affair of the brain, but of Mind.

That " to the Poet life is full of visions, to the Mystic
it is one vision ".[1] was the double rule of Francis
Thompson's practice. Having regarded the visions
and set them down, he would, in another capacity,
call them in. The Vision enfolded them all. Thus,
not long after it was written, he cancels even the
"Orient Ode," [2] and recants " his bright sciential idolatry,"
even though he had religiously adapted it to the
greater glory of God before it was half confessed.
"The Anthem of Earth" and the "Ode to the Setting
Sun " would also come under the censorship of his
anxious orthodoxy, to be in, part condemned. What
profiteth it a man, he asks in effect, if he gain the
whole sun but lose the true Orient—Christ ?

---

[1] Mr. Albert Cock in the *Dublin Review.*

[2] The ending of the " Orient Ode " seems, in the frank exultation of its
creed, to be unveiled and native pronouncement, as loud in its faith as the
last line of Patmore's " Faint yet Pursuing," where he ends by "hearing the
winds their Maker magnify."

Mysticism and Imagination

He came, even to the point of silence in certain moods, to feel the futility of all writings save such as were explicitly a confession of faith; and also of faithfulness to the institutional side of religion—the Church and the organised means of grace. "The sanity of his mysticism," says one commentator, "is the great value to the present generation. A high individual experiencing of purgation, illumination, and union, a quiet constancy in the corporate life, and discipleship as well as leadership; what combination more needed than this for our 'uncourageous day'?"

The poet is a priest who has no menial and earthly service. He has no parish to reconcile with paradise, no spire that must reach heaven from suburban foundations. The priest puts his very hand to the task of uniting the rational and communal factors of religion with the mystical. The altar-rail is the sudden and meagre boundary line between two worlds; he holds in his hand a Birmingham monstrance, and the monstrance holds the Host. He has no time to shake the dust of the street from his shoes before he treads the sanctuary. His symbolism is put to the wear and tear of daily use. As a middle-man in the commerce of souls, as the servant of the rational sides of the Church, tried by the forlorn circumstances of never-ceasing work, he may find himself shut out from the more purely mystical regions of his communion. To correct or amplify his religious experience, there are the enclosed Orders, the contemplatives of the Church. But to them, too, there must be complementary religious experience. They notch off the sum or score of the Church's experience, so that it may never be allowed to recede. It is left to the poet to prophesy or spy upon the increase of Wisdom and the multiplication of the Word.

He, too, in so far as he writes, is circumscribed by the uses of the world. The priest's ministry in infinitudes is bounded by his parish; the poet's by his language.

The Master-Key

And if religion is rightly defined as something more than communion between the man and the Almighty, as being besides the communion between man and man, and the sum of Mankind and the Almighty, then the poet is the immediate servant of God and Man.

Transfiguration is for Thompson the most familiar of mysteries. Good faith needs no Burning Bush. Or, rather, for the faithful every bush is alight. For this faithful poet the seasons were full of the promise of Resurrection. In spring he calls

> Hark to the *Jubilate* of the bird
> For them that found the dying way to life!

The rebirth of the earth after winter is the figure of the future life:

> Thou wak'st, O Earth,
> And work'st from change to change and birth to birth
> Creation old as hope, and new as sight.

and—

> All the springs are flash-lights of one Spring.

In the same poem he is seen at his daily business, the routine work of co-ordinating and synthesising. Light—the light of the sun—is also

> Light to the sentient closeness of the breast,
> Light to the secret chambers of the brain!

Arguments that go from heaven downwards are the commonplaces of his poetry; that he was ready to prove the sum of his wisdom from earth upwards is told in a passage of his prose :—

" If the Trinity were not revealed, I should nevertheless be induced to suspect the existence of such a master-key by the trinities through which expounds itself the spirit of man. Such a trinity is the trinity

203

of beauty—Poetry, Art, Music. Although its office is to create beauty I call it the trinity of beauty, because it is the property of earthly as of the heavenly beauty to create everything to its own image and likeness. Painting is the eye of Passion, Poetry is the voice of Passion, Music is the throbbing of her heart. For all beauty is passionate, though it be a passionless passion . . . Absolutely are these three the distinct manifestations of a single essence."

He had found another analogy in Pico della Mirandola, whom he thus renders :—

" 'The universe consists of three worlds—the earthly, the heavenly (the sun and stars), and the super-heavenly (the governing Divine influences). The same phenomena belong to each, but each have different grades of manifestation. Thus the physical element of fire exists in the earthly sphere ; the warmth of the sun in the heavenly ; and a seraphic, spiritual fire in the empyrean ; the first burns, the second quickens, the third loves.' Says Pico 'In addition to these three worlds (the macrocosm), there is a fourth (the microcosm) containing all embraced within them. This is Man, in whom are included a body formed of the elements, a heavenly spirit, reason, an angelic soul, and a resemblance to God.' "

" There is one reason for human confusion which is nearly always ignored. The world—the universe—is a fallen world. . . . That *should* be precisely the function of poetry—to see and restore the Divine idea of things, freed from the disfiguring accidents of their Fall—that is what the Ideal really is, or *should* be. . . . But of how many poets can this truly be said ? That gift also is among the countless gifts we waste and pervert ; and surely not the least heavy we must render is the account of its stewardship."

" Nature has no Heart "

"To be the poet of the return to Nature," Thompson continues, "is somewhat; but I would be the poet of the return to God." 'He was the accuser of Nature. He did not say

> By Grace divine,
> Not otherwise, Oh Nature ! are we thine,

but rather that by divine Grace Nature may be Man's, that he can go through it to his desire. Shut the gates of it and it is a cruel and obdurate abundance of clay, of earthworks.

"Nature has no heart. . . . Did I go up to yonder hill," he writes, "and behold at my feet the spacious amphitheatre of hill-girt wood and mead, overhead the mighty aerial *velarium*, I should feel that my human sadness was a higher and deeper and wider thing than all." "The Hound of Heaven" is full of the inadequacy of Nature. She "speaks by silences"; the sea is salt unwittingly and unregretfully. F. T. quotes Coleridge, who, he says, speaks "not as Wordsworth had taught him to speak, but from his own bitter experience":—

> O Lady, we receive but what we give,
> And in our life alone doth Nature live ;
> Ours is her wedding garment, ours her shroud !
>
> .   .   .   .   .   .
>
> I may not hope from outward forms to win
> The glory and the joy whose fountains are within.

It is at this point that F. T. strides from his fellows. He is not content with others' praise or overblame of Nature. She is dumb and hopeless, a confusion to thought. She tangles Meredith's verse and leaves Shelley drowned in body, stifled among clouds. Thompson draws away from the Pantheist and the Pagan. Coleridge's words are true of Nature's relation to ourselves— "not the truth with regard to Nature absolutely. Absolute Nature lives not in our life, nor yet is lifeless, but lives

Mysticism and Imagination

in the life of God; and in so far, and so far merely, as man himself lives in that life, does he come into sympathy with Nature, and Nature with him. She is God's daughter who stretches her hand only to her Father's friends. Not Shelley, not Wordsworth himself, ever drew so close to the heart of Nature as did the Seraph of Assisi, who was close to the Heart of God."

There, again, the complete reasonableness and sincerity of his poetry is put to the test of his prose. It is as if another and most essential witness vouched for the wisdom of "The Hound of Heaven"—a witness who, after focussing the different vision of a different art upon the same experience, swore to the same truth. He continues :—

"Yet higher, yet further let us go. Is this daughter of God mortal? can her foot not pass the grave? Is Nature, as men tell us,

> . . . a fold
> Of Heaven and earth across His Face,

which we must rend to behold that Face? Do our eyes indeed close for ever on the beauty of earth when they open on the beauty of Heaven? I think not so; I would fain beguile even death itself with a sweet fantasy. . . . I believe that in Heaven is earth. Plato's doctrine of Ideals, as I conceive, laid its hand upon the very breast of truth, yet missed her breathing. For beauty—such is my faith—is beauty for eternity."

The faith of "In Heaven is Earth" is but a tentative expression of his later gospel. At first he had been alarmed at the theory—in the form in which it had reached him—of the survival of earthly love in Heaven. He had not then read Patmore or Swedenborg. Even the tentative belief is timidly qualified :—

"Earthly beauty is but heavenly beauty taking to itself flesh. . . . Within the Spirit Who is Heaven lies

206

The Image-maker

Earth; for within Him rests the great conception of
Creation . . .

> Yet there the soul shall enter which hath earned
> That privilege by virtue. . . .

As one man is more able than his fellows to enter into
another's mind, so in proportion as each of us by virtue
has become kin to God, will he penetrate the Supreme
Spirit, and identify himself with the Divine Ideals.
There is the immortal Sicily, there the Elysian Fields,
there all visions, all fairness engirdled with the Eternal
Fair. This, my faith, is laid up in my bosom."

His belief here lies close to Swedenborg, whose *Con-
jugial Love* F. T. borrowed from my shelves with an
eagerness evinced for no other book there.

At every turn he is the devoted, intentest, faithfullest
interpreter of the material world. All his "copy"
awaited him in nature; his translations from her
tangible writings bear on every page the *imprimatur* of
his faith. The generality of the revelation made to them
did not spoil his appetite nor blur his surprising genius
for detail.

His couplings of the great and the small, not always
so sweetly reasonable as that set between the flower
and the star, sometimes need apology. The whole scale
of comparisons is unexpected in the case of one who
goes to the eating-house not only for his meals, but for
his images; who finds nothing outrageous in naming
the Milky Way a beaten yolk of stars; who takes the
setting sun for a bee that stings the west to angry
red; and, when he would express the effect of an
oppressive sunset upon Tom o' Bedlam's eye, who casts
about in the lumber-room of memory which had been
filled with oppressive images during nights endured
in a common lodging-house.

Even then he was only expressing, out of a set of

Mysticism and Imagination

accidental impressions, the poet's unremitting desire
to link up the sights and sensations of the universe.
Drummond of Hawthornden's

> Night like a drunkard reels
> Beyond the hills

may serve as a typical instance of such arbitrary simile.
From the note-books I take these unpublished lines :—

> Dost thou perceive no God within the frog ?
> O poor, poor Soul !
> Bristles and rankness only in the hog ?
> O wretched dole !
> No wry'd beneficence in the fever's germ ?
> Nor any Heaven shut within the worm ?
> Dost shudder daintily
> At words, in song, shaped so un-lovelily ?
> To school, to school !
> For does it to thee seem
> That God in an ill dream
> Fashioned the twisted horrors of the standing pool ?

Mr. Chesterton surmises the mountainous significance
of minute things. In *Tremendous Trifles*, like the lover
who writes an ode to his lady's eyebrow, or the professor
who gives his life to the study of the capillary glands,
he delights in disproportion. When Mr. Chesterton
planned a volume of poems on the things in his pocket,
but desisted because the volume would have bulked too
large, he was only formulating, in a manner acceptable to
the man who puts his hand in his pocket for a halfpenny, the old " religio poetæ." The things of the
pocket constitute a pocket dictionary in more than two
languages, a book of synonyms, a lexicon filled with cross
references, all based upon the Word. The silly silver
of men's purses is blessed, and every mortal thing
assists in immortal liturgy. St. Charles was of one
mind with those who sing the *Magnificat* of trifles.
When asked how he would die, he answered : " Playing

Words and the Word

cards, as I now do, if it should so chance." Whenever such an one dies he holds trumps. And like the priest, the poet touches mysteries with his very hand ; he makes daily communion. "To some," says Patmore, "there is revealed a sacrament greater than that of the Real Presence, a sacrament of the Manifest Presence, which is, and is more than, the sum of all the sacraments." And again we have Thompson's own

> In thee, Queen, man is saturate in God.

The Psalmist is with him :—

"If I climb up into heaven thou art there, if I go down into hell, thou art there also. If I take the wings of the morning and remain in the uttermost parts of the sea ; even there also shall thy hand lead me and thy right hand shall hold me. If I say peradventure the darkness shall cover me : then shall my night be turned into day ; the darkness and light to thee are both alike."

Thompson's own

> . . . Nay, I affirm
> Nature is whole in her least things exprest

is a splendid justification of the poet's dalliance with trifles. Vaughan confines Eternity in the scope of a night, a ring—nay, a couplet :—

> I saw Eternity the other night,
> Like a great ring of pure and endless light.

In a couplet, or a letter, literature performs her miracles. Christina Rossetti told Katharine Tynan that she never stepped on a scrap of torn paper, but lifted it out of the mud lest perhaps it should have the Holy Name written or printed upon it. That is an attitude towards literature, towards words and the Word, not unlike Francis Thompson's.

209   O

Mysticism and Imagination

In the "Orient Ode" he has addressed the sun :—

Not unto thee, great Image, not to thee
Did the wise heathen bend an idle knee ;
And in an age of faith grown frore
If I too shall adore,
Be it accounted unto me
A bright sciential idolatry !
God has given thee visible thunders
To utter thine apocalypse of wonders ;
And what want I of prophecy,
That at the sounding from thy station
Of thy flagrant trumpet, see
The seals that melt, the open revelation ?
Or who a God-persuading angel needs,
That only heeds
The rhetoric of thy burning deeds ?

   .   .   .   .   .

Lo, of thy Magians I the least
Haste with my gold, my incenses and myrrhs,
To thy desired epiphany, from the spiced
Regions and odorous of Song's traded East.
Thou, for the life of all that live
The victim daily born and sacrificed ;
To whom the pinion of this longing verse
Beats but with fire which first thyself did give,
To thee, O Sun—or is't perchance, to Christ ?

Ay, if men say that on all high heaven's face
The saintly signs I trace
Which round my stolèd altars hold their solemn place,
Amen, amen ! For oh, how could it be,—
When I with wingèd feet had run
Through all the windy earth about,
Quested its secret of the sun,
And heard what thing the stars together shout,—
I should not heed thereout
Consenting counsel won :—
" By this, O Singer, know we if thou see.
When men shall say to thee : Lo ! Christ is here,
When men shall say to thee : Lo ! Christ is there,
Believe them : yea, and this—then art thou seer,
When all thy crying clear
Is but : Lo here ! lo there !—ah me, lo everywhere ! "

"A Type Memorial"

Nature's shrines he had visited, but unavailingly :—

> Nature, poor stepdame, cannot slake my drouth.

He cries to the sun :—

> I know not what strange passion bows my head
> To thee, whose great command upon my veins
> Proves thee a god for me not dead, not dead !

He cries it to the sun, but only in the prelude to an ode that ends with the Cross.

His songs of Nature are :—

> Sweet with wild wings that pass, that pass away.

All his wild things passed, that they might be garnered in heaven. The chase of the "Hound of Heaven" ends in a divine embrace; like that ending is the ending of all his verse.

Through the symbolism of the sun all things were brought into line. Likened to the Host, with sky for monstrance; to the Christ, with the sombre line of the horizon for Rood; to the Altar-Wafer, and signed with the Cross; the Sun is to the Earth only what Christ is to the Soul :—

> Thou to thy spousal universe
> Art Husband, she thy Wife and Church.

Thompson offers his inspiration—". . . to thee, O Sun, —or is't perchance, to Christ?"[1]

He would not have his harmonies mistaken for the repetition of "fair ancient flatteries." He takes the sun, at rising and at setting, as "a type memorial"[2] :—

> Like Him thou hang'st in dreadful pomp of blood
> Upon thy Western rood ;

---

[1] "The sun is the type of Christ, giving life with its proper blood to the earth," is Mr. Edmund Gardner's concise statement of F. T.'s meaning.

[2] F. T. had a theory of the solar existence that did not stop short, with Science, at the measurement of gases and their density. "It has," Mr. Ghosh tells me he said, "a life of its own, analogous to the life of the heart, periodic in its manifestations and—," but here Francis stopped. "To Western ears it

Mysticism and Imagination

And His stained brow did vail like thine to-night,
    Yet lift once more Its light,
And, risen, again departed from our ball,
But when It set on earth arose in Heaven.

And in the After-Strain :—

    Even so, O Cross ! thine is the victory.
        Thy roots are fast within our fairest fields ;
    Brightness may emanate in Heaven from thee,
        Here thy dread symbol only shadow yields.

    Of reapèd joys thou art the heavy sheaf
        Which must be lifted, though the reaper groan ;
    Yea, we may cry till Heaven's great ear be deaf,
        But we must bear thee, amd must bear alone.

    Vain were a Simon ; of the Antipodes
        Our night not borrows the superfluous day.
    Yet woe to him that from his burden flees !
        Crushed in the fall of what he cast away. [1]

He went farther : he made the sun the type of a church service :—

        Lo, in the sanctuaried East,
        Day, a dedicated priest
        In all his robes pontifical exprest,
        Lifteth slowly, lifteth sweetly,
        From out its Orient tabernacle drawn,
        Yon orbed sacrament confest
        Which sprinkles benediction through the dawn ;
        And when the grave procession's ceased,

---

will sound ridiculous," he said, and was silent. In vain Mr. Sarath Kumar Ghosh asserted his own Eastern aptitude for such speculation. Francis grimly repeated his excommunication, and Mr. Ghosh, conscious of a frock-coat and a great command of the English idiom, was half-convinced of its stness.

[1] Compare Donne's " No cross is so extreme, as to have none "—a thought upon which many paradoxical couplets were turned in the seventeenth century. But Donne goes a little further than his fellows. He seems to have known that an image, bound up with its original, is more than a likeness :—

    Let crosses so take what hid Christ in thee ;
    And be His image, or not His, but He.

The Cross

The earth with due illustrious rite
Blessed,—ere the frail fingers featly
Of twilight, violet-cassocked acolyte
His sacerdotal stoles unvest—
Sets, for high close of the mysterious feast,
The sun in august exposition meetly
Within the flaming monstrance of the West.
O salutaris hostia,
Quæ coeli pandis ostium !

The Cross spread its arms across his world. It was never heavier on his shoulder than when he copied out Donne's lines :—

Who can deny me power and liberty
To stretch mine arms and mine own cross to be ?
Swim, and at every stroke thou art thy cross :
The mast and yard make one where seas do toss.
Look down, thou spiest our crosses in small things,
Look up, thou seest birds raised on crossed wings.

Donne had encouraged him in his own early search for its symbols. In a prayer to the Blessed Virgin Thompson speaks of the general crucifixion of man :—

O thou, who standest as thou hast ever stood
Beside the Cross, whenas it shall be said—
" It is consummated,"
Receive us, taken from the World's rough wood !

But Donne's image is the more immediate ; and the " Veneration of Images," of a living poet, in which man is addressed as—

Thou Rood of every day—

confirms both their guesses.

In his sunset Thompson found a symbol of the Crucifixion ; in Paganism his Calvary, and in Christianity an endless elaboration of Christ, so that he turns and

213

Mysticism and Imagination

wonders at himself for standing at all in the mirk of ordinary daylight :—

And though the cry of stars
Give tongue before His way
Goldenly, as I say,
And each, from wide Saturnus to hot Mars,
He calleth by its name,
Lest that its bright feet stray;
And thou have lore of all,—
But to thine own Sun's call
Thy path disorbed hath never wit to tame:
It profits not withal,
And my rede is but lame.

He regards his poetry, the poetry of unrevealed religion, of inquiry, and of hasty worship, even as he writes it, with some disfavour. But the prophetical portion of *New Poems* shows a new assurance—

I have my music bent
To waste on bootless things its skiey-gendered rain :
Yet shall a wiser day
Fulfil more heavenly way,
And with approvèd music clear this slip,
I trust in God most sweet.
Meantime the silent lip,
Meantime the climbing feet.

He saw only one possible ending to all modes of poetry, that "multitudinous-single thing" :—

Loud the descant, and low the theme,
(*A million songs are as song of one*)
And the dream of the world is dream in dream,
But the one Is is, or nought could seem ;
    And the song runs round to the song begun.

This is the song the stars sing,
    (*Tonèd all in time*)
Tintinnabulous, tuned to ring
A multitudinous-single thing
    (*Rung all in rhyme*).

The Unit and the Sum

In "Form and Formalism" Thompson says :—

"No common aim can triumph, till it is crystallized in an individual. Man himself must become incarnate in a man before his cause can triumph. Thus the universal Word became the individual Christ; that total God and total man being particularised in a single symbol, the cause of God and man might triumph. In Christ, therefore, centres and is solved that supreme problem of life—the marriage of the Unit with the Sum. In Him is perfectly shown forth the All for one, and One for all, which is the justificatory essence of that substance we call Kingship. . . . When the new heavens and the new earth, which multitudinous Titans are so restlessly forging, at length stand visible to resting man, it needs no prophecy to foretell that they will be like the old, with head, and form, and hierarchic memberment, as the six-foot bracken is like the bracken at your knee. For out of all its disintegrations and confusion earth emerges, like a strong though buffeted swimmer, nearer to the unseen model and term of all social growth; which is the civil constitution of angeldom, and the Uranian statecraft of imperatorial God."

*   *   *   *   *   *   *

"Ritual is poetry addressed to the eye," he notes. The corollary of which supports his belief that poetry was an affair of ritual—or images.

Imagination is the sense or science that discovers identities and correspondences, while fancy takes a lower place because, said Thompson, it discovers only likenesses. Imagination discerns similarity rooted or enskied; it is the origin of the symbolism that may be traced back to the heart of the truths and mysteries to which it supplies the outward shows. Imagination is the spring; Symbolism is here the manifes-

215

Mysticism and Imagination

tation of Imagination, is the identity-bearer, partaking of the very essence of the Divinity. The Symbols of Divinity are Divine ; flesh is the Word made flesh ; the Eucharist is the true Presence ; and Christ is Himself the Way to Christ. Thompson's poetry and theology abode by the Image ; it was no necessity of their nature to penetrate beyond the barriers of expression and revelation. The go-betweens of others were his essentials. Holding so grave an estimate of the functions of the imagination, he found in poetry the highest human scope and motive.

Another writer has said—

" Imagination is as the water that reflects clouds out of sight, or so near the sun that they may not be viewed save in the darkening mirror."

And images enlarge and qualify ; they create, too, in so far as they bear and nourish thoughts that can only be expressed through them. They belong, F. T. maintained, to the highest poetry, the poetry of revelation and the intellect. In this idea he was confirmed ; for its sake he surmounted the opposition of the thinker in poetry to whom he was most dutiful in admiration. " It is false," he declared with his whole heart, "that highest or supremest poetry is stripped of figure. Purely emotional poetry at its height is bare of imagery, not poetry of supremest flight. . . . Supreme emotion is not supreme poetry." And yet just in its own measure is the estimate he contested. It is set forth by A. M. in the *Nation*, 23 Nov., 1907 :—

" Imagery is not, it may be held, the last, or inmost, word of poetry. There is a simplicity on the yonder side. The simplicity of the hither side may be natural and pleasing enough, though it may also be 'natural' as is the village fool. But the simplicity of the further poetry is a plainness within those splendid outer courts of approach where imagery celebrates ritual and ceremony. A

At the Junction-lines

few poems abide in that further place—a further place, did we call it ? It is far, indeed, from the access of the suitor, but closest of all things to the warm breast of the very Nurse. Francis Thompson dealt almost altogether in imagery ; and it is because of this that his less sympathetic readers accuse him of a lack of simplicity. And he himself, in a manuscript note, says : ' Imagery is so far from being " all fancy " (which is what people mean by saying it is " all imagination ") that the deepest truths—even in the natural or physical order—are often adumbrated only by images familiar, and yet conceived to be purely fanciful analogies. . . .' No ' lack ' was among his faults. Where he might be charged or questioned was in his commission, not in his omission—his commission of the splendid fault of excess. How many poets might be furnished, not from the abundance, but from the overabundance, of his imagery, and the prunings and the chastenings of his ' fancy.' The spoils of such a correction as would have made a few of his odes more ' classical ' might have been gathered up, a golden armful, by poets who need have stooped for nothing else, twelve basketsful of fragments, after the feeding of a chosen multitude."

One is for the idea, the other for vision ; one for the word, the other for its conception.

" He stood at the very junction-lines of the visible and invisible, and could shift the points as he willed," said F. T. of Shelley. And the lever was imagery ; the signals were images ; the sleepers were images—all the machinery that made and marked the way. It binds the universe ; it expresses " the underlying analogies, the secret subterranean passages, between matter and soul ; the chromatic scales, whereat we dimly guess, by which the Almighty modulates through all the keys of creation."

That modulation through time, also, Thompson traces in the transition from antiquity to the future, from Paganism to Christianity, from the Old Law to the New :—

> On Ararat there grew a vine ;
> When Asia from her bathing rose,
> Our first sailor made a twine

Mysticism and Imagination

Thereof for his prefiguring brows.
Canst divine
Where, upon our dusty earth, of that vine a cluster grows ?

On Golgotha there grew a thorn
Round the long-prefigured Brows.
Mourn, O mourn !
For the vine have we the spine ?   Is this all the Heaven allows ?

On Calvary was shook a spear ;
Press the point into thy heart—
Joy and fear !
All the spines upon the thorn into curling tendrils start.

He had intended to show in an essay that symbolism
is no arbitrary convention.   He bids himself expound
its elements by leading examples, and, had he done so,
we should have known more of the geography of that
region where symbols and their principles are merged.
"All things linkèd are" ; the daisy is the signature of the
star ; for the poet all terrestrial minutiæ were signed, nay,
scribbled all over with reference marks and sealed with
the likeness of larger things.   From an old commentator on St. Thomas Aquinas, F. T. copied :—

"The angelic intellect contains the things which
belong to universal nature, and those also which are
the principles of individuation, knowing by science
divinely infused, not only what belongs to universal
nature, but also individualities of things, inasmuch as
these all form multiplied representation of the one
Simple Essence of God."

The ancient school of Herbalists believed that natural
remedies were stamped with the likeness of the parts to
which they would bring healing, as walnuts, which,
because they "have the perfect signature of the head,
are profitable to the brain."   Poisons show something
like contrition by taking to themselves colours and odours
plainly evil ; vipers, as proper scholars of the alphabet,
wear V for venom on their heads.   The Herbalists took

Blake's Definitions

the narrowing road, from vision down to practice. They pounded their discoveries to powder with the bald-head pestle of literalness. The mortar of the herbalist is the chalice of the poet. It is the difference again between illusion and imagination, or, as Blake figured them, between Adam and Christ.

Blake's conception of the identity of and correspondence between the Complete or Divine Mind and Humanity led him to further definitions which are of weight in general consideration of the poetry of imagination. Our world, he held, was a contraction of our mind from the mind of God of which it is a part. To illusion—the perception and acceptance of the erroneous deductions of the contracted personality, or Adam—he gave the name Satan. Besides Perception (here I have recourse verbatim to Mr. Edwin J. Ellis's invaluable disquisition) :—

" Besides perception, always tempting us to error, by leading through narrow to mistaken personality, there is ' imagination,' always inviting us to truth. For this Blake took the name of Saviour, or Humanity free from Adam's narrowness and Satan's falseness."

Of the more purely literary aspect of imagery Thompson has written :—

" How beautiful a thing the frank toying with imagery may be, let 'The Skylark' and 'The Cloud' witness. It is only evil when the poet, on the straight way to a fixed object, lags continually from the path to play. This is commendable neither in poet nor errand-boy."

And again :—

" To sport with the tangles of Neæra's hair may be trivial idleness or caressing tenderness, exactly as your relation to Neæra is that of heartless gallantry or love. So you may toy with imagery in mere intellectual ingenuity, and then you might as well go write acrostics ;

Mysticism and Imagination

or you may toy with it in raptures, and then you may write a 'Sensitive Plant.'"

In all the poetry belonging to the period of "The Mistress of Vision" Patmore is the master of vision. He leads the way to "deific peaks" and "conquered skies," the Virgil of a younger Dante.

Their thoughts chimed to the same stroke of metre and rhyme;[1] for each of the mystical poems may be found suggestions in Patmore. For the "Dread of Height" we find among "Aurea Dicta" the following :—

"'Searchers of Majesty shall be overwhelmed with the glory.' Blissfully overwhelmed; ruined for this world, yet even in this enriched beyond thought; happy searchers, consumed by the thunder of divine instructions and the lightning of divine perceptions, but surviving as new creatures in the very flesh of the destroyer."

And again :—

"The spirit of man is like a kite, which rises by means of those very forces which seem to oppose its rise; the tie that joins it to the earth, the opposing winds of temptation, and the weight of earth-born affections which it carries with it into the sky."

Patmore's "Hate pleasure, if only because this is the only means of obtaining it" is the root paradox of the many found in the lines beginning—"Lose, that the lost thou may'st receive," and the rest.

But go through the whole of the two poets, and even while recognising the twin enterprises of imagination you will end in the enjoyment of their dissimilarity. Patmore has quoted St. Paul—"Let each man abound in his own sense," and has said himself :—

"When once he has got into the region of perception, let him take care that his vision is his own, and not fancy he can profit himself or others much by trying to appropriate *their* peculiar variations of the common theme."

---

[1] "The metre in my present volume," wrote the author in a suppressed preface to *New Poems*, "is completely based on the principles which Mr. Patmore may be said virtually to have discovered."

To Each his Vision

Patmore may have given Thompson a metre and a score of thoughts, but above everything else he gave him the freedom of his imagination. Having led him to a point of vantage, he looked in the same direction, but the revelation varied as the view varies to two men who walk along a road towards the same sunset. They are a few paces apart; to one an intervening tree may be black and sombre, to the other streaked with fire. The height they reached may have been the same, but the dread of height was to each a thing of his own.

From Patmore, August 1895 :—

" I see, with joy, how nearly we are upon the same lines, but our visions could not be true were they quite the same ; and no one can really see anything but his own vision."

Again, in November of the same year :—

" It is always a great thing to me to receive a letter from you. My heart goes forth to you as it goes to no other man ; for are we not singularly visited by a great common delight and a great common sorrow ?   Is not this to be one in Christ ? "

Later :—

" You dissipate my solitude and melancholy as no other, but one, can."

Again from Patmore :—

" In the manner of your verse you are gaining in simplicity, which is a great thing.   But I will speak more of that bye-and-bye. In the matter, I think you outstrip me.   I am too concrete and intelligible.   I fear greatly lest what I have written may not do more harm than good, by exposing Divine realities to profane comprehensions, and by inflaming ' popular esotericism.' "

"The Mistress of Vision" is described by F. T. as " a phantasy with no more than an illusive tinge of psychic significance."   It is a masque in which he and his Muse observe the formalities of dialogue, but before

Mysticism and Imagination

the poem is finished the truth is out; as when, dawn breaking upon dancing lovers, their steps cease, and for a moment their embrace is real. So in the poem : the phantasy is not maintained; the masque is up. Christ, before one is aware, is treading the land of Luthany, is walking on the waters. Following, in carefully considered sequence, is "Contemplation," and, afterward, the true fruits of *The Unknown Eros*. "I felt my instrument yet too imperfect to profane by it the highest ranges of mysticism," he had said, and, in "The Mistress of Vision," "The Dread of Height," and particularly in "The Orient Ode," something is withheld. As the rood-screen shields the altar, language screens revelation.

Although the spirit of reservation in the literature of religious experience has apology in the saying that they who know God best do not seek to define Him, that is not the leading argument for reticence. Patmore said that in such matters the part is greater than the whole, and in any case

"No great art, no really effective ethical teaching can come from any but such as know immeasurably more than they will attempt to communicate."

And, beyond that, they recognised truths "which it is not lawful to utter," but knew that the poet may express them in ways that shade them to the eye, or make them invisible as the too-bright disc of the sun. Sufficient rays may pass through cloudy speech to diffuse life-sufficing warmth. "See that thou tell no man" is an injunction of which the poets keep the letter but break the spirit.

"Not only among the Hebrews," writes F. T. in a review of a paper on St. Clement, "but among the Egyptians and Greeks, prophecies and oracles were delivered under enigmas. The Egyptian hieroglyphics, the apo-

Reservation

thegms of the wise men of Greece, are instances of the practice of throwing a kind of veil around important truths in order that the curiosity of men may be aroused and their diligence stimulated. All who treated of divine things, whether Greeks or Barbarians, concealed the principles. . . . Whatever has a veil of mystery thrown around it, causes the truth to appear more grand and awful."

St. Clement speaks of an *unwritten* tradition of blessed doctrine, handed down from SS. Peter, James, John, and Paul. St. Clement's own account of these sacred doctrines is, he himself says, incomplete; some he has forgotten, others he would be unwilling to allude to even in speech, much more unwilling in writing, lest they who met them should pervert them to their own injury, and he should thus be placing, according to the proverb, a sword in the hand of a child.

We may suspect Patmore and Thompson of this mystical knowledge, since they exercised St. Clement's caution. So does the Eastern teacher of the day; and all of these conform in not being thinkers of the scientific or material order. The Socratic definition of the true philosopher " who in his meditations neither employs his sight nor any of his senses, but a pure understanding alone," must, with Blake's "Cultivate imagination to the point of vision," be printed on page 1 of the first *First Reader* in mysticism.

Thompson dwells also on St. Paul's unspoken message, which, designated by the name of *wisdom*, he withheld from many of the Corinthians because they were not fit to hear it. He communicated it to the *spiritual* not to the *animal* man. Origen says that that which St. Paul would have called *wisdom* is found in the " Canticle of Canticles." Thompson dwells further on the hidden meanings of the Pentateuch, believing that there was " an inexhaustible treasure of divine wisdom concealed

223

Mysticism and Imagination

under the letter of Holy Writ." Thompson saw wise men whispering, and guessed that there were secrets; their presence discovered, they were open secrets for such as he. "You have but to direct my sight, and the intentness of my gaze will discover the rest." Of the poet who is religious it may be said : "There hath drawn near a man to a deep heart, that is, a secret heart." Look not at a star if you wish to see it : avert your gaze and it is clearer to you. So with the rockets and flashes of revelation. The Mass has secrets, and so have children. It must be remembered that the greater part of F. T.'s seeming reservations are only such as exist between the Church and the outer world. For instance :—

"The personal embrace between Creator and creature is so solely the secret and note of Catholicism, that its language to the outer sects is unintelligible—the strange bruit of inapprehensible myth."

During walks at Pantasaph and Lymington, Thompson penetrated on the one hand to places where thought is singed and scorched, on the other to healing regions of light ; at one time deep in melancholy, at another buoyantly content. A. M. observed that during certain drives with Coventry Patmore he would sit looking at the floor of the carriage with the harrowing expression that one gathers from Rossetti's "Wood Spurge."

Imagination is onerous. Christina Rossetti points to more than a problem in artistry when she writes :—

"At first sight and apparently the easiest of all conceptions to realise, I yet suppose that there may, in the long run, be no conception more difficult for ourselves to clench and retain than this of absolute Unity ; this oneness at all times, in all connexions, for all purposes."

But once grasped it may never be relinquished. And it is a commonplace of the mystics that contemplation is painful. St. John of the Cross's warning of the deso-

lation that follows the dwelling in the neutral land
between the temporal and the spiritual is one of many.

There is no escape. Conscience is another name for
consciousness. " If men understood clearly they would
sin at every step, wherefore they understand grossly, that
sin may not be imputed to them," wrote F. T., half
protesting against the disabilities of clear understanding.
And again :—

"Life is an Inkermann, fought in the mist. If men
saw clearly, they would despair to fight. Wherefore the
Almighty opens the eyes only of those whom He has led
by special ways of gradual inurement and preparation."

The futility of Francis's conversational repetition was
a by-word ; but when he said a thing twice in verse or
prose it probably mattered more than most other things.
"The Dread of Height" states the burden of knowledge,
and John ix. 41., quoted as the poem's motto, is made to
enforce it too :—"If ye were blind ye should have no
sin ; but now ye say We see, your sin remaineth."
What John said (in ix. 41, or elsewhere) he would generally have thought sufficiently said. But in this matter he
repeats John, and then more than once repeats himself.

A man does not, because he is as conscious of his
God as were the disciples who really had Him on the
road to Emmaus, find the road an easy one. Bunyan
holds good ; the better way is the roughest. The more
excellent landscape is that which is seen against the
sun. But it is rigid in its splendours ; every cock of
hay, every clod, is a shadow. Is the ear that hears " the
winds their Maker magnify " happier than that which
can note only rattling of windows and the cracking of
boughs ? During sound perhaps, not certainly during
pauses in sound :—

"I never found any so religious and devout, that he
had not sometimes a withdrawing of grace. There was
never Saint so highly rapt and illuminated, who before

or after was not tempted. For he is not worthy of the
high contemplation of God who has not been troubled
with some tribulations for God's sake."

The commonplaces of the *Imitation* are sound sense.
" Thou visitest him early in the morning ; and suddenly
Thou provest him."

> I do think my tread,
> Stirring the blossom in the meadow-grass,
> Flickers the unwithering stars.

Such treading may be better than the asphalt of every
day, but it is not easy going.

Of futurity he wrote in a letter to A. M. :—

" You must know this thing of me already, having
read those Manning verses, which I do not like to read
again.   You know that I believe in eternal punishment :
you know that when my dark hour is on me, this
individual terror is the most monstrous of all that haunt
me.   But it is individual.   For others—even if the
darker view were true, the fewness is relative to the
total mass of mankind, not absolute ; while I myself
refuse to found upon so doubtful a thing as a few
scattered texts a tremendous prejudgment which has
behind it no consentaneous voice of the Church.   And I
do firmly believe that none are lost who have not wilfully closed their eyes to the known light : that such as
fall with constant striving, battling with their temperament, or through ill-training circumstance which shuts
them from true light, &c. ; that all these shall taste of
God's justice, which for them is better than man's mercy.
But if you would see the present state of my convictions
on the subject turn to the new Epilogue of my ' Judgement in Heaven ' (you will find it in the wooden box)."

His correspondent has written :—

" As a thinker, Francis Thompson is profoundly meditative,
and, if pessimistic, then pessimistic with submission and fear, not

The Heart of Woman

with revolt. His thought must not be called gloomy, even when
it is dark as night, for in the darkness there is a sense of open and
heavenly air."

The most natural thing in the world (although at first
he did not see it, having been a seminarist, a person
not always apt to be in the secret) was that the singer of
the Church—the Church that defined the Immaculate
Conception—should be a poet of woman-kind—one of
the Marians. Seminary training did not prepare him for
a world of women. A note on the Marriage of Cana,
which proves, he avers, that "much wine is needed
before a man may go through with matrimony," is
characteristic of his schooling. In humour the schooling lasted when all else had been outlived. His unpublished comedy "Man Proposes, Woman Disposes" is full
of ready-made gibes, and his "Dress," printed in the *Daily
Mail*, is threadbare comic verse on a subject he treated
reverently enough when there was no joke to crack.
It is still, perhaps, as the seminarist that he notes: "In
Burmah the monks complain that women are natively
incapable of any true understanding of religion." But
it is a later Thompson who adds the comment: "The
heart of woman is the citadel, the *ultimum refugium* of
true religiosity." Genesis gives him the heading for
several pages of a note-book devoted to such subjects:
"I will put enmity between thee and the woman."

Rod, Root, and Flower set him to work in the same
nursery-garden. His note-books reflect Patmore's aphor-
istic habit. He himself defended or denied the "fragmentary" nature of Patmore's book. "It might as well
be said that the heavens are fragmentary, because the
stars are not linked by golden chains. You are given the
stars—the central and illuminative suggestions ; you are
left to work out for yourself, by meditations, the system
of which they are the nodal points." This, it will be
seen, is his rewriting of Patmore's own comment on the
book, quoted at p. 201.

Mysticism and Imagination

I can do no more than bring together his scattered notes on Woman. He himself could hardly have fitted them into any satisfactory sequence.

In a note-book I find :—

" The function of natural love is to create a craving which it cannot satisfy. And then only has its water been tasted in perfect purity, if it awakens an insatiate thirst of wine."

His hope is made known in his poetry :—

> The Woman I behold, whose vision seek
> All eyes and know not ; t'ward whom climb
> The steps of the world, and beats all wing of rhyme.

And his prose :—

" When the federation of the world comes (as come I believe it will) it can only be federation in both government and religion of plenary and ordered dominance. I see only two religions constant enough to effect this : each based upon the past—which is stability ; each growing according to an interior law—which is strength. Paganism and Christianism ; the religion of the Queen of Heaven who is Astarte, and of the Queen of Heaven who is Mary." (Note by F. T. : " ' We offer sacrifice to the Queen of Heaven ' " (Jer. xliv. 19).

Once he turns the subject with a stock phrase of playfulness—

> Daughter of the ancient Eve,
> We know the gifts ye gave—and give.
> Who knows the gifts which *you* shall give,
> Daughter of the newer Eve ?
> You, if my soul be augur, you
> Shall—O what shall you not, Sweet, do ?

But before he is through with the poem he is led to

greater explicitness, and, finally, to the solemn manner of
concealment—

> When to love *you* is (O Christ's spouse !)
> To love the beauty of His house ;
> Then come the Isaian days ; the old
> Shall dream ; and our young men behold
> Vision—yea, the vision of Thabor-mount,
> Which none to other shall recount,
> Because in all men's hearts shall be
> The seeing and the prophecy.
> For ended is the Mystery Play,
> When Christ is life, and you the way ;
> When Egypt's spoils are Israel's right,
> And Day fulfils the married arms of Night.
> But here my lips are still.
> Until
> You and the hour shall be revealed,
> This song is sung and sung not, and its words are sealed.

> In thee, Queen, man is saturate with God.
>   Blest period
> To God's redeeming sentence. .So in thee
> Mercy at length is uttered utterly.

In human passion, as in sun-worship, he relates everything to the Deity. It is within forbidden degrees if it
cannot be referred back to Divine Love. His series " A
Narrow Vessel," he describes as " being a little dramatic
sequence on the aspect of primitive girl-nature towards
a love beyond its capacities." Opening with a "rape of
the lock," the whole breadth of the centuries and of the
human mind apart from Pope's, the girl bemoans the
gift of her hair :—

> My lock the enforcèd steel did grate
>   To cut ; its root-thrills came
> Down to my bosom. It might sate
>   His lust for my poor shame.

Here is unwonted attention to the minutiæ of sensation ; and the third poem of the second series is the one

that comes nearest in all Thompson's work to the many
love poems of the many modern poetry-books. The likeness is startling. It is the only poem of his which the
illustrators of "Tennyson" of 1857 would have relished
to put upon wood. The girl was an actual girl named
Maggie Bryan, of the Welsh village; his photograph
was long kept in her narrow room, and her grave, made
in the October following the poet's death, is near the
scene of that love-making that was so incongruous and
timid that it had little real existence in word or look.
"Love Declared," the poem that sinks to the commoner
level of love-poetry, is fiction and reads like it; the rest
reality—only a little more than the reality.

But Thompson did not leave it at reality. No sooner
has an unwary reader, who, on other pages, had been
clutching at his poet, made sure, on this one, of his man
than the creature of bone and muscle slips from him.
The sequence, it is confessed in the last poem, is written
solely in the interests of allegory. Here for once is
actuality, one had said; but only to learn that no actuality bulks so large for the poet himself as the actuality
of religious speculation. His own Pantasaph drama, a
thing that passed in the high-street, hemmed in by
cottages, noted by gossipers, with strong hill winds
blowing in the faces of the actors, was most personal to
the hero for its allegorical meaning—

"How many," he asks, "have grasped the significance
of my sequence, *A Narrow Vessel?* Critics either overlooked it altogether or adverted to it as trivial and discon-
nected. One, who prized it, and wished I had always
written as humanly, grieved that the epilogue turned it
into an unreal allegory. He could not understand that
all human love was to me a symbol of divine love; nay,
that human love was in my eyes a piteous failure unless
as an image of the supreme Love which gave meaning
and reality to its seeming insanity. The lesson of that

The Girl and the Allegory

sequence is just this. Woman repels the great and pure love of man in proportion to its purity. This is due to an instinct which she lacks the habits and power to analyse, that the love of the pure and lofty lover is so deep, so vast in its withheld emotion, as her entire self would be unable to pay back. Though she cast her whole self down that eager gulf, it would disappear as a water-drop in the ocean. And though the lover ask no more than her little tremulous self may think fit to give, she feels that so vast a love claims of right and equity her total surrender. Though the lover be generously unexacting, that wonderful gift, she feels, exacts no less than all, and then she cannot with her entire potency and abandonment of love adequate the hungry immensity poured around it. So, with instinctive fear, she recoils from a love which her all cannot equal. Though the lover asks no more than she ,please to give, his love asks her very being, demands a continual upward strain. The narrow vessel dreads to crack under the overflowing love which surges into it., She shrinks with tremor ; she turns to the lover whose shallow love has nought to frighten her ; she can halt where she pleases, far short of total surrender. It is an easy beginning, which seems to involve so little and involves—how much ! For she does not understand that once she begins to love, her nature will not rest short of supreme surrender (I assume an average nature capable of love), and that she will end by wasting her whole self on this thin soil, which will reject and anticipate it (while) she recoiled with dislike and fear from the great love which would have absorbed and repaid it an hundred-fold. Now this is but the image and explanation of the soul's attitude towards only God. The one is illustrated by the other. Though God asks of the soul but to love him what it may, and is ready to give an increased love for a poor little, the soul feels that this infinite love demands naturally its whole self, that if it begin to love God it

may not stop short of all it has to yield. It is troubled,
even if it did go a brief way, on the upward path ; it fears
and recoils from the whole great surrender, the constant
effort beyond itself which is sensibly laid on it. It falls
back with relieved contentment on some human love, a
love on its own plane, where somewhat short of total
surrender may go to requital, where no upward effort is
needful. And it ends by giving for the meanest, the
most unsufficing and half-hearted return, that utter self-
surrender and self-effacement which it denied to God.
Even (how rarely) if the return be such as mortal may
render, how empty and unsatiated it leaves the soul.
One always is less generous of love than the other. Now
this was the theme and meaning of my sequence. It
did not (as it should have done) follow on to the facile
welcome of a light love. But that was by implication
glanced at in the epilogue, which drew what I have
shown to be the real conclusion of the entire study—
even to the possible most tragic issue of all, in the soul
which has taken the kiss of the Spouse (so to speak) only
to fall away from Him, 'the heart where good is well
perceived and known, yet is not willed.' "

That sequence, he said, was written solely in the
interests of allegory. Obviously the episode was not
sufficient unto itself. Only once had he known love
really sufficient for love poetry.

CHAPTER XI: PATMORE'S DEATH AND "NEW POEMS"

In July, 1896, the year of his death, Patmore made an offer of service memorable from a man, called arrogant and harsh, to a man who might well, in personal matters, have stirred his prejudices :—

"You were looking so unwell when we parted, that, not having heard from you, I am somewhat alarmed. Pray let me have a post-card.

"If, at any time, you find yourself seriously ill, and do not find the attendance, food, &c., sufficiently good, tell me and I will go to Pantasaph to take care of you for any time you might find me useful. It would be a great pleasure and honour to serve you in any way."

Thompson answered :—

". . . You have been most generously kind to me ; and I can truly say that I never yet fell from any friend who did not first fall from me. I thank you for the great honour you have done me by your offer to come up and look after me if I needed nursing. Fortunately it has not come to that yet.

"I have not seen Meredith's article[1]—I am so entirely cut off from the outside world."

When the Laureateship fell vacant Patmore wrote to the *Saturday Review* proposing my mother's name. Francis wrote to him :—

"I think your *Saturday* letter very felicitously put. But alas ! small are the chances of any government acting on it. I fear the compliment to 'journalism' points too surely to Edwin Arnold. I have not received the

[1] "Mrs. Meynell's Essays" in the *National Review*, Aug. 1896.

233

Patmore's Death

Selections.[1] A. M. has only once in my life sent me a book of hers—her essays. I should indeed like to see the book. The selections in themselves must possess a peculiar interest for me ; and the Preface I am most eager to read."

The appointment made, Francis again wrote to the point :—

"What a pity you could not uphold the dignity of the Laureateship in the eyes of Europe."

Patmore died in November, 1896. To Mrs. Patmore Francis wrote :—

"I am shocked and overcome to hear of your—and my—bereavement ; there has passed away the greatest genius of the century, and from me a friend whose like I shall not see again ; one so close to my own soul that the distance of years between us was hardly felt, nor could the distance of miles separate us. I had a letter from him but last Monday, and was hoping that I might shortly see him again. Now my hope is turned suddenly into mourning.

"The irrevocableness of such a grief is mocked by many words ; these few words least wrong it. My friend is dead, and I had but one such friend.—Yours in all sympathy of sorrow, FRANCIS THOMPSON."

At the same time he wrote to Palace Court :—

"CRECCAS COTTAGE, PANTASAPH.

"DEAR WILFRID,—I send you my lodging account for the last two months.

"Of nothing can I write just now. You know what friends we had been these last two years. And I heard from him but the Monday before his death. There is no more to say, because there is too much more to say. Yours always, FRANCIS THOMPSON."

[1] *Poetry of Pathos and Delight*, being selections made by Alice Meynell from the poetry of Coventry Patmore.

234

"Oceanic Vast of Intellect"

"*P.S.*—I am fearful about the *Athenæum* project. I told Coventry I had altered the sub-title to prevent identification, lest the poem[1] should offend his friends ; and since he did not dispute it, I conclude he took my view that it might give displeasure. To dwell on the harsher side of his character now has an ungracious air."

Of the same poem he wrote again to W. M. :—

"I am sorry I could not wire the correction in time. I did not see your letter till too late on Thursday to do anything. I would rather have had the phrase altered, and hope Mrs. Meynell may have taken on herself to do so, since it only affected the poem temporarily. In my book I shall retain the original phrase, which Coventry would have objected to have altered in permanent record. He accepted and justified my use of the phrase, in a poem drawing only an aspect of his character. But where it was connected with him as a funeral poem, I would certainly have wished it replaced by something else. About all things I trust soon to have personal talk with you. Always yours affectionately,

FRANCIS THOMPSON."

The high-pitched phrases of the obituary poems confess the strain he put upon himself to publish his grief. He dropped into private prose while he was at the task. "Age alone will grasp in some dim measure what must have been the unmanifested powers of a mind from which could go forth this starry manifestation ; and what 'silence full of wonders' interspaced his opulent frugality of speech." "It remains a personal (and wonderful) memory that to me sometimes, athwart the shifting clouds of converse, was revealed by glimpses the direct vision of that oceanic vast of intellect." "The

---

[1] "A Captain of Song," addressed to Patmore before his death, and at his death published in the *Athenæum*, December 5, 1896.

basic silence of our love" and the "under-silence of love" are other phrases that tell of something not to be expresssed in the obituary column. There are scraps, also, of private verse which tell his sorrow:—

> O how I miss you any casual day !
> And as I walk
> Turn, in the customed way,
> Towards you with the talk
> Which who but you should hear ?
> And know the intercepting day
> Betwixt me and your only listening ear ;
> And no man ever more my tongue shall hear,
> And dumb amid an alien folk I stray.

He grieved for Patmore as a wife grieves for the husband who dies before the birth of her child. "This latest, highest, of my work," he says of a portion of *New Poems*, "is now born dumb. It had been sung into his sole ears. Now there is none who speaks its language." His loss made a visit to his friends in London desirable.

Of the dedication he had previously written to Patmore:—

"The book (A. M.'s *The Colour of Life*) is dedicated to you, and just a fortnight ago I sent to London a volume of poems—the product of the last three years—which I had also (knowing nothing then of her intention, or even that she had a book on the point of appearing) taken the liberty of dedicating to you."

That dedication to Patmore runs :—

> Lo, my book thinks to look Time's leaguer down,
> Under the banner of your spread renown !
> Or if these levies of impuissant rhyme
> Fall to the overthrow of assaulting Time,
> Yet this one page shall fend oblivion's shame
> Armed with your crested and prevailing name.

A Dedication

The tribute is handsomely conceived without any of the insincerity that cowered behind the handsomeness of eighteenth century dedications. It was an occasion for setting forth the humility which was a very real part of Thompson's character. In a printed note the author explains :—

" This dedication was written while the dear friend and great Poet to whom it was addressed yet lived. It is left as he saw it—the last verses of mine that were ever to pass under his eye."

To Francis, Mrs. Patmore wrote just before the publication of the book :—

" In to-day's *Register* I see that you have decided to retain the dedication of the poems you are now bringing out to my husband. I cannot resist thanking you and also letting you know how much pleasure the mark of your friendship gave him before he died. He was also looking forward to your visit to him with great delight."

Before the publication of *New Poems* a preface was written and cancelled, and a dozen titles mooted and rejected. In one MS. the name *Poems, partly mystical* is followed by an Introduction :—

" This book represents the work of the three years which have elapsed since my first volume was prepared for the press, my second volume having been a poem of comparatively early date. The first section exhibits mysticism in a limited and varying degree. I feel my instrument yet too imperfect to profane by it the higher ranges. Much is transcendental rather than truly mystic. The opening poem (" The Mistress of Vision ") is a fantasy with no more than an illusive tinge of psychic significance. And of the other poems some are as much science as mysticism! but it is the science of the Future, not the science of the scientist.

"New Poems"

And since the science of the Future is the science of the Past, the outlook on the universe of the "Orient Ode," for instance, is nearer the outlook of Ecclesiastes than of, say, Professor Norman Lockyer. The "Orient Ode," on its scientific side, must wait at least fifty years for understanding. For there was never yet poet, beyond a certain range of insight, who could not have told the scientists what they will be teaching a hundred years hence. Science is a Caliban, only fit to hew wood and draw water for Prospero ; and it is time Ariel were released from his imprisonment by the materialistic Sycorax." [1] In a letter to Patmore, he had written :—

"The bits of science that crop up in your essays remind me of little devils dancing among rose trees."

The list of possible titles insists upon his regard for one aspect of his later work :—*Songs of the Inner Life ; Odes and other Poems ; New Things and Old ; Songs of a Sun-worshipper ; Music of the Future ; Night before Light ; At the Orient Gates ; The Dawn before the Day-Star.* In the event *New Poems* was chosen ; and on the eve of publication, F. T. writes to W. M. :—

"Herewith I send the book. Now, if Alice and you, after you have read it in proof, say 'this is bad poetry,' I will cut out half the book ; but not half a line to please a publisher's whim for little books and big margins. I was cabined and confined over my first book ; with my spurs won, I should be at liberty to make the book comprehensive. It will be a book as long as the *Unknown Eros*, for if the *Unknown Eros* has about twenty more poems,

---

[1] "Many a bit of true seeing I have had to learn again, through science having sophisticated my eye, inward or outward. And many a bit I have preserved, to the avoidance of a world of trouble, by concerning myself no more than any child about the teachings of science. Especially is this the case in regard to light. I never lost the child's instinctive rightness of outlook upon light because I flung the scientific theories aside as so much baffling distortion of perspective. 'Here is cart for horse,' I felt rather than saw, and would nothing with them. . . . Though scientists in camp stand together against me, I would not challenge the consensus of the poets."

238

The Contents Table

none of them are so long as one half-dozen of mine. Treated in the sumptuous style, it would make a book about the size of Rossetti's first volume; but there is no reason why it should be got up more than just well and simply. I believe it will be my last volume of poetry—in any case my last for some years—and I am determined to make it complete, that I may feel all my work worth anything is on record for posterity, if I die. . . . I have sacrificed something to the levity of the critics. I have put a whole section of the lightest poems I ever wrote after the first terribly trying section, to soothe the critics' gums. If they are decent to the measure of their slight aim, that is all I care for; they aimed little at poetry. That they are true to girl-nature I have a woman's certificate, besides the fact that I studied them —with one exception—from an actual original. . . . Again I have put a batch of four 'simple' poems at the opening of the miscellaneous section to catch the critical eye, though their importance is not such as to give them a place so prominent. So I have done what artifice could do to lighten a very stern, sober, and difficult volume. 'Tis more varied in range than my former work; and by my arrangement I have done my best to emphasize and press into service this, the solitary redeeming fact from the popular standpoint.

"From the higher standpoint I have gained, I think, in art and chastity of style; but have greatly lost in fire and glow. 'Tis time that I was silent. This book carries me quite as far as my dwindling strength will allow; and if I wrote further in poetry, I should write down my own fame."

New Poems found the critics, in 1897, more hostile than before. Perhaps the *Saturday Review* was the most severe :—

" He has been, from the first, unfortunate in being shielded from sincere criticism. He has been persuaded by his friends that

239

he is a genius, divinely inspired, whose wildest utterances are his best. . . . In no poet of reputation is it (order) more strikingly absent than in Mr. Thompson. Beautiful fancy, sonorous and picturesque diction we find here, indeed, but no motive power. These odes begin on one key, are shifted to another, take up a fresh subject, drop it, and, at length, as if merely wearied of their aimless flight, drop suddenly, and cease in the air."

" These, and the rest, are nonsense-verses," the same writer says of " The Mistress of Vision," but finds elsewhere "a touch of genuine sublimity." The former *British Review* picks out several examples of " his barbarous jargon " (a phrase also used by Horne of Meredith's " Song of Queen Theodolinda ") and prescribes for him Ben Jonson's pill for the poetaster and that he be shaken free of " the praises with which his friends now mislead him." The *Literary World* also sees need of doctoring, saying, " Nothing can be stronger than his language, nothing weaker than the impression it leaves on the mind. . . . It is like a dictionary of obsolete English suffering from a fierce fit of delirium tremens." *The Critic,* of New York, takes Thompson's ignorance of religion and symbolism for granted ; the *Times* finds fault with both his poetry and Catholicism ; the *Morning Post* is unfavourable ; the *Daily Chronicle,* the *Speaker,* and the *Guardian* all begin severely but leave scolding before they ended to give generous praise. The *Sheffield Daily Telegraph* was handsome. The poet's obscurity was the chief cause of displeasure, since from thinking a man's meanings difficult it is fatally easy to go on to say he is meaningless. The case they make is startlingly good ; one reaches for one's Thompson from the shelves to see if he is in truth so great as one had thought before spending an hour with his early critics. If one pauses before quoting them, it is not for fear of dealing unkindly with them. They are convincing ; only the Thompson of scraps they condemn is not the

" A Terrible Poem "

Thompson we know by the book. When the *Pall Mall* says

"There is a terrible poem called 'The Anthem of Earth' without form and void, rhymeless and the work of a mediæval and pedantic Walt Whitman,"

the point may be conceded, as between that particular critic and his particular Thompson; it is even possible to share with the *Pall Mall* its "deep-rooted irritability" when one has to contemplate on its pages tortuous and steep passages torn from their text.

Against the adverse may be set many good criticisms. Mr. Richard Whiteing wrote finely in the *Daily News*, for he cleared the hurdle of initial distaste—"It is idle to throw the book to the other end of the room. You have to pick it up again." He hates such "outrageous conceits" as "The world's unfolded blossom smells of God"; or "Soul fully blest to feel God whistle thee at heel." It is the old hatred, probably, of overhearing the "little language" of lovers or whispered prayers. But Mr. Whiteing admits that "to put him in order might only be to spoil him. He must have his way."

In the *Speaker*, Sir A. T. Quiller-Couch, after commenting, as usual, on the precipitate and defiant eulogies of the poet's "friends," continued :—

" . . . On the other hand, to be stung into denying that he is a poet, and an extraordinarily fine one, is to lose one's head just as wildly and less pardonably. . . . Of 'The Mistress of Vision,' I can only say that it recalls, after many days, the wonder and delight with which as a boy I first read ' Kubla Khan.' "

The *Daily Chronicle*, where Mr. Le Gallienne had given place to Mr. Archer, on a first reading, recognised "a man of imagination all compact, a seer and singer of rare genius"; the *Athenæum* "a singular mastery of verse"; the *Edinburgh*, with ponderous speed, "a great poet," and the *Academy* and *Bookman* gave handsome welcomes. Notwithstanding these, the impression on public and poet was discouraging. The book sold badly, and soon died, so that for the first half of the year in 1901 it brought in six shillings' worth of royalties : four copies had been sold. During the first half of 1902 the book found five buyers.

F. T. so far felt depressed by the bulk of adverse criticism as to write his thanks to one of the few kindly reviewers of the new book. He got in answer, June 7, 1897 :—

" I simply expressed (very inadequately) the pleasure your work had given me, without the least thought as to what anyone else thought or might think. That, however, is not strictly true. Your letter reminds me that I read some extracts to a friend, and then said, ' This is not work which can possibly be *popular* in the wide sense ; but it is work that will be read and treasured centuries hence by those who really care for poetry.' This comes back to me as you speak of the reaction. I assure you no conceivable reaction can wipe out or overlay such work as yours. It is firm based on the rock of absolute beauty ; and this I say all the more confidently because it does not happen to appeal to my own specu-lative, or even my own literary, prejudices.—Yours very truly,
WILLIAM ARCHER."

Later F. T. met Mr. Archer casually at Mr. Doubleday's house in Westminster, and his poetry and portrait figured in Mr. Archer's *Poets of the Younger Generation*. He was not put out of humour by small royalties :—

" DEAR WILFRID,—It strikes me that the cheque (2/11) has a very unseemly tail, which would be much improved by a piece grafted on to it, to give it a trifle more handsome proportions. Perhaps the thing might not be impossible to a patient operator (to speak ex-medical-studently).—Yours ever,   F. T."

He could be tragic too. His interruption during a reading of " Othello " at our house is never to be forgotten. Desdemona was in death agony, when an

Mr. Garvin to the Rescue

emphatic voice proclaimed :—"Here's a go, Mrs. Meynell ; I have lost my *Athenæum* cheque." But he found it in another pocket.

If buffers had been needed between the unfavourable reception of *New Poems* and the sensibility of the author they were supplied at this time by Mr. Garvin's splendid appreciation of his previous works, *Poems* and *Sister Songs,* in the *Bookman,* March 1897 :—

" Even with the greatest pages of *Sister Songs* sounding in one's ears, one is sometimes tempted to think the ' Hound of Heaven' Mr. Thompson's high-water mark for unimaginable beauty and tremendous import—if we do damnably iterate Mr. Thompson's tremendousness, we cannot help it, he thrusts the word upon us. We do not think we forget any of the splendid things of an English anthology when we say that the 'Hound of Heaven' seems to us, on the whole, the most wonderful lyric (if we consider *Sister Songs* as a sequence of lyrics) in the language. It fingers all the stops of the spirit, and we hear now a thrilling and dolorous note of doom and now the quiring of the spheres and now the very pipes of Pan, but under all the still sad music of humanity. It is the return of the nineteenth century to Thomas à Kempis. In *Sister Songs* Mr. Thompson has passed from agonies to exultations. Of pure power he had not more to reveal. But *Sister Songs* has the very sense of Spring : there is some lovely renaissance of spirit in the book, a melting of snows and all dewy germinations of delight. What rhythms are so lissome and persuasive as those of the first part ? In dainty and debonair invention it is altogether incomparable. *Sister Songs* opens with all the lyrical *élan* of Shelley perfectly married with the full and definite vision, the pure and vivid phrase of Keats. Thus in two of Mr. Thompson's many passages on childhood—

> Or if white-handed light
> Draw thee yet dripping from the quiet pools,
> Still lucencies and cools,
> Of sleep, which all night mirror constellate dreams ;

and again—

> . . . bubbles from the calyces
> Of the lovely thoughts that breathe,
> Paving like water-flowers thy spirit's floor beneath.

243

"New Poems"

"The second part of *Sister Songs* is in a greater mood. It is the high ritual of beauty, a very apocalypse of poetry, and one should only labour the futility of terms in attempting to praise it. The primary things of poetry are newly and immortally said. But Mr. Thompson's receptive mind is saturated with modern thought, and he uses it in a singular way to deepen the ancient interpretations. He touches Darwinism, and it becomes transmutable in a lovely and poignant lyric—

> In pairing-time, we know, the bird
> Kindles to its deepmost splendour,
>   And the tender
> Voice is tenderest in its throat.

"May we not dare to say of this passage (beginning—'Wild Dryad ! all unconscious of thy tree' in *Sister Songs*) that it almost arrives at that ultimate thing, that 'one thought, one grace, one wonder at the least,' which for Marlowe was beyond the furthest reach of words, and which poets have been seeking to declare from the beginning of song ? Mr. Thompson's poetry scarcely comes by way of the outward eye at all. He scarcely depends upon occasions. In a dungeon one imagines that he would be no less a poet. The regal air, the prophetic ardours, the apocalyptic vision, the supreme utterance—he has them all. A rarer, more intense, more strictly predestinate genius has never been known to poetry. To many this may well appear the simple delirium of over-emphasis. The writer signs for those others, nowise ashamed, who range after Shakespeare's very Sonnets the poetry of a living poet, Francis Thompson."

CHAPTER XII: FRIENDS AND OPINIONS

THE friends he found for distraction in London were few, his acquaintances still fewer; thus his biographer, in falling back on such slight records as would go unnoticed in a life more thickly peopled, believes that they have at any rate the value of rarity.

But in any case the chapter of his meetings could be more than matched with the chapter of his evasions. Thus ran the excuses:—

"Dear Wilfrid, I could not come in to tea with Blunt and Yeats, for I had to go down to the *Academy*, and was back much too late. Had I known on Thursday I would have altered my arrangements so as to accept your invitation. I am very sorry to have missed this chance of meeting Yeats, as I have long desired to do. You know I heartily admire his work."

Meredith's invitations he could not permanently resist. At Box Hill he spent a night in June 1896. Meredith had written to A. M., "You and the poet will have Heaven's welcome to the elect. But the cottage will be wounded if you desire not to sleep in it after having tried its poor resources. Be kind." To dine and sleep and wake in that small cottage was to be at very close quarters with nature and a man. With birds at the window, trees bowing and rustling at the back door, and at the front the vivid grass ready for his feet, Francis was thrust into the presence of a showy bit of nature, and was hardly more easy than if he had been thrust at the theatre into a box directly adjoining a crowded stage. He would pull at his necktie, and

245

smooth his coat, and be most warily conscious of his companion's eye, microscopic, like a husband's, for defect. The singing of Meredith's blackbirds would be no less confusing than the stream of Meredith's talk; the nodding flowers and the thousand shadows, the sunshine and the talker, were too strange to him. For years he had evaded nature and an eye; here he was forced to be seen and to see in the unclouded atmosphere of this garden on a hill, and during a long drive. Talk and caviare for breakfast were alike foreign to him, who never breakfasted even on toast. To be on tremendously good terms with Nature for her own sake, with talk for its own sake, with French literature, with the Celt, was Meredith's triumph; Thompson was shy of all these.

Meredith's method was one of acceptance, of bird's song and of Burgundy. Thompson's method was of refusal because he was not hardy enough for one or the other. With that mixture of precision and involved evasion that was his habit, Meredith praised "Love in Dian's Lap," quoting the lines—

> And on this lady's heart, looked you so deep,
> Poor Poetry has rocked himself to sleep;
> Upon the heavy blossom of her lips
> Hangs the bee Musing; nigh her lids eclipse
> Each half-occulted star beneath that lies;
> And in the contemplation of those eyes,
> Passionless passion, wild tranquillities.

The lady, too, was in the garden to hear.

In his written comments on *Poems*, Meredith had fastened on the misprinted passages as if they were evidences of the wilfulness of the poet, and he recalled these in talk, slow to relinquish an opportunity for his golden chaff. With the *Edinburgh* praise of Thompson he proclaimed himself in agreement, writing (July 19, 1896) "I subscribe to the words on Francis Thompson's verse." But he also called Thompson turgid, on the eve of passing to the writing of his own ode on the French Revolution; *Sister Songs* he had called at first sight a "voluntary."

He discovered no consecutive argument in *Sister Songs;* but for his banter he found an immediate opening; he invented a landlady for Thompson— Amelia Applejohn—to whom imaginary sonnets were addressed. He told how Amelia was summoned to Thompson's room to listen to the latest, rolling down her sleeves the while, and brushing the flour from her elbows.

After Thompson's death, Meredith wrote to W. M.:—

"Box Hill, *February* 3, 1909.

" Dear Mr. Meynell,—The love of all the Meynells, let all the Meynells know, is precious to me. And the book of the poems (*Selected Poems*) was very welcome, though a thought of the poet's broken life gives pain. What he might further have done hangs at the closing page. Your part in his history should help to comfort you. What we have of him is mainly due to the Meynell family.

Our Portia I may suppose to be now in Italy, and Italy seems to me her natural home. For me, I drag on, counting more years and not knowing why. I have to have an arm when I would walk. I am humiliated by requiring at times a repetition of sentences. This is my state of old age. But my religion of life is always to be cheerful; though I see little of my friends, I live with them.—Ever to be counted yours,

George Meredith."

One of the few occasions on which Francis entered a friend's house (always excepting W. M.'s) in London was when, in December 1896, he spent some weeks with Mr. and Mrs. Doubleday. Like a little boy, he posted word to W. M., as to a father, across the few intervening miles of London, of his safe arrival there, of his friend's kindness, and of his admiration of Mrs. Doubleday's music making:—"Mrs. Doubleday is very kind, and she is a simply exquisite pianist. Doubleday and I have fraternised over music."

"My friend Alfred Hayes," he used to say, almost with ostentation. And the phrase remains because he so rarely proclaimed or could proclaim a relationship of the sort. That he paid a visit and wrote letters and verses to Mr. Hayes were, even if he forgot to despatch one of the letters, unusual marks of consideration. The visit planned, it followed that he did not turn up in the expected way, so that his host, in his anxiety, asked W. M. for news, and later wrote:—

"20 CARPENTER ROAD, EDGBASTON,
October 13, 1896.

"DEAR MR. MEYNELL,—I am very sorry that, as all turned out well, I wrote to you in some apprehension as to Thompson. He turned up at the wrong railway-station and performed some other singular feats, but those were mere details, and we enjoyed his visit very much. I hope it did him good in spite of the fact that owing to its happening to be a very busy week for me at the office, I was obliged to leave him a good deal to his own devices, which consisted mainly in smoking innumerable pipes over the books he found in my study. The weather was so forbidding that we were only able to make two excursions afield. I hope he will come again in the summer when no infant daughter must again bar the way.—Yours, ALFRED HAYES."

Mr. Hayes gives me a reminiscence of his guest:—

"In the Autumn of the year 1896 Francis Thompson was my guest for a week at Edgbaston. The evenings were veritable *Noctes Ambrosianæ ;* but though the general impression of deep insight and opulent imagination, of many a flash of inspiration and radiant turn of speech, lingers as a precious recollection, the details of his conversation have vanished, for the most part, from memory, as completely as the precise hues and cloud-shapes of the sunsets of those memorable days.

"One indelible impression, however, remains—his amazing range of reading, the infallibility of his literary memory, and the consequent wealth of allusion he had at his command.

"My Friend Hayes"

"At meals he would sit mostly silent, sometimes quitting the table, his food half consumed, as if at some imperious mandate, but somehow without leaving behind him the slightest suspicion of discourtesy. These sudden disappearances, whose cause I never sought to discover, soon came to be expected, and only provoked a smile—it was Thompson's way. But let it not be supposed that he was uncouth or affected ; his manner was that of a great child ; he was simply incapable of pose or unkindness.

"His personal appearance is deeply engraved on the tablets of my memory. He was a pathetic figure. His form and face bore, only too clearly, the marks of those grim years of tribulation of soul and torment of body from which he had so recently been delivered. His appearance smote me with deep pity, but even deeper respect ; and within a few hours he had won my affection. I was struck, as were the few intimate friends who once met him at my house, with a strange other-worldliness about him, as if he were conscious of making only a hasty sojourn on earth in the course of an illimitable journey. . . . I remember how the discoloured face would suddenly light up, and the dazed eyes flash, in such moments of happy excitement, as if a volcanic eruption of delight had broken through the crust of his soul. He gave me the impression of concealing within him two inexhaustible reservoirs of sorrow and joy ; ebullitions from each appear in his poetry ; but in his long talks with me he rarely drew except from the fountain of joy."

Some time after this visit he wrote to Mr. Hayes of his journalism, his book, and his desire to see his friend again :—

"I met Norman Gale, for a brief moment, at my publishers', in January or thereabouts. I was charmed with him. Alas, I am farther off from you than ever ; it is not likely that I can visit you again for an unknown time to come. And I entertain such a happy recollection of you, your dear wife, and your charming children ! Let us pray for the unexpected, which always happens, you know !—Always yours, dear Hayes,

FRANCIS THOMPSON.

"I am very busy, or I would write at more length to you. Believe me, that I do not forget you ever."

Friends and Opinions

From her invalid's couch Mrs. Hamilton King sent Francis treasured messages of trust and commendation, and, guessing his need, wrote him many things that sounded bravely to one who accused himself of something worse than futility in friendship :—

" It is true that everyone must live out his own life, and I am not sure that it is good that another should live it for him ; but you at least have done much for your friends. Coventry Patmore relied on you ; and when I last saw Mr. Wilfrid Meynell he told me that both he and Mrs. Meynell felt themselves entirely your debtors—your poetry was so much for them. And you may have much more to do. I wish it were possible for you to live nearer and within reach of your friends. . . . It is a great consolation to feel that one has ministered to the most sensitive and precious among the children of God, and also it is a great joy and privilege to me to have your friendship."

Between 1896 and 1900 he also had correspondence with one who was especially his friend, Miss Katharine Douglas King, Mrs. Hamilton King's daughter. Before meeting her he had written to W. M. :—

"Do you know that Miss K. Douglas King is—together with Winifred Lucas—one of the few women I ever desired particularly to meet ? She has a temperament of genius heaped up and running over. I read through all her *Merry England* stories some months ago, and was startled by their individual and impressive note."

Her book, *The Child who will never Grow Old*, published two years later, bears on its first page his line, "The heart of Childhood, so divine for me." Miss King played with the Palace Court children, and worked among the poor children of the East End who often figure in her stories. Francis once visited her and her charges at the hospital in Leonard Square. Writing subsequently, Miss King says :—

" I count you as an old friend, but I know now I did not really know you until Saturday. When you were by your little ' genius's '

With Sick Children

—Harry's—bed, and the baby boy Percy with the white shoes was at your knee, that was to me a revelation! I think of you now with that infant's serious, confiding face upturned to you. It was all so natural. To some people a child is a pretty ornamental *addition*. Your personality now seems incomplete without the child as the natural and exquisite finish to the whole man. Adieu, dear friend."

A later letter announces her impending marriage :—

"FOREST HALL, *April* 1900.

" MY DEAR FRANCIS,—I have been wanting to write to you for so long, and yet have not been able to find time until now ; and now I find it a little difficult, because one feels reluctant to speak of one's own great happiness to one whose life has been so sad and lonely as yours, even though that one should be so firm and true a friend as you have ever been to me. My marriage is fixed for the early part of July. Although my new home will be far away, we both hope that in time we may come to live nearer London, and I hope that my marriage will not bring me less, but more, in touch with my friends, amongst whom, Francis, I hope that I may ever count you as one of the first and nearest, and may God bless you.—Believe me, Your always affectionately,　　　　KATHARINE D. KING."

It was after this that he wrote the following description of his friend :—

" There is no need of courage in the feminine woman, and I love her for the fact. Yet my dear friend (now removed by marriage) was a brave woman, and I loved her for it against all my wont. Perhaps, because she took me by surprise ; perhaps because—who knows why? She was not self-reliant with all her bravery, and I suppose the combination made her real femininity the more piquant. Perhaps it was rather her crystal truth than the courage which (I think) came from it, not caused it, that won me at sight. Truth—*integrity* (or *oneness*) *of nature*—is what calls to me."

In the matter of his close friendships, he wrote to

251

Friends and Opinions

Miss Agnes Tobin,[1] a lover of his poetry and herself a translator of Petrarch's sonnets :—

"Of what you say of me in relation to your spiritual development I dare not trust myself to write, lest I offend the modesty of words : it comes as a great prop to a life very lonely of support."

Mrs. Vernon Blackburn is elsewhere named; but of other acquaintances among women he had none, or only such as lasted during one or two meetings. The Duchess of Sutherland's invitations were found retained among his dusty papers like adventurous Sisters of Charity, stiff and clean in the ragged company of a neglected correspondence, old pipes and newspaper-cuttings.

The people he did not know yet counted for something in his history; he has been associated with some he might have known, but did not, and with others he could never have known. Oscar Wilde, on hearing some of *Sister Songs* read aloud, said, "Why can't I write poetry like that ? That is what I've wanted to do all my life." The two, however, did not meet. In a letter from Mrs. Wilde, January 1895, I find, "I so enjoyed Mr. Thompson's visit to me on Friday," and in another, June 1894, "Oscar was quite charmed with the lines you read him of Francis Thompson." "Of the living poets whose work I like, he is one of the very few whom I like as well as their work," wrote Mr. Vincent O'Sullivan after meeting him at about the same time.

Of the invitations he did not accept were those from Mrs. Louise Chandler Moulton that he should sometimes go to her "for a quiet talk *à deux*"; from Elliot and Fry that he should be photographed "in his study"; from a *World* writer that he should be interviewed as a subject for one of the "Celebrities at Home."

---

[1] To this lady's "genius for friendship" the dedication of Mr. Joseph Conrad's *Under Western Eyes* bears witness.

Mr. Whitten's Portrait

In 1897 Mr. Lewis Hind found that the *Academy* might welcome something every week from Thompson, and wrote telling him so. Then he came into touch, slowly as was his way, with the office staff. "I saw what I concluded was Clarence Rook at the *Academy* on Wednesday, but we did not even exchange a look, for Hind did not introduce us. So I left convinced that Hind meant to get out the *Academy* by hook or by C. Rook." From this time began his friendship with Mr. E. V. Lucas and Mr. Wilfred Whitten. All these, along with the "management," learnt how to smile on the trials provided by this contributor. Mr. Lucas is quoted on an earlier page devoted to cricket. Mr. Whitten has written :—

" I first met Francis Thompson at the *Academy* office in Chancery Lane, in 1897, the year in which, with his *New Poems*, he took farewell of poetry and began, I fear, to look on life as so much dead lift, so much needless postscript to his finished epistle. . . . We gave Thompson as many books of theology, history, biography, and, of course, poetry as he cared to review. It was a usual thing, in reading the proofs, for one of us to exclaim aloud on his splendid handling of a subject demanding the best literary knowledge and insight. Thompson came frequently to the office to receive books for review, and to bring in his ' copy.' Every visit meant a talk, which was never curtailed by Thompson. This singer, who had soared to themes too dazzling for all but the rarest minds ; this poet of the broken wing and the renounced lyre had not become moody or taciturn. At his best he was a fluent talker, who talked straight from his knowledge and convictions, yet never for victory. He weighed his words, and would not hurt a controversial fly. On great subjects he was slow or silent ; on trifles he became grotesquely tedious. This dreamer seemed to be surprised into a kind of exhilaration at finding himself in contact with small realities. And then the fountains of memory would be broken up, or some quaint corner of his *amour propre* would be touched. He would explain nine times what was clear, and talk about snuff or indigestion or the posting of a letter until the room swam round us.

" A stranger figure than Thompson's was not to be seen in London. Gentle in looks, half-wild in externals, his face worn by

253

Friends and Opinions

pain and the fierce reactions of laudanum, his hair and straggling beard neglected, he had yet a distinction and an aloofness of bearing that marked him in the crowd; and when he opened his lips he spoke as a gentleman and a scholar. A cleaner mind, a more naïvely courteous manner, were not to be found. It was impossible and unnecessary to think always of the tragic side of his life. He still had to live and work in his fashion, and his entries and exits became our most cheerful institution. His great brown cape, which he would wear on the hottest days, his disastrous hat, and his dozen neglects and make-shifts were only the insignia of our 'Francis' and of the ripest literary talent on the paper. No money (and in his later years Thompson suffered more from the possession of money than from the lack of it) could keep him in a decent suit of clothes for long. Yet he was never 'seedy.' From a newness too dazzling to last, and seldom achieved at that, he passed at once into a picturesque nondescript garb that was all his own and made him resemble some weird pedlar or packman in an etching by Ostade. This impression of him was helped by the strange object—his fish-basket, we called it—which he wore slung round his shoulders by a strap. It had occurred to him that such a basket would be a convenient receptacle for the books which he took away for review, and he added this touch to an outward appearance which already detached him from millions. . . . He had ceased to make demands on life. He ear-marked nothing for his own. As a reviewer, enjoying the run of the office, he never pounced on a book; he waited, and he accepted. Interested still in life, he was no longer intrigued by it. He was free from both apathy and desire. Unembittered, he kept his sweetness and sanity, his dewy laughter, and his fluttering gratitude. In such a man outward ruin could never be pitiable or ridiculous, and, indeed, he never bowed his noble head but in adoration. I think the secret of his strength was this: that he had cast up his accounts with God and man, and thereafter stood in the mud of earth with a heart wrapt in such fire as touched Isaiah's lips."

He had no valet of whom to make a conquest; but a friendly editor, at any rate, was at his feet, even when they were unpunctual. Mr. Lewis Hind writes:—

"During the seven years that I edited the *Academy*, I knew the poet intimately, seeing him two or three times a week. It amused him to write articles, and to know that his landlady was

In Chancery Lane

being paid, although such matters were of no real importance to him ; but the weekly wage gave him pocket-money to buy the narcotics of his choice, and that *was* important.

" In memory I see him one miserable November afternoon communing with the Seraphim, and frolicking with the young-eyed Cherubim in Chancery Lane. The roads were ankle-deep in slush ; a thin, icy rain was falling ; the yellow fog enwrapped the pedestrians squelching down the lane ; and, going through them in a narrow-path, I saw Francis Thompson, wet and mud-spattered. But he was not unhappy. What is a day of unpleasant weather to one who lives in eternity ? His lips were moving, his head was raised, his eyes were humid with emotion, for above the roof of the Chancery Lane Safe Deposit Company, in the murk of the fog, he saw beatific visions. They were his reality, not the visible world.

" He was on his way to the office of the *Academy* with the manuscript of a book review, and on his damp back was slung the weather-worn satchel in which he would carry away volumes for the ensuing week. A Thompson article in *The Academy* gave distinction to the issue. What splendid prose it was ! Reading the proofs, we would declaim passages aloud for the mere joy of giving utterance to his periods. He wrote a series of articles on ' Poets as Prose Writers ' which must some day be recovered from the files ; he wrote on anything. I discovered that his interest in battles,and the strategy of great commanders was as keen as his concern with cricket. So the satchel was filled with military memoirs, and retired generals ensconced in the armchairs of service clubs wondered. Here was a man who manipulated words as they manipulated men. Once or twice in those seven years of our intercourse a flame of his old poetic fire blazed out, and once I was able to divert the flame into the pages of the *Academy*. When Cecil Rhodes died I telegraphed to Thompson to hasten to the office. That was on a Monday. He appeared on the Tuesday. I asked him point blank if he would write an ode on Cecil Rhodes for the next issue of the paper, and without waiting for his refusal talked Rhodes to him for half an hour, roused his enthusiasm, and he departed with a half promise to deliver the ode on Thursday morning. Thursday came and nearly passed. I sent him three telegrams, but received no answer. It was necessary to go to press at eight o'clock. At half-past six he arrived, and proceeded to extract from his pockets a dozen and more scraps of crumpled paper, each containing a fragment of the ode. I pieced them together, sent

255

the blurred manuscript to the printers, gave him money for his dinner, and exacted a promise that he would return in an hour to read the proof. He returned dazed and incoherent, read the proof standing and swaying as he read, and murmured : 'It's all right.' It was all right. I am prouder of having published that ode than of anything else that the *Academy* ever contained. In 1904, when I resigned the editorship of the *Academy*, we no longer met regularly ; but I saw Thompson at infrequent intervals at Mrs. Meynell's house. He would come to dinner at any hour that suited his mood, take his bite and sip, and pace the room with a book in his hand, striking innumerable matches, never keeping his pipe alight, rarely taking part in the general conversation, but ever courteous and ever ready to laugh at the slightest pleasantry."

Of his editor, and to his editor, Thompson writes :—

> " 39 GOLDNEY ROAD, HARROW ROAD,
> *Sunday Night.*

" DEAR HIND,—Since I was betrayed so unfortunately into putting a hasty definition into clumsy words, I beg to be allowed to define my intended meaning—to define my definition, in fact. I called you, I believe, 'a man of the world with a taste for letters.' It would be nearer my meaning if I had called you a man of action with a love for letters—and art. Wilfrid Blunt, Wyndham, &c., are examples of the class. I might also say Henley. It is true that you no more than Henley have ever been a man of action like Blunt or Wyndham. Some more inclusive term is needed. The essential thing is, that *life* occupies the principal place in your regard —not life as it should be lived, the ideal of life in other words—but actual everyday life, 'life as she *is* lived.' This is foremost, letters or art second. Raleigh and a host of the great Elizabethans belonged to the same school. 'Man of action first' is perhaps the nearest I can get to it. 'Man of the world' is bungling because it bears so many significations. Anyway, *now*, I hope, you have some idea of my meaning. It was an antithesis between the pure thinker and recluse, on one

Francis Thompson
a sketch at Palace Court
E.M.

"Mr. Thompson of Fleet Street"
Drawn by Everard Meynell, 1903

Late Copy

hand; the man interested in action for its own sake, yet with a foothold in letters, on the other.—Yours ever,

F. T."

Scruples in criticism, anxiety over ten shillings overdrawn from the *Academy's* cashier, and the imaginary coldness of his editor in consequence, brought Mr. Wilfred Whitten letters a column long, and though abbreviated (as most given in this book are), they are sufficiently characteristic of a profuse manner :—

"DEAR HIND,—I muddled up the time altogether today. How, I do not now understand. I started off soon after 2. Thinking I had time for a letter to the *Academy* which it had been in my mind to write, I delayed my journey to write it. When I was drawing to a conclusion, I heard the clock strike 3 (as it seemed to me). I thought I should soon be finished, so went on to the end. A few minutes later, as it appeared, the clock struck again, and I counted 4. Alarmed, I rushed off—vexed that I should get in by half-past 4 instead of half-past 3, as I intended—and finished the thing in the train. I got to the *Academy*, and was struck all of a heap. There was nobody there, and it was ten past six! How I did it, I do not even now understand. I will be with you in good time to-morrow. But that cannot make amends to myself for such a *fiasco* and waste of time.—Yours, F. T."

At other times his copy is late because he has no stamp; or, thinking he has delivered an article, the next day he finds half of it still in his pocket; but illness is his stand-by, his most robust excuse.

The two following letters tell of books lost on either side :—

"16 ELGIN AVENUE, W.
November 2, 1897.

"MY DEAR HIND,—I will do as you wish about the Crashaw. I think you are right, but in the absence of

Friends and Opinions

any notification I kept to the stipulated length of two columns.

"I received the letter you forwarded from Arthur Waugh ; but the book which should have accompanied it has not been sent me. Will you please see what has become of it, and have it forwarded at once. I am afraid it may have got mixed with the books for review ; and it is a book I value, sent me as a gift by Waugh, in recognition of my last 'Excursion.' Please let the matter be looked into without delay.

"I am glad to hear that Wells has given you well-deserved recognition in the *Saturday*.—Yours sincerely,

FRANCIS THOMPSON.

"*P.S.*—For fear of any confusion, I may add that Waugh's book is a volume of 'Political Pamphlets,' belonging to the same 'Library' as the volume noticed in my last 'Excursion.'"

"DEAR HIND,—I regret exceedingly to find that the Menpes was disposed of along with an accumulation of back review books, nor can I get it back, for it sold almost at once. I am very sorry it should have happened ; because it should not and would not have been sold, had it not gone among others when I was in a hurry, and my mind occupied only with the work I had in hand. Of course, under such circumstances, I hold myself responsible for replacing it as soon as I can. Or if you cannot wait, I would suggest you get the book and dock it out of my extra money. The only alternative is for me to pick oakum (if they do that in debtors' gaols). And I have not the talents for oakum-picking. Though I enjoyed the distinguished tuition of a burglar, who had gone through many trials—and houses—in the pursuit of this little-known art, I showed such mediocre capacity that the Master did not encourage me to persevere. Besides, seeing how overcrowded the profession is, it would be a pity for me to take the oakum out of another man's fingers.

258

More " Academy "

"Seriously, I am very upset that this should have happened. I can think of nothing but what I have suggested.—Yours sincerely,   F. THOMPSON."

"DEAR HIND,—I was taken sick on my way to the station, not having been to bed all night, and having been working a good part of to-day; and though I came on as soon as I could pull myself together again, I was too late. So I leave here the Dumas article, which I brought with me, and will be down to-morrow morning, when I am told you will be here.—Yours in haste,

F. THOMPSON.

"*P.S.*—You had another very interesting article last week; but I had qualms whether your art of artistic romance, or of the Thing Seen, or the Thing which Ought to have been Seen if it Wasn't, was taking me in again with its realism more real than fact."

"DEAR HIND,—I was so unwell yesterday that I could not come—neuralgia in the eye. I am the more sorry because the Watson article was ready to bring with me, as you desired. The acute pain drove it out of my head. Nor could I see to write an explanation of my absence. To-day, when I remembered the unsent article, I thought it of course too late to be of use to you this week. So, my eye being still weak, I decided to bring it (not the eye) to-morrow, with personal explanation. But getting your telegram I send it herewith. A really fine Ode [1]— though close (in point of style) to my 'Nineteenth Century' Ode in the *Academy*. Thorp perceived it, without any 'lead' from me; so it is not merely my own fancy. But it is, on the whole, a better poem than the original. If all made such fine use of the model, I would not mind imitation.—Yours in haste,

F. THOMPSON."

[1] William Watson's on the Coronation of Edward VII.

259

Friends and Opinions

"16 ELGIN AVENUE, W.
Monday.

"MY DEAR HIND,—I was taken very ill last week, and was totally unable to get in my work for the *Academy.* Having pulled round, I send you herewith the Wordsworth, and trust to let you have the Fiona Macleod in the course of to-morrow, or at any rate by Wednesday morning by the latest.

"With regard to your request for articles on Shelley, Browning, and Tennyson, I am sorry that, after careful consideration, I must ask you to hand them over to someone else. Considering the importance—the great importance—of what I am asked to treat, I do not feel that I could do justice either to my subject or my own reputation within the limit of 1000 words proposed. In the case of such minor men as Landor, or even possibly Macaulay, I should not object to the limitation —biographical details being omitted. But I simply cannot pledge my name to a disposal of Tennyson or Browning in about two columns. It would be a mere clumsy spoiling of material which I might to greater advantage use elsewhere. I could only undertake it on the terms that the length of the article should be determined by the organic exigencies of my treatment alone. Of course I have never dreamed of anything beyond five columns as what you could reasonably allow me for important articles. If some have extended to more, it has been the result of miscalculation, and I should have quite acquiesced in your cutting such excessive articles down.—Yours very sincerely,
FRANCIS THOMPSON."

Of the ethics of reviewing he writes at length, to the Editor :—

"I regret that—in pressure of work and ill-health— Miss Frances Power Cobbe's letter, which you forwarded

260

The Reviewer

me, has not received the immediate attention which it deserved. I regret that my review should strike her as a personal attack. But I cannot see that it exceeded the limits of impartial criticism. Miss Power Cobbe seems to imply that I in some way found Miss Shore's poems 'morally objectionable.' I am unaware of any sentence which could create such an impression. For the rest, I was necessarily unaware of Miss Shore's personal circumstances. I was not even aware of its being her first book of poems. When a book comes before a reviewer for criticism, he cannot be expected to know or take account of personal matters—of anything outside the book itself. Many things might plead that he should be very gentle with the author, but he has no knowledge of them. The book is an impersonal thing to him ; and the author who publishes a book becomes impersonal, and must expect to be treated as a mere name at the head of so many printed pages ; it is the inevitable consequence of publication.

"The critic can but register his impressions, coldly impartial by his very function. Did he abstain from the blame he thought just, because (for example) of the writer's sex, it would be equivalent to abdicating criticism where women are concerned, extending the privileges of the drawing-room to the reviewing-column. But women of literary power would be the first to protest against the insincerity of 'letting them off' because of their sex."

But it may be judged that reviewing is not always so strict a business :—

"16 ELGIN AVENUE, W.
Saturday.

" MY DEAR HIND,—I have been very unwell for the last two or three weeks, or your urgent requests should have been better attended to. The Dunlop article was finished on Monday week, when I got your letter from

261

Friends and Opinions

Henley, and consequently had partly to re-write it. And unluckily an attack of sickness which confined me to bed prevented my getting it in yesterday, although it was actually done. But I trust I am now much better all round, and shall be able to give the *Academy* proper attention. It is cutting my own throat for me to neglect it, and you may be sure I should not wilfully keep you waiting as I have done the last two or three weeks. I trust I have met Henley's wishes in the article as it now stands. I had no notion, to begin with, that there was so much to do over the book; and so I had treated it slightly. I will call in on Monday, in case you have anything you might wish to say in regard to it.

"With much regrets for my delay (but really I have been having a pretty beastly time of it)—Yours sincerely,
FRANCIS THOMPSON."

This was no longer the Henley of the great time, when every issue of the *Scots Observer* contained a poem or essay fit to make a beginning of fame for one of the "young men"; when this week the new cadences of Mr. Kipling's "Barrack-Room Ballads" sent city readers swinging and chanting back from their offices towards suburban sunset and supper. Those contributors fronted a famous future, their organ observed of all observers, their editor the instantaneous boisterous welcomer of the talent that served his turn. All the precious persons of his choice made the bluff figure of the chief the more defined. "I am the Captain of my Soul" was his boast, but others knew him as the captain of a newspaper staff. Famous for the young men he made his own, he is here recalled for the young man he rejected. My father sent him a poem by Francis Thompson which, consistently enough, he refused. Indocile, he would probably still have resolution to refuse verses "reeking of Shelley, whom I detest." It is proof of his perception that from the first he knew

A Rejection

the newcomer was no shipmate for the Captain Silver of the literary weeklies. In the description of the lame pirate of *Treasure Island* the likening of his face to a ham suggests that the image of the editor, more massive than those of any two contributors, was before Stevenson as he wrote; pirate and editor had each a crutch, and each threw it at an intruder. Thompson's words of Henley and his last book impute to him, too, a Silver's grip:—

". . . We know exactly the best he has done, and resent instinctively the slightest deflection from it. Well, here there are such deflections—that is all which can be said; and we feel them in exact proportion to our love of the Henley who took us masterfully by the throat of old. He still takes us by the throat, but his grip is not compulsive. Yet now and again the old mastery thrills us, and we remember. It is good to remember."

And Henley on his side learnt to admire. Where the poet had failed, the journalist writing about *The Centenary Burns* had his strong approval:—

"*March* 7, 1897.

"DEAR HIND,—Thompson's article, which came in this morning, is quite masterly throughout. The worst I can say against it is, indeed, that it anticipates some parts of my own terminal essay, so that I shall have to quote it instead of writing out of my own stomach. All manner of compliments to him, and a thousand thanks. I know not which to admire the more: his critical intelligence or his intellectual courage.

"To one point only must I take exception. The book is referred to throughout as 'Mr. Henley's.' This it is *not*; so, in justice to Henderson (who feels the slight the more keenly because of the uncommon brilliancy of the work) I must ask you to find room for the protest herewith enclosed. . . .—Sincerely yours,
W. E. H."

Henley's half-capitulation shows a streak of unsuspected tolerance. F. T. reeked of so many things, besides Shelley, that Henley detested. The Burns article itself, to which Henley makes allusion, says uncompromising things of Burns :—

"Imagination and tenderness demand either the refinement of education or the refinement of pure and sweet life. These things *might* be in peasant song. They are in the songs of the Dimbovitza, which are higher as absolute poetry than anything within Burns' compass. Not because these songs are the outcome of greater genius, but because they are the outcome of a healthier and sweeter rustic state ; a state in which the women were chaste and tender, the men brave and sober. Burns could well have sung it had he known it."

Writing a year later, Henley, on the defensive, said :—

" My dear Hind,—What a jackass is your F. Thompson ! I have never babbled the *Art for Art's Sake* babble. If I have, I'll eat the passage publicly. *What* I've said is, the better the writer the better the poet : that, in fact, good writing's better than bad. That is my only formula, and that I'm no more likely to swallow than F. T. is to write invariably well.—Yours ever sincerely,
W. E. Henley."

But Henley and Thompson were to make friends :—

" My dear Thompson,—I saw Henley on Saturday. He wants us to call on him next Friday afternoon. Will you be here at three *sharp* ? Henley said some very nice things about you, and is quite anxious to meet you. He also bids me say that he is looking forward to your excursions on the Prophets. So do hurry them up. He tells me that many of the lyrics in his Anthology are from the Old Testament. This is *entre nous*.—Sincerely yours,
Lewis Hind."

His only encounter with the sage of Muswell Hill followed, but not at three *sharp*. To his escort, Mr. E. V. Lucas and Mr. Hind, Henley was the mighty overseer of men who had not found, save through him, their journalistic souls. The escort still marvels at F. T.'s unpunctuality. Francis owed neither his soul nor hours to any man, and was late. "I have had no time to eat, Hind," was his gloomy beginning. Mr. Hind has described what followed a meal at the station :—

"Suddenly he became rigid, his body swayed, and a film came over his eyes. A minute or two passed; then he recovered, lighted his pipe, and did not refer to the episode. We arrived at Henley's house two hours late."

Doubtless his timorousness was as great as theirs, only his timeliness was less. But it was he who fronted and appeased the wrathful master with talk of "London Voluntaries" and Henley's influence. Instead of reeking of Shelley he showed himself reeking of Henley, who was not abhorrent. The escort were left well to the rear in flatteries no less sincere than theirs. Thompson's admirations were always well set up and bright-eyed because they were so well reasoned. No prepossessions, whims, or sloths made up his opinion. No author was carelessly shelved or unshelved; he did not put Swinburne aside although his angels and Swinburne's never rested nor flew on the wing together. His attention was widely inclusive. Often would he come with some cutting of fugitive verse and tender it for what it was worth, reading it aloud and expecting from his audience the controlled and properly adjusted pleasure he himself experienced. So tolerant was he, that anybody's complaint that there "was nothing in it," would cause him to reconsider his cutting; the "anybody" of poetry or criticism was the recipient of his constant courtesy. He was very slow—too slow for the short span of his life to alter his allegiance to the literature that had ever seriously contented him. The novels of Lord Lytton he read again at the end of his life because he had early cared for them, and reasonably, he found. So with Hardy; of one passage I remember him to have often spoken with particular admiration—that in which Sergeant Troy thralls a woman by sword play and the swinging of his flashing steel round and round her person. So with Meredith, over whose novels I have found him sitting in a Westbourne Grove confectioner's, with, I am sure, "review" books unreviewed in his bag, and in his pocket telegrams from Hind. Of Meredith's poetry his admiration was of the established sort that needs no questioning. And Jacobs had his laugh, always readier than his tear, for pathetic print is more liable to stand suspect on the page than humorous. Whatever modern author he discussed it was his relish rather than his distaste that flavoured his opinion.

Henley and he were amiable for an afternoon; but the difference between them could hardly have been bridged for longer. The differences between them were made up of crude difference of speech, of the actual lipping of feelings and phrases. Thompson writes lightly in the following note-book comment, but he is treading lightly because the ground beneath quakes with radical conflict :—

"We are convinced Mr. H. has been misled by a false report. It is the more probable because Spring, of late years, has been flighty, and given rise to dissatisfied comment. We are aware that C. P. has spoken of 'all amorous May,' and yet another poet has gone so far as to call the same lady 'wanton.' But 'the harlot spring'—Captain, these be very bitter words. Why in the name of wilfulness, why must poor Spring—of all seasons, poor Spring—be a harlot ? Even the author of *Dolores*, with all his disrelish for 'lilies and languors,' has not committed defloration of the poor young maid—'the girl child Spring'; he leaves her as he found her. If she escaped the dangerous society of Mr. S. (whose verse would 'thaw the consecrated snow that lies on Dian's lap') we cannot believe she should later make this slip."

Bunyan

Of Henley's "fads, blindnesses, wilful crotchets" as also of his critical prose, "the swift and restless brilliance of a leaping salmon in the sunlight," F. T. wrote in the *Academy* and brought, in doing so, the thought to one's mind of his own dissimilarity.

Perhaps nowhere in all the thousand columns F. T. contributed to the Press is a single wilful word. The unexpected must never be expected of him. His views on the general literature of the past may be taken for granted, or sought in their proper place. He will seldom be found at variance with the accepted estimates. Perhaps only once does he stand nearly alone. One of his earliest essays—"Bunyan in the Light of Modern Criticism"—approved Mr. Richard Dowling's assault upon *The Pilgrim's Progress*. Thompson could not tolerate the dulness and insufficiency of Bunyan's descriptions :—

"In the account of the Valley of Despair he does flicker into a meagre glimmer of description ; but its only effect is to leave the darkness of his fancy visible, and he flickers feebly out again. The Mouth of Hell is by the way ; and, after his usual commonplace manner of vision, he introduces this tremendous idea with a dense flippancy, such as never surely was accorded it before."

If he essayed other reversals of conventional opinion, he did so in good faith. But one goes to his critical work, not for its consistent good faith and sound sense, but for the few dominant, vital enthusiasms that hold him and would have been written of, even if he had never contributed to the papers. The "Shelley" has been quoted incidentally in these pages ; his "Crashaw," in its carefully critical tone, seems to deny an admiration often obvious in Thompson's work. As a reviewer he put by some of his impulsive affection. De Quincey and Patmore entered into his life ; to place them among the

Friends and Opinions

"reviewer's" authors would be absurd. Rossetti's name got into Thompson's criticisms from every quarter; it is in "Paganism Old and New," in the "Don Quixote," in "Crashaw," and in a dozen other papers; it dogs de Quincey's in and out of all the prose work.

He professed no learning, boasted no single proficiency. In a young family that was finding its way about in journalism and painting and other professions, he offered no unfriendly criticism, and seemed to know of none. I wonderingly remember now how he let me help him in an article on Hardy. At first there had been a difficulty about the re-reading of the novels; "No, Wilfrid, it's no good. As I thought, it's no good, Wilfrid," he had said after searching the shops of Kilburn for the books he wanted. "Your own copies are gone—gone from the shelves, and I've no way of procuring others." Even when supplied with copies he needed help, and wrote, as I know from the printed article, a thing of patchwork, with a centre-piece of his own well-knit prose, and a beginning and end ; the rest the bedraggled fringes, which I recognise with reluctance as I read them now for my own.

His earlier admiration of Swinburne is restated with reserves in his *Academy* review of the collected works of that poet, of whom it was rumoured that he disapproved of Thompson's liberties with the English language. Many younger poets might have been made the happier had they been aware whose was the pen that praised them in print. In *Hand in Hand, Verses by a Mother and Daughter*, F. T. makes the discovery of a sonnet with a last line that "is a touch of genius"— a sonnet by the daughter, Mr. Rudyard Kipling's sister, and called "Love's Murderer." Under the heading "Above Average," 1901, he deals with the books of Mr. Aleister Crowley and Mr. Madison Cawein. Mr. Crowley he had reviewed before. "The Mother's Tragedy" contains the "old vigour and boldness, the sinewy phrase

Contemporaries

that draws the praise out of you." At less length we read of Mr. Cawein, whose "strength lies in luxuriant descriptive power. . . . Assuredly, in this single gift, Mr. Cawein shows very great promise and no small accomplishment." He welcomes in the *Academy* the poetry of Mr. Sturge Moore, Mr. Alfred Noyes, and Lord Alfred Douglas; and anticipating George Meredith, he praises Dora Sigerson Shorter for her gifts of metrical narrative, adding: "Her ballads touch a deep and poignant feeling. The unconsciousness of a child contrasted with the sorrow of its earthly lot—this is a familiar theme, yet Mrs. Shorter handles it with unfamiliar freshness and power." He pulls the ropes for Mr. Newbolt's *Admirals All;* he ducks his head to Mr. Owen Seaman's parodies. He gathers "the teeming felicities" from the *Studies in Prose and Verse* of Mr. Arthur Symons. F. T. was one of the few critics who "lived by admiration." At the end of a day of reviewing he would still have the spirit to cut occasional verses from his evening paper and carry them for approbation to friends far quicker than he to shrug fastidious shoulders.

Aubrey de Vere, a man mellow in ancient stateliness, he met at Palace Court. The obituary notice of de Vere in the *Academy* was written by him. From the "Ode to the Daffodil" and "Autumnal Ode" he quotes enough to justify, with reservation, a high admiration :—

"Of warmth he was capable, especially in his younger days, but not of pathos or subtle suggestion. His general manner, it must be owned, was somewhat coldly grave. One of his odes is fine, with passages of absolute grandeur ; some of his sonnets are only not among the best in that kind."

His appreciations were not ordered by papers committed to a policy of praise. On the contrary, he wrote : "My editors complain that I don't *go* for people—that

I am too lenient." For all that, he knew the distress
of the vapid verse that came his way, and he stopped
to note it in rhyme :—

> Of little poets, neither fool nor seer,
> Aping the larger song, let all men hear
> How weary is our heart these many days !
>
> Of bards who, feeling half the thing they say,
> Say twice the thing they feel, and in such way
> Piece out a passion . . .
>
>   .   .   .   .   .   .
>
> Of bards indignant in an easy chair
> (Because just so great bards before them were)
> Who yet can only bring
> With all their toil
> Their kettle of verse to sing,
> But never boil,—
> How weary is our heart these many days !

But the solace he had to the drudgery of reviewing
was generally ancient. When he could set to and write
a solid *Academy* page on the "clod-paced Drayton,"
note the sluggishness of "his thick-coming ideas in the
strait pen of a defined stanza," chaff him for the room
he needs to turn about in, and cry "hear, hear!" to
his minor metres, he was doing lively work and was
lively at it. Or when Samuel Daniel comes up for
judgment, the critic is manifestly happy—happier than
in the presence of Mr. Maurice Hewlett or Mr. Kipling.
A review of an Elizabethan is touched with a quicker
interest than that of the weightiest in contemporary
literature. The evenness of his judgment, the unbiassed
distribution of his attention makes for fairness, but
somewhat spoils the current and local effectiveness. He
enjoyed getting at Butler's wit more than getting at
Oscar Wilde's. *Hudibras* was a book of the moment
for him, whereas *The Yellow Book* was not. St. Francis
de Sales might tempt him on a bookstall, but he never

bought a new work. D'Annunzio and publishers' announcements did not catch his pennies; nor were his borrowings much more modern. The authors he had from my shelves were Swedenborg and Shakespeare, with W. W. Jacobs, in whose jolly company he spent a few of the last hours of his life.

CHAPTER XIII: THE LONDONER

On days when London is cracked and bleared with cold, and passengers on the black pavement are grey and purple and mean in their distress, whipped by the East Wind and chivied by the draughts of the gutters; when lamp-posts and telegraph poles and the harsh sides of the houses ache together and shiver, Thompson would be the most forlorn and shrivelled figure in the open. It always seemed to be a necessity of his to be out in rough weather. I have never known him to stay in on its account; and at times when even riches lack confidence, and an universal scourge of cold and ugliness lashes the town, he was about. Even within, beside a fire, he was a weathercock of a man. The distress of his hands, and the veering of his hair from the comparative orderliness of other times would instantly proclaim an East wind. It was written all over him, and, though come to the shelter of four walls, the tails of his coat seemed still to be fluttering. One thought of him when East winds blew as the Pope of Chesterfield's description—". . . his poor body a mere Pandora's box, containing all the ills that ever afflicted humanity." Sensitive beyond endurance, Francis yet made nought of his pains so long as the keener sensitiveness of his conscience was undisturbed. Of all men the least fit to endure physical suffering, he endured it forgetfully and even light-heartedly unless, his spiritual assent being thwarted, he felt the chills of estrangement from God.

He was not more comfortable in the sun, and against the particular heat of 1906 he had particular ill-will. " Most people expatiate on the excellence of this summer,

Spring in Kilburn

though the angry and malignant sun is as unlike the
true summer sun as the heat of fever to the heat of
youth." It was his habit to go forth in August in an
ulster—threadbare, perhaps—but his own fever alone
explains his distress.

Sister Songs opens with a complaint against the spring
season of 1891 :—

> Shrewd winds and shrill,—were these the speech of May ?
> A ragged, slag-grey sky—invested so,
> Mary's spoilt nursling, wert thou wont to go ?

"To my Godchild" opens in the same manner. The
early months, drenched with icy rain, had meant misery
and dumbness. Breaking of silence came with the
breaking of the frost, and the poetry which returned
with the warm weather is full of acknowledgments. It
is something more than the small-talk of his verse ; it is,
like the dedications of the eighteenth century, a formal
obeisance to a patron—"Sun-god and song-god."

The Spring found him happiest. The May of his
poems is the May known to the Londoner. After
deploring, in the proem of *Sister Songs*, the lateness of
the season, it is suddenly upon him. He discovered
it for certain round a street corner not far from his
lodgings in Elgin Avenue—

> Mark yonder how the long laburnum drips
> Its jocund spilth of fire, its honey of wild flame.

That is the signal best known to the Londoner. Most
of the details of his description in *Sister Songs*, from the
stars to Covent Garden clock, are metropolitan. From
his high room, down steep stairs, a faded oilcloth at his
feet, the coiling patterns of a varnished wall-paper at his
restricted elbow ; through the muffled light and air of
the hall, and past the broken stucco of the front steps,
he would emerge on a morning of good fortune, to see,

not a dismal street of other lodgings exactly like his own, but

> A garden of enchanting
> In visionary May,
> Swayless for the spirit's haunting,
> Thrice threefold walled with emerald from our mortal
> mornings grey.

We may imagine that St. Francis cared not overmuch for the look of the Assisi streets ; it is doubtful whether Francis of Kilburn cared at all about the aspect of Kilburn. The gayest thoroughfare caught his eye no more than the most dismal—and Brondesbury is not gay. To "And your new lodging, Francis, what of it ? " he would give a good account of the rights and lefts that led there, but he would make no picture of it for you, having none himself. I do not suppose he found the soot and stucco architecture of Elgin Avenue any more or less entertaining than the red brick of Palace Court, and, while he might describe Oxford Street as "stony-hearted," I doubt if he could have described to the satisfaction of a builder the nature of its exterior stone. Manchester could hardly do less than blind the civic eye. Certainly Francis was no observer, and had retained the ignorance, rather than the innocence, of his Vision.

At this time, after his return from Pantasaph, his days were mostly spent at Palace Court and nights passed in the region which at first by accident and later by habit was his own. When, many years before, he came from Storrington, he was lodged at Fernhead Road, Paddington, and afterwards at various houses in Elgin Avenue with Landlady Maries, the wife of my father's printer. Faithful to the northern town, his last lodging was at 128 Brondesbury Road, Kilburn. At the junction of Elgin Avenue and Chippenham Road is the " Skiddaw " public-house, by whose parlour-fire he often spent nocturnal hours in preference to the hearths of the critics. Mr. Pile, the

In the Edgware Road

tobacconist next door, is remembered for the support
that he gave to Francis's tremulous claims to a place
next the fire. Francis seldom failed to receive kindness
at the hands of rougher men ; his constant courtesy of
speech and his humility were to the liking of a class quick
to know a gentle man. From the whispered hints of
Mr. Pile it was understood that the frail, shabby man of
many platitudes and an abstracted eye was privileged.

From the situation of his lodgings it came about that
the Edgware Road was his Rambla, his Via dei Palazzi,
his Rue de Rivoli ; and at the end of it, the site of
Tyburn Tree. No local allusion, however, finds place
in his " To the English Martyrs," which is another sign of
his aloofness. But when he writes of the Tree that—

> The shadow lies on England now
> Of the deathly-fruited bough,
> Cold and black with malison
> Lies between the land and sun ;
> Putting out the sun, the bough
> Shades England now,

his voice rose from the frozen and fogged pavement that
marks the very spot.

Browning, too, knew, and far better, the "cheap
jewellery and servants' underclothing" of the Edgware
Road. Unlike Browning, F. T. had no eye for values.
And among night-caps, he would never have known
that they were cotton, and hardly that they were red.
As soon as say whether jewellery or clothing was cheap,
he could have argued with Browning on the vintages.
A connoisseur in his books by right of imagination, his
connoisseurship would not have passed muster in the
shops ; it was nailed to the counter. His waggon of
wares ran smoothly enough in starry traces ; but hitched
to cart-horses in Edgware Road he could not have
driven it ten yards. Perhaps when Patmore, a collector
of rubies and sapphires, drew specimen stones from his

waistcoat, Thompson was thrilled with the real presence ;
but not so much as by the love of immaterial jewels.
Not even Meredith's burgundy could teach him—who
had written of grapes against the sun without ever entering a vineyard—anything of wine-merchant's wine. Before Hedges and Butler were in partnership, before the
chateaux were a-building, his own cellar had been laid
down.

His inattention in the Edgware Road was out and out ;
one marvels that he ever turned the right corner, and
not at all that he was knocked down by a cab. But
instinctively his eyes would open in fair presences ; the
things that made poetry struck through his closed lids,
as daylight through a sleeper's. But inattention in the
Edgware Road made the place blank as a railway tunnel.
He could look upon the raiment of his sitter in "Love
in Dian's Lap," and pay his compliments, but never a
word had he for the bonnets of mistress or maid upon
the highway. Riding in an omnibus he would not know
whether Polaire or a Sister of Charity were at his side.

He was constantly alone ; and, often as I have met
him in the streets of London, I have seldom surprised
him in a conscious moment. He would walk past,
looking straight before him, and if he was always late
for his appointments, and took longer, by several hours,
to get home at night than the average man, it was because he would retrace his steps, and go to and fro
upon a certain beat as if indefinitely postponing the evil
moment when he would have to confine himself for
food, or sleep.

The lamps of the town bring moths from the dark
fields. They had no attraction for him. I never heard
him talking of the beauty of London. There is no
pleasure in his lines, which like others here quoted are
put forward, not as poetry, but as biography—

> The blear and blurred eyes of the lamps
> Against the damps,

The London Book

or in the commentary on a London dawn from another note-book :—

> The dreary scream of stable cocks
>   Comes ghastly through the dark,
> The salty blues of day
>   Slant on the dreary park ;
> The houses' massèd fumes
>   Against the heartless light
>   Hold the black ooze of night.

He never went sight-seeing; the town was the dun
background of his own visions, but certain actualities
were etched vividly or heavily massed upon his mental
canvas. Certain things he knew more completely than
the practised desultory observer, and when, in 1897, he
was asked by Messrs. Constable for a book on London,
he could at once fetch out of the studio of his memory
a great number of pictures that had been stored there,
their faces to the wall. Although "my London book"
and the work on it made for several months his password
to late meals at our house, he never wrote it. His
letters to Mr. William Hyde, whose drawings were to
make half the book, were, as it proved, Francis's only
contribution to the scheme :—

"47 PALACE COURT, W.

"DEAR MR. HYDE,—I regret to have delayed my
answer to your letter so long. Firstly, I was occupied by
unavoidable business ; secondly, when I was free to consider your notes, it took me some time really to master
them, and consider my plan in relation to them. In
the first place, I do not design a consecutive narrative
of any kind. I do not design to treat either topography
or the life of London, for both of which I am utterly
unqualified. My design is to give impressions of
London, such as present themselves to a wanderer

277

The Londoner

through its streets. I intend to divide the book into parts, which—by way of provisional title—I might describe as Fair London and Terrible London. For Fair London, the plates you have already done will supply sufficient material in the way of illustration. The other part will consist of studies of London under its darker aspects—weird, sordid, and gloomy—being drawn from its appearance rather than its life. Under this section would come some of the plates already done; and I have marked others among your notes, any of which would fall into my ideas. Since the darker aspect of London is particularly evident to a houseless wanderer, it is my idea to include in this section a description of the aspect of London from midnight to early dawn—for which my own experiences furnish me with material. I intend to take my wanderer through the Strand, Covent Garden, Trafalgar Square, perhaps part of Piccadilly, the Embankment, Blackfriars Bridge, &c., bringing him round to Fleet Street opposite St. Paul's at dawn; and to describe the night effects and the effects of gradual dawn in the streets. You can see for yourself that some of your suggested drawings would be embraced in this, perhaps some of those already done—for example, "Coffee Stall, early morning"; the "houseless wanderer sleeping in the streets" and even the "Factory at Night," since I have in my mind such a factory across Westminster. Also, as regards the general section, I have in my mind a bridge near a railway station, with long shafts of electric lights, mingled with other lights, utilitarian, and a river; which suggests sufficiently your goods depôt with electric light effects. In the same section I should dwell on such a neighbourhood as New Cut. Your suggestion as to this or Clare Market will therefore be certain to come *à propos*, whether by night or day; though I think night exhibits such neighbourhoods most impressively and characteristically. And I intend

278

The Landladies

to describe a night fire; and the effects of vistas of lamps in such a neighbourhood as Pall Mall. Locality, you will see, is unimportant. It is *effect* I wish to dwell on; the *character*—of horror, sombreness, weirdness, or beauty—of various scenes. My own mind turns especially towards the gloomier majesties and suggestiveness of London, because I have seen it most peculiarly under those aspects."

The book was written, but, as Francis's copy was never produced, by another author.

Thompson's landladies were his faithful, patient, and puzzled friends. He disliked their food, broke their rules, burnt their curtains, but seldom rebuked them. They, on their part, found in him none of the virtue of a good lodger. Notwithstanding, they showed a gentleness of regard and manner that did credit to their liberality. I have known them show an unwillingness to lose him quite out of proportion to his value as a lodger, and he showed himself more reluctant to move away from them than was always consistent with their excellence as landladies. Of one of these he was genuinely fond, and her feeling for him she sought to explain when she said, " I can sympathise with him, you know, having a son in the profession myself."

It was she who sought to mend his unsociable ways by subtle attacks upon his solitude, saying, " It's very nice for Mr. Thompson; he's got the trains at the back every half hour and more, when he's in his bedroom. But then the trains, when all's said, aren't the same as the company he could get downstairs. Many a time I've asked him to have his bit of lunch in with me and the other 'mental'—O yes, she's a mental case, as I may have told you." On a few occasions she did entice him to her table, but more often he was content with the conversation of the District Railway engines at the bottom of the garden. His own comment on the trains was among the random manuscripts found in that same bedroom:—

> The very demon of the scene,
> The screaming horror of the train,
> Rushes its iron and ruthless way amain,
> A pauseless black Necessity,
> Along its iron and predestined path.

One landlady's memories of him are supported by the carpet in his room, which is worn in a circle round his table. All night long he would walk round and round; in the morning he would go to bed. There was, she observed, a delicate precision in his manner that forbade all familiarity. His prayers, pronounced as if he were preaching, she often heard.

An interior glimpse comes from a fellow-lodger :—

" I will tell you things as I remember them at the Elgin Avenue establishment. There was a Bengali, who showed me how to play poker ; there was a convert parson, a dramatic critic, and a man who acted. I seem to remember playing cards with them better than anything. It was generally then that Thompson would come in at the front door, and call down the kitchen-stairs for his porridge and beer. Coming into the room, he would talk of something he had seen or read ; or of food, cricket, or clothes. He wished he had bought a suit in a shop-window, because he had given more for those he wore. I fancy he was not exactly rich ; I suppose none of us were. He would eat ; then walk up and down the room talking at any ear that might be listening or at none ; then he would write under the gas-jet. He would leave as he came. I don't suppose he ever gave me a look, and I had no idea he was a great man. But I *remember* him ; though for the rest, I only know they existed."

Mr. Wilfred Whitten tells of the rare—perhaps the only—occasion on which F. T. dined in a restaurant with a friend, after the common fashion :—

" Some seven years since we dined together at the Vienna Café. You remember how, in the one conversation which Boswell felt himself powerless to report, Johnson ' ran over the grand scale of human knowledge.' Thus it was that night. Thompson called up the masters of poetry, and their mighty lines. I shall never forget his repeating this, from ' Comus,' as one of the things in all English verse that he relished—

> Not that nepenthe which the wife of Thone
> In Egypt gave to Jove-born Helena.

These words fell on my ear like the music of all poetry, and I turned to see Thompson's eyes humid with a vast understanding. He dealt in these great names and antiquities. The arts, the rites, the mysteries, and the sciences of eld gave him their secrets and their secret words. But I think he loved the pomp of facts only that he might transmute it into the pomp of dreams, and where his dreams ended let his poetry tell."

Mr. Whitten's, like Patmore's, is the testimony of one who knew him familiarly enough to know his better sort of talk. The impressions of those who met him once or twice generally agree with Mr. William Hyde's :—

" I remember that he was so shy and nervous that I felt anxious not to say anything that would increase his diffidence. The tragedy of his aspect was obvious. Of the glorious moments he must have lived in when the soul was master very few external traces could be seen, save his eyes."

Which were his churches; where the roof to his piety? When the cross-roads did not make his transept and the shops his aisle, he made shift with thin modern Gothic, with rigid varnished bench and Belgian Madonnas. His altars were decked with brass vases and huddled bunches of the disconcerting flowers of commerce. Being a late and irregular comer, he would often find the charwoman dryly banging her broom among the chairs. In the Harrow Road, between a printing-shop and a tobacconist's, was the church nearest the lodging of several years. To St. Mary of the Angels, Bayswater, he also went upon occasion. There was a friend, a second Mezzofanti for languages, with the language of poetry, in addition, very familiarly known;

The Londoner

and there, too, were other friends. At Lymington he would quite naturally become a more timely church-goer. At the foot of the steep High Street, past shuttered town-hall and boarded shops, and along a resounding passage, was the little church attended by Coventry Patmore. Here, in a Roman camp as formidable as Cæsar's, but uncatalogued save in the Catholic Directories, these two followed the Mass. The Church at such moments had no need of architects. Her son, St. Francis of Assisi, had cathedrals and towers at hand, but put them to no use; Francis Thompson had none at hand and was no poorer. He seemed the last person on earth to have noted if the candlesticks came not from Cellini, but Birmingham; if the altar-rails were soap-stone travesties of antiquity. And yet he had, at any rate in verse, his preferences. In "Gilded Gold," he refers to

> Degenerate worshippers who fall
> In purpled kirtle and brocade
> To 'parel the white Mother-Maid.

And he decides that her image as it stood arrayed

> In vests of its self-substance wrought
> To measure of the sculptor's thought

is "slurred by these added braveries."

It is doubtful whether he would have crossed the road to hear one preacher in preference to another, or to hear any; it is certain that he was as content to go to his prayers through a slit in a thin brick wall as under the tympanum of Chartres. If instead of being a Londoner, with the English climate, the disciplined and formal rows of benches, to dishearten him, he had had his lodging near St. Mark's or St. John Lateran, he might have become a more punctual church-goer.

Lionel Johnson, who couples Francis with the Martyr Southwell for "devout audacity," has said the things

that are to say of the sacred poet's familiar attitude.
He quotes the gentleman who confuted the view that
man's attitude towards God must necessarily be abject
—"Not abject! Certainly, it should be deferential, but
not abject." Against the deferential gentleman he
ranges all saints and poets, "His carollers and gay
minstrels—His merry men."

And he had, besides a devotional familiarity, his own
very strictly observed devotional formalities. Every
notebook from Ushaw days till his death is dedicated
with some such holy device as this :—

DEO IN QUO ET PER QUEM MEDITATIONES
EJUS REMEDITO.

He had his triumphs at the Vatican, his victories at
Farm Street; a Pope's messenger sought him in the
Harrow Road with his Holiness's thanks for his translation of a pontifical ode, and of course did not find
him. There is a legend that about this time he wrote
an "Ecclesiastical History"—no less!—put the MS.
into the hands of Cardinal Vaughan to beguile the way
to Rome, and so lost it. The disappearance of the book
might pass for fact, but I find no line about it among
his papers, either before or after its alleged existence.
His habit was to herald any attempt with written notes
and exhortations to himself to begin, as thus :—" Mem.
(ink in) I might, Deo Volente, one day try my hand at
a version of the Imit. in Biblical style, so far as it is
given to my power." Or "Revise Pastoral; and get
buttons, if any possible chance."

Francis himself did not doubt his position as a Church-
man. The boast he makes in "The Lily of the King"
is more than any bishop would venture.

St. Francis, dining one day on broken bread, with a

The Londoner

large stone for table, cried out to his companion : "O brother Masseo, we are not worthy so great a treasure." When he had repeated these words several times his companion answered : "Father, how can you talk of treasure where there is so much poverty, and indeed a lack of all things ? For we have neither cloth, nor knife, nor dish, nor table, nor house ; neither have we servant nor maid to wait upon us." Then said St. Francis : "And this is why I look upon it as a great treasure, because man has no hand in it, but all has been given us by Divine Providence, as we clearly see in this bread of charity, in this beautiful table of stone, in this clear fountain."

Did Francis Thompson mate so happy a Poverty? She whom he took in marriage was a very shrew in comparison. In place of rocky platforms she gave him the restaurant's doubtful table-cloth, or maybe he ate from paper bags. Broken bread that is appetising in Umbria is heavy in Soho; and Francis never drank from the clear stream. But for all that I remember his asserting, with utmost conviction in his voice, the excellence of the viands set before him in a shop in Westbourne Grove. "Here, Ev., I get what I like," I can hear him say; "here the beef is always good; excellent, Evie, excellent, I say." [1]

Both Francises said that happiness was stored in self-denial, but Francis of Assisi was the quicker to make good his statement by immediate happiness. The same desires, the same secret, the same grace possessed two men wedded at least into the same family. The contrast

---

[1] It may also be observed in passing that, while he was more experienced in privation than were any of his friends, Francis could be fastidious. It is still told of him in Sussex, where a clever cook attended his invalided appetite, that he would make great demonstrations at the mere sight of a dish he disapproved. Laying down his knife and fork this frank guest would proclaim against one of the several viands. "Miss Laurence, I *hate* mutton!" The piled-up emphasis of his voice made such a sentence tremendously effective. "Wilfrid," he once said to my father, "Wilfrid, the Palace Court food is *shocking!*"

The Two Poverties

is between their two ladies rather than themselves. She
whom the Saint courted in the stony fields

> Where clear
> Through the thin trees the skies appear
> In delicate spare soil and fen,
> And slender landscape and austere

was not the modern maiden—

> Ah ! slattern, she neglects her hair,
> Her gown, her shoes. She keeps no state
> As once when her pure feet were bare—

with whom the poet of London kept company.

At times when he was most ill and thin and cold and
lonely, his laugh, on joining friends, would outdo theirs
for jollity, and with the unjoyful appetite of a man whose
every organ was out of order, he offered a grace far
longer than customary among the grateful and pious, a
grace so long that his meat would get cold while he
muttered, so long that he would sometimes seem to
imagine it was at an end before the rightful moment,
and take up his knife and fork to start his meal, only, on
remembering an omission, to lay them down again until
the end.

His sense of possession and privacy in possession of
the beauties of nature exceeds Traherne's, whose ecstasy
in the belief that he owned the world's treasuries was
trebled by the thought that everybody else owned them
too. Thompson is more selfish :—

> I start—
> Thy secrets lie so bare !
> .   .   .   .   .   .
> With beautiful importunacy
> All things plead, ' We are fair ! '   To me

The Londoner

The world's a morning haunt,
A bride whose zone no man hath slipt
But I, with baptism still bedript
Of the prime water's font.

On the other hand, let it be noted that all he left
at his death was a tin box of refuse—pipes that would
not draw, unopened letters, a spirit lamp without a
wick, pens that would not write, a small abundance
that remained merely because he had neglected to throw
it away. The Prayer of Poverty had been half answered
unto him :—

"Of thee, O Jesus, I ask to be signed with this
privilege; I long to be enriched with this treasure;
I beseech Thee, O most poor Jesus, that for Thy sake, it
may be the mark of me and mine to all Eternity, to
possess no thing our own under the sun ; but to live in
penury so long as this vile body lasts."

That he was no snatcher of review-books is already
noted. To the Serendipity Shop—the venture of a
friend in Westbourne Grove—he would often go, but
never with any curiosity as to the varied prints, books,
and autographs with which it was stocked. Some one
thing would catch his eye, and be discussed, but nobody
I have known had less of the mere passion for acquisi-
tion. He collected nothing, and presents were acceptable to him but as the outward signs of kindliness: the
meaning having once reached him, he had little use for
the means. At no time did he possess a book-case, nor
sufficient books to crowd the slenderest shelf. A man
less encumbered could hardly be discovered in this
work-a-day world. His inclination was to love the
impersonal riches—the free flames, uncaged air, water
without the pitcher, and the wandering winds. His
authors were no less his own because he had not put

them on his shelf and clapped his autograph upon the fly-leaf.

Physical self-denial, disregard of personal luxuries, are but the manifestations of a spiritual state, of the state recommended by Christ: "Blessed are the poor in spirit for theirs is the Kingdom of Heaven." For the Saint this state has its pressing calls. He puts his virtue to the proof; he embraces the leper, he lectures the birds, he is a man of action; his remotest and most spiritual experiences take on actuality; the Passion puts its mark upon his hands, and feet, and side. The poet, also pierced, has no credentials. A man of inaction, he also renounces personal prides, ambitions, pleasures. The leper would pass Thompson unnoticed, and he was too shy, too little a man of the world, to preach to the practical sparrows of the Edgware Road. Though nearly a Franciscan, and learned in the difficult arithmetic of subtraction, he was necessarily not apt in the good works that marked the Master.[1]

The seclusion which, despite the bond between reader and writer, oppresses the poet, makes him impotent for actual good works. In a world where many things are ripe for the doing, he remains unaware of the duties of citizenship. On his behalf, as for the enclosed monk or nun, it may be urged that retreat from all worldly operations, even beneficent, is retreat from an entanglement of purposes and cross-purposes, of paradoxical and slipshod good; from a field where humility is vanity and strength goes to seed in abject poverty or abject riches. This alone were insufficient reason for withdrawal. There is a more positive motive. The poet's works are absolute good works. He is a missionary even if he never helps with gift or speech or touch another man's distress. The prayers of the Trappist

---

[1] There were exceptions to this habitual carelessness; in 1898 he asked his sister for prayers that a friend might join the Church. She gave them and begged his, for her own purposes, in fair return.

neither clothe the naked, nor feed the hungry, but are not, even if judged by the laws of expediency, the less valuable. They preserve two joyful possessions—the art of prayer and the standards of austerity. They glorify God. So too does Poetry. Song, like Prayer, is for ever re-stating and re-establishing the permanent values. Francis Thompson's consciousness of Good and Evil is alone as profitable as the Bills of half a dozen Ministries. And his consciousness of Good and Evil had been less strong, had he known only the alloyed good and mitigated evil of active life, instead of knowing, in contemplation, their primaries.

Something, as rigorous as the vows of a monk, bound him to his manner of life. He misused all the conveniences of existence; sought no shelter from cold, kept no easy hours, mismanaged his food, his work, his rest. He was without the Silurist's daily ecstasies and special Sunday " shoots of bliss: Heaven once a week." Thompson's Sundays were as dreary as Kilburn and a missed Mass could make them, as dreary as a sweated worker's. He knew, but neglected, as by a set purpose, the domestic economy of felicity observed by his fellows —Herbert, Vaughan, Crashaw, and Traherne—

> That Light, that Sight, that Thought
> Which in my Soul at first he wrought. . . .
> My bliss
> Consists in this ;
> My Duty too
> In this I view.
> It is a fountain or a spring
> Refreshing me in everything.

As to health, if he was careless of it in himself and others, he is excused by St. Bernard's description of God " as the final health."

" To our generation uncompromising fasts and severities of conduct are found to be piteously alien ; not because, as rash

Crumbs of Actuality

censors say, we are too luxurious, but because we are too intricate, nervous, devitalised. We find our austerities ready-made. The east wind has replaced the discipline, dyspepsia the hair-shirt. . . . Merely to front existence is a surrender of self, a choice of ineludibly rigorous abnegation."

Such is the main argument of *Health and Holiness*. But it is probable that he generalised too liberally from his own disabilities. Tortures were not invented and practised because a robuster past could make light of them. The rack was always agonising, or it had never been used. The sailor who bore his 300 lashes in 1812 probably felt them as keenly as a sailor would feel them now. East winds penetrated hair-shirts. Man was the same, save that in greater saintliness he was ready to endure, and in greater cruelty was willing to inflict, more pain.

Capitulation such as Thompson's to a sordid environment may mean too great a severance from other things :—

"The perceptions of the spirit," as he confessed, "are not indefinitely credible and sufficing without the occasional confirmation and assurance of the body."

The confirmation made to him was fined down to the minimum. True, one sunrise sufficed for five years of idolatry. He could strike a fair balance for his spiritual load with a few crumbs of actuality. It would seem that the greater the spiritual load the smaller the range of corporeal experience necessary for the nice adjustment of the scales. Yet the adjustment must be perfect. One of his many analogies for the interlocking of our complementary natures is as follows :—

"Holiness is an oil which increases a hundred fold the energies of the body, which is as the wick. Important that this wick shall not needlessly be marred during preparation through some toughening ascetic process which must inflict certain injury. The flame is dependent after all on the corporeal wick."

He argued, further, from Manning's longevity and energy, that the more copious and pure the oil, the more persistently and brightly does the wick burn. The energising potentialities of sanctity he illustrates in the great works accomplished by St. Francis despite the constant hæmorrhage of the stigmata.

CHAPTER XIV: COMMUNION AND EXCOMMUNION

RENUNCIATION is the better part of possession : Francis states very clearly that compulsion must have no hand in it if it is to be profitable. He writes under the heading, "A distraught maiden complaineth against enforced virginity "—

> Cold is the snow of the thawless valleys,
> Chill as death is the lily's chalice,
> Only she who *seeks* the valleys
> Groweth roses amid the snow.

And he reiterated that spiritual experiences do not endure without from time to time falling back upon their base for supplies, " the confirmation and assurance of the body." [1] That the lines of communication were cut was a pressing grief. I have seen the sense of isolation come up against him, hold him, and shake him. At such times he would be within sight of children, and though no angels then " snatched them from him by the hair," he could be conscious that he was less near them than their relatives. His praises of domestic relationships ring with the note of one whose comprehension is sharpened by the desire of things out of

[1] " Bodily being is the analogy of the soul's being ; our temporal is our only clue to our spiritual life " ; our fleshly senses the only medium for our divine experience. We are the symbols of ourselves. To such thoughts he adds disjointed notes in confirmation from the ancient mythologies : " Bird-heads to gods with man-bodies."—" Zeus = Sky."

Communion and Excommunion

reach.   In an incomplete " Ballad of Judgement " a man, marvelling at his rewards in Heaven, asks :—

> O when did I give thee drink erewhile
> Or when embrace Thine unseen feet ?
> What gifts Thee give for my Lord Christ's smile,
> Who am a guest here most unmeet ?

and the answer comes :—

> When thou kissedst thy wife and children sweet,
> (Their eyes are fair in My sight as thine)
> I felt the embraces on My feet
> (Lovely their locks in thy sight, and Mine).

Other verses of the same unpublished ballad, though imperfect, enforce the idea :—

> If a toy but gladden his little brothers
> (A touch in caress to a child's hair given)
> Young Jesus' hands are filled with prayers
> (Sweep into music all strings of Heaven).

and further that

> . . . . for his sweet-kissed wife
> God kissed him on his blissful mouth.

Allegories of a happy road from bodily to heavenly experience fill many a more complex passage ; here it is given with Chap-book directness.

Elsewhere he closely regrets his loneliness, and repudiates the merit of its heroism in this epitaph on the writer of " Love in Dian's Lap " :—

> *Here lies one who could only be heroic.*
>
> How little, in the sifted judgement, seems
> That swelling sound of vanity !   Still 'tis proved
> To be heroic is an easier thing
> Than to be just and good.   If any be
> (As are how many daily ones !) who love
> With love unlofty through no lofty days.
> Their little simple wives, and consecrate

The Grief-Erudite Heart

Dull deeds with undulled justice : such poor livers,
Though they as little look to be admired
As thou look'st to admire, are of more prizeful rate
Than he who worshipped with unmortal love
A nigh unmortal woman, and knew to take
The pricking air of snowy sacrifice.

Being without the occasional " confirmation," he
yearned for it ; without that particular chance of being
daily just and good, he saw in it the sum of life's purpose. And when he was threatened with the approach
of too close affection, he grew alarmed, crying :—

Of pleasantness I have not any art
In this grief-erudite heart.

   .   .   .   .   .

O Sweet ! no flowers have withered on my hair,
For none have wreathed them there ;
And not to me, as unto others' lots,
Fell flowerful youth, but such the thorns that bare
Still faithful to my hair.
O sweet ! for me pluck no forget-me-nots,
But scoop for me the Lethe water dull
Which yields the sole elixir that can bless—
Utter forgetfulness—
And I shall know that thou art pitiful.

Another form of his painful, elaborate, and even dis-
ingenuous attitude towards happiness was distrust.
" All life long he had been learning how to be wretched,"
he quotes from Hawthorne, " and now, with the lesson
thoroughly at heart, he could with difficulty comprehend
his little airy happiness " ; then, continuing in his own
verse :—

In a mortal garden they set the poet
With mortal maiden and mortal child ;

   .   .   .   .   .   .

In a mortal garden they set the poet ;
As a trapped bird he breathed wild.
He had smiled in sorrow : not now he smiled.

   .   .   .   .   .   .

Communion and Excommunion

But into the garden pacing slowly,
Came a lady with eyes inhuman. . . .
And the sad slow mouth of him smiled again,
This lady I know, and she is real,
I know this lady, and she is Pain !

The Lady Pain figures, in one sense, in " Love in Dian's
Lap." His only real love was itself a thing most strictly
circumscribed ; it existed only to be checked :—

"I yielded to the insistent commands of my conscience and uprooted my heart—as I supposed. Later,
the renewed presence of the beloved lady renewed the
love I thought deracinated. For a while I swung
vacillant. I thought I owed it to her whom I loved
more than my love of her finally to unroot that love,
to pluck away the last fibres of it, that I might be beyond
treachery to my resolved duty. And at this second
effort I finished what the first had left incomplete.
The initial agony had really been decisive, and to
complete the process needed only resolution. But
it left that lady still the first, the one veritable, full-
orbed, and apocalyptic love of my life. Through her
was shewn me the uttermost of what love could be—
the possible divinities and celestial prophecies of it.
None other could have taught them quite thus, for none
other had in her the like unconscious latencies of utter
spirituality. Surely she will one day realise them, as by
her sweet, humble, and stainless life she has deserved
to do."

Of one consolation he writes to her :—

"The concluding words of your letter, 'friend and
child,' reminded me of some lines written at the time
I was composing " Amphicypellon." They were written
hastily to relieve an outburst of emotion ; and, not
thinking there was any poetry in them worthy of you,
I never showed them you. But when I read those con-

Pain

cluding words of your letter, I resolved to transcribe them that you might see you could not have addressed me more according to my wish."

These verses were :—

> Whence comes the consummation of all peace,
>   And dignity past fools to comprehend,
> In that dear favour she for me decrees,
>   Sealed by the daily-dullèd name of Friend,—
>   Debased with what alloy,
>   And each knave's cheapened toy.
> This from her mouth doth sweet with sweetness mend,
> This in her presence is its own white end.
>   Fame counts past fame
>   The splendour of this name ;
> This is calm deep of unperturbed joy.

> Now, Friend, short sweet outsweetening sharpest woes !
>   In wintry cold a little, little flame—
> So much to me that little !—here I close
>   This errant song. O pardon its much blame !
>   Now my grey day grows bright
>   A little ere the night ;
> Let after-livers who may love my name,
> And gauge the price I paid for dear-bought fame,
>   Know that at end,
>   Pain was well paid, sweet Friend,
> Pain was well paid which brought me to your sight.

Pain he proclaimed a pleasure. Why, then, did he call his pains a sacrifice ? "Delight has taken Pain to her heart" was the sum of St. Francis's teaching on a subject dear to the guest at the Franciscan monastery-gates. He himself wrote a commentary on St. Francis :

"Pain, which came to man as a penalty, remains with him as a consecration ; his ignominy, by a Divine ingenuity, he is enabled to make his exaltation. Man, shrinking from pain, is a child shuddering on the verge of the water, and crying, 'It is so cold !'

Communion and Excommunion

How many among us, after repeated lessonings of experience, are never able to comprehend that there is no special love without special pain? To such St. Francis reveals that the Supreme Love is itself full of Supreme Pain. It is fire, it is torture; his human weakness accuses himself of rashness in provoking it, even while his soul demands more pain, if it be necessary for more Love. So he revealed to one of his companions that the pain of his stigmata was agonising, but was accompanied by a sweetness so intense as made it ecstatic to him. Such is the preaching of his words and example to an age which understands it not. Pain. is. Pain is inevadible. Pain may be made the instrument of joy. It is the angel with the fiery sword guarding the gates of the lost Eden. The flaming sword which pricked man from Paradise must wave him back."

The something awry, the disordering of sympathy, the distorting perspective, is hard to name. Perhaps loneliness, perhaps disease, perhaps his poetry, perhaps the devil. But it was there—a distemper, with his own discomfort for its worst symptom. Like the child that meditates upon the sweet it sucks, while it watches the progress of a squabbling world in the back-yard, he could be above the control of his environment; but the sweet once sucked, the poetry gone, he heard and saw and felt, and was sad and sore.

> To each a separate loveliness,
> Environed by Thy sole caress.
> O Christ the Just, and can it be
> I am made for love, no love for me?
> Of two loves, one at least be mine;
> Love of earth, though I repine,
> I have not, nor, O just Christ, Thine!
> Can life miss, doubly sacrificed,
> Kiss of maid and kiss of Christ?
> Ah, can I, doubly-wretched, miss
> Maid's kiss, and Thy perfect kiss?

Reticence

Not all kisses, woe is me !
Are kissed true and holily.
Not all clasps; there be embraces
Add a shame-tip to the daisies.
These if, O dear Christ, I have known
Let all my loveless lips atone.

In a letter to A. M :—

" . . . I have suffered from reticence all my life : the opening out of hearts and minds, where there is confidence, puts an end to so much secret trouble that would grow monstrous if it were brooded over."

. And in his verse :—

. . . The once accursèd star which me did teach
To make of silence my familiar.

And again, from Elgin Avenue :—

" DEAR MRS. MEYNELL,—I have been musing a little on the theme mentioned between us this afternoon ; and some frequent thoughts have returned to me—or, I should say, recollections of frequent experience. (The theme I mean is the difficulty of communicating oneself. By the way, R. L. S.'s theme is more distinct from yours than I quite realised this afternoon. His is sincerity of intercourse, yours is rather adequacy of intercourse, and the two, though they may overlap and react on each other, are far from identical.)

" But the thoughts of which I speak (they are but one or two) are as useless to myself as pebbles would be to a savage, who had neither skill to polish them nor knowledge whether they were worth the polishing. So I am moved to send them to the lapidary. If anything should appear in them worth the saying, how glad I would be that it should find in you a sayer. But it is a more possible chance that poor thoughts of mine may, by a beautiful caprice of nature, stir subtle thoughts in you. When branches are so thickly laden as yours, a child's pebble may bring down the fruit.

297

Communion and Excommunion

"First, then, there is one obstacle to communication which exists little, if at all, for the generality, but is omnipresent with the sensitive and meditative who are destitute of nimble blood. I mean the slow and indeterminate beginnings of their thought. For example, such a person is looking at a landscape. Her (suffer me to use the feminine pronoun—it takes the chill off the egotism of the thing, to assume even by way of speech, that in analysing my own experience I am analysing yours) companion asks her, 'What are you thinking of?' A child under such circumstances (to illustrate by an extreme antithesis) would need no questioning. Its vivid, positive thoughts and sensations have to themselves a glib and unpremeditated voice. But she? She is hardly thinking: she is feeling. Yet 'feeling' is too determinate and distinctive a term: nay, her state is too sub-intellectual for the term to be adequate. It is sensoriness instinct with mind; it is mind subdued to sensoriness. She feels in her brain. She thinks at her periphery. It is blended twilight of intellect and sensation; it is the crepuscular of thought. It is a state whose one possible utterance would be music. Thought in this subtle stage cannot pass into words because it lacks the detail; as the voice, without division, cannot pass into speech; as a smooth and even crystal has no brilliance. To that 'What are you thinking of?' she can only answer 'Nothing' or 'Nothing in particular,' and not unlikely, her companion, seeing that she was full of apparent thought, is discouraged at what seems her unsympathetic reticence. Yet she longed to utter herself, and envied the people who, at a moment's notice, can take a rough pull of their thoughts. If one could answer, 'Stay a while, till my thoughts have mounted sufficiently to burst their dykes.'—But no: by that time his interest would have faded, and her words would find him listless. She towers so high to stoop on her quarry, that the spectator loses sight of her, and thinks

Least Imperfect Sympathy

she has lost sight of *it*. And the habit so engendered makes one slow of speech apart from slowness of thought. One cannot at the first signal *mobilise* one's words. How one wonders at the men, who, with an infinitely smaller vocabulary, have it always on a war-footing, and can instantly concentrate on a given subject.

"Another point is that power of communication in oneself is conditioned by power of receptiveness in others. The one is never perfect; neither, therefore, can the other be. For entire self-revelation to another, we require to feel that even the weak or foolish impulsive things we may let drop, will be received without chill,— nay, even with sympathy, because the utterer is loved. That priceless 'other's' principle must be (to parody Terence without an attempt at metre) *Tuus sum, nil tuum mî alienum puto.* But such an 'other' is not among men—no, nor women either. The perfectest human sympathy is only the least imperfect.

"Then again, when we *can* communicate ourselves by words, it may often become a sensible effort to a sensitive person through the mere dead weight of language, the gross actualities of speech:—exactly as to delicate *you* a lovely scene loses half its attraction, if it must be reached by the fatigue of walking to it.

"Finally, I think there is the fact that, in what concerns their veritable spirit, all mortals are feminine. In the mysteries of that inner *Bona Dea*, speech is male, and may not enter. We feel that we could only admit to them the soft silence of sight. But then—we cannot say: 'Draw aside my flesh and see.' Would we could!

"That reminds me of what you alluded to about the inefficiency of the eyes. I am so glad you mean to touch on that. I see much about the superior eloquence of eyes, &c. But it always seems to me they have just the eloquence of a foreign tongue, in which we catch only enough significance, from the speaker's tone and the casual sound of some half-familiar word to make us

pained and desperate that we can comprehend no more.
There is a turn in Seneca—

> Illi mors gravis incubat,
> Qui, nimis notus omnibus,
> Ignotus moritur sibi.

'On him death lies heavy, who, too known of all, dies
unknown to himself'—'Too known of all!'—with
myself I am but too intimate; and I profess that I find
him a dull boy, a very barren fellow. Your Delphic
oracles notwithstanding, a man's self is the most unprofitable acquaintance he can make; let him shun such
scurvy companions. But, 'nimis notus omnibus!' If
this were the most likely terror death could yield, O
Lucius Annæus!—who is known to *one*? In that *Mare
Clausum* of our being, sealed by the conventing powers
of birth and death, with life and time acceding signa-
tories, what alien trafficker has plied? Far heavier,
Luci mi, death weighs on him, who dies too known of
himself, and too little of any man. I have bored
you, I feel, unpardonably. Repentantly your Francis
Thompson. But my repentance does not extend to
suppressing the letter, you observe. A most human
fashion of penitence!"

But though "too little known of any man," the poet
has faith in the reader's understanding greater than the
reader's faith in his meanings. As for the reader, the
best probe for seeming obscurity is faith. Let an example be taken from the parish priest who read "The
Hound of Heaven" six times before he understood.
Faith in divine meanings, and many blindfolded readings,
are better beginnings than explanations. Sign articles
with your master-poets; sit, idly perhaps, in their work-
shops, and one day you find yourself promoted from
apprentice to partner. Their obscurities are your limitations, your limitations their obscurities, and you and
they must have it out between you. And even at the

Hearer and Utterer

moment when the Poet is most obscure, he is most plain with you, most intimate, most dependent on your personal understanding and acceptance. Then most of all does he give you his confidence, have faith in your faith; then, most of all, does the anchor of his meaning need the clutch of your understanding, the kite of his fancy need the tail of your comprehension. He is riding such waves and flying in such winds of thought that he were lost without you—

> We speak a lesson taught we know not how,
> And what it is that from us flows
> The hearer better than the utterer knows.

And his confession of his dependence on you as his colleague makes a laureate of you. See that you be a Wordsworth rather than a Nathaniel Pye among readers.

The silence in which he was most unhappy was a silence in poetry. Comparing his case to the earth's life in winter, "tearless beneath the frost-scorched sod," he writes :—

> My lips have drought, and crack,
> By laving music long unvisited.
> Beneath the austere and macerating rime
> Draws back constricted in their icy urns
> The genial flame of Earth, and there
> With torment and with tension does prepare
> The lush disclosures of the vernal time.

His second period of melancholy was the more severe; he thought he saw in it, against all his convictions in regard to the rhythm or the resurrections of life, the signs of his poetry's final death. He suffered the torment and the tension in preparation for what he was convinced would be still-born song.

The depression first came upon him with the publication of *New Poems*—

"Though my aims are unfulfilled, my place insecure, many things warn me that with this volume I am probably closing my brief poetic career."

Communion and Excommunion

He had already written of himself as one

> Whose gaze too early fell
> Upon her ruinous eyes and ineludible.
>
> . . . . . .
>
> And first of her embrace
> She was not coy, and gracious were her ways,
> That I forgot all Virgins to adore.
> Nor did I greatly grieve
> To bear through arid days
> The pretty foil of her divine delays ;
> And one by one to cast
> Life, love, and health,
> Content, and wealth
> Before her, thinking ever on her praise,
> Until at last
> Nought had I left she would be gracious for.

In "The Sere of the Leaf," an early poem written at the end of 1890, and published in *Merry England*, January 1891, he answers Katharine Tynan, a poet who had spoken of a full content :—

> I know not equipoise, only purgatorial joys,
> Grief's singing to the soul's instrument,
> And forgetfulness which yet knoweth it doth forget ;
> But content—what is content ?

He makes a like protest in the "Renegade Poet on the Poet" :—

" . . . Did we give in to that sad dog of a Robert Louis, we must needs set down the poor useless poet as a son of joy. But the title were an irony more mordant than the title of the hapless ones to whom it likens him— *Filles de joie ?* O rather *filles d'amertume.* And if the pleasure they so mournfully purvey were lofty and purging, as it is abysmal and corrupting, then would Mr. Stevenson's parallel be just ; but *then*, too, from ignoble victims they would become noble ministrants.

302

"Needy with a Double Need"

... Like his sad sisters, but with that transfiguring difference, this poet, this son of bitterness, sows in sorrow that men may reap in joy. He serves his pleasure, say you, R. L. S.? 'Tis a strange pleasure, if so it be."

Forsaken, his complaints were doubled. Of many lamentations for his muse, the following lines to W. M. have a personal bearing:—

> Ah, gone the days when for undying kindness
> I still could render you undying song!
> You yet can give, but I can give no more;
> Fate, in her extreme blindness,
> Has wrought me so great wrong.
> I am left poor indeed;
> Gone is my sole and amends-making store,
> And I am needy with a double need.
>
> Behold that I am like a fountained nymph,
> Lacking her customed lymph,
> The longing parched in stone upon her mouth,
> Unwatered by its ancient plenty. She
> (Remembering her irrevocable streams),
> A Thirst made marble, sits perpetually
> With sundered lips of still-memorial drouth.

"I shall never forget when he told me," writes Mr. Wilfred Whitten, "under the mirrored ceiling of the Vienna Café that he would never write poetry again."

At one time he would declare "Every great poem is a human sacrifice"; but at another:—

"It is usual to suppose that poets, because their feelings are more delicate than other men's, must needs suffer more terribly in the great calamities which agonise all men. But, omitting from the comparison the merely insensible, the idea may be questioned. The delicate nature stops at a certain degree of agony, as the delicate piano at a certain strength of touch."

Communion and Excommunion

And at another, in an early note-book:—

"The main function of poetry is to be a fruitful stimulus. That is, to minister to those qualities in us which are capable of increase. Otherwise, it is a sterile luxury. Nor should it be made to minister to qualities which are mischievous by much increase. Sought mainly to provoke waning emotion, it is a sterile luxury; sought mainly to stimulate crescent emotion a pernicious luxury."

In view of these various accounts of the poetic function one must ask: Were the sorrows necessary? were they real? One mistrusts the poet, to whom joy must necessarily often come in the affirmation of distress.

One may argue that Thompson must have been happy on the score of his poetry. As a poet, no doubt, he was; but not necessarily as a man. The two states did not overlap. He says in a letter to a friend that he did not realise that *Sister Songs*, so poor a thing, would give pleasure; whereas in verse he speaks of sending it exultingly.

His "I have no poetry," like the communicant's "I am unworthy," is but the prelude to the embrace. In the "To a Broom Branch at Twilight" (*Merry England*, November 1891), he declares that there are songs in the branches—

> I and they are wild for clasping,
> But you will not yield them me.

The thought that silence is the lair of sound was his own ample consolation for other unproductive periods: but now as he grew ill and really silent, he felt that silence could nurture only silence.

His pride faces his distress; they stare each other out of countenance. It is certain that he often joined in

" Curse of Destinate Verse "

George Herbert's address to a Providence who has made man "the secretary of her praise," though "beasts fain would sing," and "trees be tuning on their native lute" :—

> Man is the world's high-priest ; he doth present
> The sacrifice for all ; while they below
> Unto the service mutter an assent
> Such as springs use that fall, and winds that blow.

And against the many contrary passages of Francis's may also be set his on the poet's happiness :—

> What bitterness was overpaid
> By one full verse ! world's love, world's pelf
> I fillipped from me, and but prayed
> Boon of my scantly yielded self.

Here the " curse of destinate verse " reads like a blessing. Yet, strictly speaking, he found that unwritten predestinate verse means an ill case :—

> For ever the songs I sing are sad
> With the songs I never sing.

His complaint is not against the verse that gets written, which even when sad of origin is a boon : "Deep grief or pain, may, and has in my case, found immediate outlet in poetry."

To his view of others on previous pages must be added his attitude towards the author of "The Anthem of Earth," of "The Hound of Heaven," of "Shelley." One who went to the task of reviewing his contemporaries heavy, not with distaste, but with pent-up potential admirations, who had an appetite at once insatiable and fastidious for all literature, must needs have enjoyed in relaxation the splendours of his own

Communion and Excommunion

verse.[1] But not merely as critic did Francis Thompson realise the greatness of Thompson. The innermost chambers of his consciousness buzzed with the certainty of his poetic gravity and significance. He trusted the quality of the poetry within him as an ordinary man trusts the beat of his pulse and counts upon it. There were anxieties of composition and, of course, the ebb and flow of satisfaction in himself and a final despair. But before that he had known that he was, and he still knew that he had been, a poet. That is why he is so often the laureate of his own verse—

> Before mine own elect stood I,
> And said to Death :—' Not these shall die.'
>   I issued mandate royally.
> I bade Decay :—' Avoid and fly ;
>   For I am fatal unto thee.'

> I sprinkled a few drops of verse,
> And said to Ruin, ' Quit thy hearse ' :
>   To my loved, ' Pale not, come with me ;
> I will escort thee down the years,
>   With me thou walk'st immortally.'

These vaunting rhymes were written that he might go on to declare his undoing, being now stripped of his songs. It was true, of course, that he lost, not the poetry, but the functions of the poet., In exquisite lines he begs his muses to stay their flight, and his exquisite

---

[1] With nothing that he has to say of another poet is it so impossible to agree as with his own estimate of the relative importance of the sections of *New Poems*—

"CRECCAS COTTAGE, PANTASAPH, *November* 1896.

"MY DEAR DOUBLEDAY,—I regret that I cannot consent to the omission of the translations. If anything is to be left out, it must be the section *Ultima*, not the translations. I said at Pantasaph that I would keep these, whatever I left out. They were held over from my first book, and I will not hold them over again. I regard the ' Heard on the Mountain' as a feat in diction and metre ; and in this respect Coventry Patmore agrees with me. But I do not at all mind leaving out the section *Ultima*.—Yours, F. T."

His Confidence

lines belie the convention that they have flown, that the shrines of his heart are empty.

In Mr. Wilfred Whitten's obituary notice of Thompson there is report at first hand of the poet's satisfaction in that his poetry was immortal.   He quotes :—

> The sleep-flower sways in the wheat its head,
> Heavy with dreams, as that with bread ;
> The goodly grain and the sun-flushed sleeper
> The reaper reaps, and Time the reaper.
>
> I hang 'mid men my needless head,
> And my fruit is dreams, as theirs is bread :
> The goodly men and the sun-hazed sleeper
> Time shall reap, but after the reaper
> The world shall gleam of me, me the sleeper !

And he adds : " When Francis Thompson wrote these verses, he did not indulge a fitful or exalted hope ; he expressed the quiet faith of his post-poetic years. Thompson knew that above the grey London tumult, in which he fared so ill, he had hung a golden bell whose tones would one day possess men's ears.   He believed that his name would be symphonised on their lips with Milton and Dryden and Keats.   This he told me himself in words too quiet, obscure, and long ago for record.   But he knew that Time would reap first."

CHAPTER XV: CHARACTERISTICS

THE poet is important, present, manifest to the poet. His poetry is an addition to his state, which yet is complete without it. The state of poetry, the state of the poet, has superfluity escaping into song. It is this superfluity that makes, not the poet, but the poetry-book. If Thompson had only written of his experiences as a poet, he would have written fine poetry; when he wrote of the poet's songs he made songs, when he wrote of the poet's communings with God and Nature he made more songs, and, to make songs, need never have written directly of God and Nature. In one sense his descriptions of the poet's throes are out of all proportion to their product. He tells you so often of his Song, that it might be complained he had no time for singing. He will compose a poem to show he is Muse-forsaken, or to establish the fact that his lady is immortal only in his verse; it hardly matters whether he wrote otherwise of her or not. He will tell you, with supremest diction, that his poppy and he lie safe in leavèd rhyme. The great bulk of his poetry is about his poetry—that is, you might read his three volumes and think they were but prefaces to thirty-three. Really they are the index not to forty-eight other volumes, but to the forty-eight years of the poet's existence—to the Poet, that is.

"The more a man gives his life to poetry, the less poetry he writes," was Thompson's own experience.

This harping upon himself is notable. His preoccupation is poetry—and the poet. It is not a matter of

The Maker

selfishness but of difference. *New Poems* meets with many objections on this score, for sharp distinctions within the species are always resented. The presence of the man is resented, and the presence of the poet, or prophet, is resented. But that he has his own place in creation he knows well enough. Isaiah knew it ; and when one of his kind says—

> This dread Theology alone
> Is mine,
> Most native and my own ;
> And ever with victorious toil
> When I have made
> Of the deific peaks dim escalade,
> My soul with anguish and recoil
> Doth like a city in an earthquake rock,
>
> .   .   .   .   .   .
>
> With deeper menace than for other men,

he is proclaiming a family egoism that can no more be "pooh-poohed" than a racial pigment or tribal distinction, the stature of the pygmies or the stripe of the zebra. The tribal segregation of the spirit is distrusted, however, because it defies scientific classification. It is known as madness, saintliness, obscurity, affectation, "nerves," mania, fanaticism, conceit, according to its symptoms in a Blake, or a Jacopone da Todi ; all its kinds are labelled, but it is never brought to exact order. The variousness of degree in the poetic character is a necessity of the case. The poet makes the difference because he makes his own world, his own scope, his own experience. If he is one of a tribe, he is always the head of it—a chief, like every other, with a tent as large as the sky, as large as the horizon which his own intellectual stature may command.

The poet is conscious of his status as the " maker "— the maker who presumes upon the common advantage of being made in the likeness of God, and gives point to the likeness. It is plainly stated by F. T. in "Carmen

Characteristics

Genesis" and in an unpublished note written in support
of the poem :—

> Poet ! still, still thou dost rehearse,
> In the great *fiat* of thy Verse,
>   Creation's primal plot ;
> And what thy Maker in the whole
> Worked, little maker, in thy soul
>   Thou work'st, and men know not.
>
> Thine intellect, a luminous voice,
> Compulsive moved above the noise
>   Of thy still fluctuous sense ;
> And Song, a water-child like Earth,
> Stands with feet sea-washed, a wild birth
>   Amid their subsidence.

And in prose repetition of the " Poet or Maker " :—

"In the beginning, at the great mandate of light, the
sea suddenly disglutted the earth : and still in the
microcosm of the poetic, the *making* mind, Creation
imitates her august and remembered origins. Still, at
the luminous compulsion of the poet's intellect, from
the subsidence of his fluctuant senses emerges the
express and founded consistence of the poem ; confessing, by manifold tokens, its twofold parentage,
quickened with intellectual light, and freshened with the
humidities of feeling. Of generations it shall endure the
spiritual treading and to generations afford its fruits,
a *terra firma* which may scarce wear out before the
prototypal earth itself. This is the function of the
maker since God first imagined : though poetry's Book
of Genesis is yet unwritten which might be written, and
its Moses is desired and is late. An art not unworthy
the Seraphic Order and the handling of Saints. For
the poet is an Elias, that when he comes makes all things
new. It is a converse, alas, and lamentable truth, that
the false poet makes even new things old."

Pride of Poetry

Of the Poet's powers of Creation or Transfiguration Wordsworth held an advanced estimate :—

" The objects of the poet's thoughts are everywhere ; though the eyes and senses of men are, it is true, his favourite guides, yet he will follow wheresoever he can find an atmosphere of sensation in which to move his wings. Poetry is the first and last of all knowledge—it is immortal as the heart of man. If the labours of the men of science should ever create any material revolution, direct or indirect, in our condition, and in the impressions which we habitually receive, the poet will sleep then no more than at present. . . . If the time should ever come when what is now called science, thus familiarised to men, shall be ready to put on, as it were, a form of flesh and blood, the poet will lend his divine spirit to aid the transfiguration, and will welcome the Being thus produced, as a dear and genuine inmate of the household of man."

Pride of poetry, when Francis was forgetful of pride of pain, crops up in a hundred places ; he writes, for instance, of Davidson's " The Testament of an Empire Builder " :—

" We still lament that here, as in the preceding poems of the series, there is far too much metrical dialectic, argument in verse, which is a thing anti-poetic. Poetry should proclaim, poetry is *dogmatic ;* when it stoops to argue, it loses its august privilege and becomes, at the best, a K.C. in cloth of gold."

It was easily perceived he was not candidly and fully himself in common conversation. He was as much shut within his repetitions as the last little Chinese box is shut within a series of Chinese boxes. Lift all the lids and you find emptiness in the last. Francis insisted on your putting all the little boxes back again, fitting the right lid on each, for, having made his point, he seldom failed to prove it backwards. Had he been of another age and race, he would have had an hermitage and been sought by those who wished instruction—the instruction that is not seldom done in silence. But who was ready to listen to Francis's silences in London? It is possible that if a child had sought him in Kensington Gardens, as he sat oblivious of the sparrows and the leaves and the nursemaids, and had asked for knowledge, revelation might have followed. We know that in the study at Lymington Patmore came to the conclusion that his visitor's prose was better than his poetry, his talk better than his prose. The windows of that Lymington study were thrown open to the ample airs of Heaven; in London lodgings the east winds made the noise outside, and Thompson's talk about the weather filled the air within. The Eastern must have communion, even the communion of silence, before he lights the lamp of common knowledge; Plato needed the magnetism of listeners and learners. Francis needed none but the absent, perhaps the unborn, reader. The shares he issued were all deferred shares.

And every stanza was an act of faith; every stanza a declaration of good-will. It is optimism that compels the poet to give the superfluity of his inner song to the world. He knows, perhaps against all common-sense, that the world will some day be fit for it. He launches the utmost treasures of his rare estate upon the nondescript audience. The pessimist either ceases writing (what is the use?), or, if he writes, cannot always be trusted to give his best to a posterity he despises. But Francis gave out no secrets unless he had wrapt them in poetry. He bore them secretly, and set them free only when he had decked them in imagery. He was too busy making clothes against their birth for other companionship. Also, he was shy of his own inability to be communicative and shy of his own ardent emotions towards his friends:—

"I know how it must tax you," he wrote to A. M., "to endure me; for you are a friend, a mother; while I, over and above these, am a lover—spiritual as light, and

A Habit of Life

unearthly as the love of one's angelic dreams, if you will
—but yet a lover ; and even a seraph enamoured must
be a trying guardian angel to have to do with."

And again :—

" I am unhappy when I am out of your sight, but
you, of course, can have no such feeling in reference
to me. Now my sense of this inspires me with a
continual timidity about inflicting my society on you
in any way, unless you in some way signify a desire
for it."

He inflicted his society on nobody. What he did inflict
was the unaccomplished proxy of himself. Of the
manner of his detachment he writes :—

" I do not know but, by myself, I live pretty well as
much in the past and future as in the present, which
seems a very little patch between the two. It has been
more or less a habit through life, and during the last
fifteen years, from the widened vantage of survey then
gained, it has come to dominate my mental outlook.
So that you might almost say, putting it hyperbolically,
I view all mundane happenings with the Fall for one
terminus and the Millennium for the other. If I want to
gauge the significance of a contemporary event of any
mark, I dump it down as near as I can, in its proximate
place between these boundaries. There it takes up very
little room."

His very backwardness was benevolent ; his eye, often
pre-occupied, was never indifferent ; neither careless nor
trivial, it never sought an easy exchange of confidences,
nor made friends by suggestion of either tact or intelligence. He was a man who, if he entered not into
much intercourse, did not stand aloof through contempt
or active disinclination, but for other friendlier reasons.

313

Characteristics

He was a man to be observed, not to observe; to be seen, not to see. Neither he nor his room-mates would, as a rule, be at great pains to come together; but, even if you held no talk with him, he was sufficiently interesting or endearing to take your eye.

It was after an evening divided between silence and explanations that, wondering how well he covered the fires of his imagination, one went to the door to help with hat and coat. Some final repetition, unblushingly proclaimed with "As I have said before," would still longer delay his return to himself; but once he had begun to go down the flights of steps in Granville Place, where we had taken a flat, he would find himself face to face again with the realities of life that he chose to keep private, and be loudly talking to himself in a style more meaningful and threatening than any speech of his in company. Then the hall door would be slammed; and still in the silent street, past puzzled policemen, he would stride away in fierce agitation, but less solitary than when he sat among us. But a certain sweetness went with him; he did not need to talk to stimulate that grateful mood of charity and peace that some know only when they can actually do works of mercy with their tongues and eyes. His gentle eye proved that not all his silent thoughts were troubled; and often his gaze would climb to some invisible and fair peak of contemplation, resting there content in silence. Sometimes he was obviously happy in small-talk and his companionships, but that was when commonplaces were not used solely as a shelter from the inconvenience of thoughts not commonplace. Even his halfpenny paper, as he read it over in his tea-shop, was a root of happiness. He was fair game for the journalist of Lower Grub Street. Here is a random list of the things he cut from the *Daily Mail*: "Maria Blume's Will," "Insurance of Domestic Servants," "Help for the Householder," "*Mikado* Airs on Japanese Warship

314

Cuttings

—Amusing Scenes," "Freaks of Weather: Startling Changes of Temperature," "The Milk Peril, What hinders Reform," and "Joy," a poem by Mr. Sturge Moore—with a little more margin to it, and straighter scissors-work.

CHAPTER XVI: THE CLOSING YEARS

As F.T. grew busier with journalism, and was helped to bread by it, he grew peevish with his prose, as other men do with a servant :—

"Prose is clay ; poetry the white, molten metal. It is plastic, not merely to gross touch, but to the lightest breath, a wish, a half-talent, an unconscious feather-passage of emotional suggestion. The most instantaneously perfect of all media for expression. Instant and easy as the snap of a camera, perfect as star in pool to star above, natural as breathing of sweet air, or drinking of rain-fresh odours ; where prose asks a certain effort and conscious shaping. But prose can be put in shafts (to its slow spoiling) ; verse, alack ! hears no man's bidding, but serves when it lists,—even when it consents to lay aside its wings."

"Poetry *simple* or synthetic ; prose analytic."

"It might almost be erected into a rule that a great poet is, if he pleases, also a master of prose," he writes in one of several studies of "The Prose of Poets"—including Sir Philip Sidney's, Shakespeare's, Ben Jonson's, and Goldsmith's, first published in the *Academy.*

At times the every-day difficulties of journalism seemed insurmountable. Then would he write desperately to W. M. of the necessity for cowardice on his part and a return to a mode of life that had no responsibilities :—

"Things have become impossible. B—— did not out-right refuse me an advance on my poem, but told me to

316

The Life Mask
1905

Money Matters

call again and 'talk it over.' . . . The only thing is for me to relieve you of my burthen—at any rate for the present—and go back whence I came. There will be no danger in my present time of life and outworn strength that I should share poor Coventry's complaint (that of outliving his ambition to live). . . . For the reverse of the medal, you have Ghosh who has just been promised £220 odd for a series of tales.

" . . . For the present, at any rate, good-bye, you dearest ones. If for longer—

Why, then, this parting was well made.

—Yours ever and whatever comes,
FRANCIS THOMPSON."

During the years when such despairs were common W. M.'s favours were forced upon a spasmodically reluctant poet, whose earnings seemed never at best to leave him a margin for incidental expenses :—

" To have to talk of money-matters to you is itself a misery, a sordidness. How much worse in its way all this must press on you is comprehensible to anyone. We are no longer as we were ten years ago. You have grown-up children to launch in life. . . ."

For W. M. there was never a doubt of the honour and pleasure of his position. If Francis's rent fell sometimes in arrears, it was not because there was any falling-away in willingness, but because it had taken its place among the many liabilities of the master of a large household, and had to wait among them for its turn to be met.

After a desperate letter foretelling the end, a little conversation with my father would correct his despair, and he could return to his landlady with the most

obvious remedy, or some suggestion equally effica-
cious :—

"You are right. Mrs. Maries has given way, on the
understanding that you will make some arrangement
with her before the end of the month."

Again, to W. M. :—

". . . As for poetry, I am despondent when I am
without a poetical fit, yet when I have one I am miserable on account of my prose. I came lately across a
letter of Keats' (penned in the præ-Endymion days),
which might almost word for word be written by myself
about myself. It expresses exactly one of the things
which trouble me, and make me sometimes despair of
my career. 'I find' (he says) 'I find I cannot do
without poetry—without eternal poetry; half the day
will not do—the whole of it. I began with a little, but
habit has made me a leviathan. I had become all in a
tremble from not having written anything of late : the
sonnet over-leaf did me good ; I slept the better last
night for it : this morning, however, I am nearly as bad
again.' I, too, have been 'all in a tremble' because I
had written nothing of late. I am constantly expecting
to wake up some morning and find that my Dæmon has
abandoned me. I hardly think I *could* be very vain of
my literary gift; for I so keenly feel that it is beyond
my power to command, and may at any moment be
taken from me."

This nervousness for his muse, like to Rossetti's for
his sight, came upon him more hardly in later years.

Misrepresentation—it is easy to trace its origin—was
busy before his death. The word went round that the
streets had put a worse slur than hunger, nakedness,
and loneliness upon him. In 1906 a pamphlet reached
him from the University Press, Notre Dame, Indiana,

in which he read that he "had been raised out of the depths":

"No optimism of intent can overlook the fact of his having fallen, and no euphemism of expression need endeavour to cloak it. Down those few terrible years he let himself go with the winds of fancy, and threw himself on the swelling wave of every passion, desiring only to live to the full with a purpose of mind apparently like that of his contemporary, Oscar Wilde, but in circumstances now vastly different from those the brilliant young Oxford dandy knew. He said, 'I will eat of all the fruits in the Garden of Life,' and in the very satisfaction of his desire found its insatiableness."

With gossip turning the pages, that reader found the proof of Thompson's wrong-doing in "The Hound of Heaven."

I fled Him down the nights and down the days,

could only mean that the runaway was a criminal, and the Almighty the policeman who hurries when he is sure of a crime. "The Hound of Heaven," a study in the profound science of renunciation, was said to be the work of a man who had "thrown himself on the swelling wave of every passion." It mattered nothing that in the poem we read only that the poet had "clung to the whistling mane of every wind," had turned to children "very wistfully," had "troubled the gold gateway of the stars." There is really nothing in it to support the blacker theory. A better way to understand the poetry and know the poet is to believe the poet and the poetry. This pamphleteer and the writer of the obituary notice in the *Times* were strangers, their knowledge was based on hearsay. In face of such misunderstanding, at the time of his death it was hardly surprising to read in the *Mercure de France* that "he went mad, and death happily put an end to his miseries."

The Closing Years

A Professor of Romance Languages in Columbia University may be right in thinking that Thompson does not ever sink so low as Verlaine, nor ever rise quite so high, and that greater poets than Thompson, from Collins to Coleridge, have often failed in the ode-forms, but he is inaccurate when he says that, " like Verlaine, he is the poet of sin."

Since there was so little to go upon, it is hardly surprising that the alien onlooker's conception of Francis Thompson was a misconception. His poor living, his unknown lodging, his fugitive seclusion encouraged the legend that he was still an outcast. Since this alien had never heard him laugh, and to the ear's imagination it is easier to frame a cry, the subject of the ready-made legend never even smiled ; there were no *fioretti* connected with his name, and the weeds were taken for granted. The heavy remorsefulness of his muse seemed, to such as are unfamiliar with the *confiteor* of the saints, to mark a more real repentance, and therefore real misconduct, than does the ordinary, facile *peccavi* of modern poetry-books. We notice that at his death the writers of the obituary notices who were ready with suggestions of evil days were equally ready with the usual liberal condonation. " No such condonation was called for—though by some it was offered—in the case of Francis Thompson," wrote A. M. in the *Dublin Review*, January 1908. " For, during many years of friendship, and almost daily companionship, it was evident to solicitous eyes that he was one of the most innocent of men."

To *The Nation*, November 23, 1907, W. M. wrote his protest :—

" I see in the *Times* a paragraph about Francis Thompson, against which I will ask you to let me make appeal. It comes from ' A Correspondent,' who ' writes to us ' ; and I am just such another, writing to you. But I knew Thompson, and no pen but

320

Misrepresentation

an alien's could have written this to Printing House Square:
' There are occasions on which the conventional expression of
regret becomes a mockery, and this is one of them. What the
world must regret is not the release of Mr. Thompson, but the fact
that the cravings of the body from which he is released should
have had power to ruin one of the most remarkable and original
of the poetic geniuses of our time.' I know what the writer in-
sinuates. I know, too, that he has overshot his mark. But the
public will only too greedily infer from his words that Thompson
was a degraded man—he who carried dignity amid all vicissitude ;
that he was a debauchee—he who lived, as he sang, the votary
of Fair Love. Nor need I adopt in his regard the fine passage in
which Mr. Birrell defends Charles Lamb's ' drinking.' For Mr.
Francis Thompson did not ' drink.'

" The ' genius ' of Francis Thompson was not ' ruined,' or we
should not have the evidence of it on every page of three volumes,
presenting together a body of best poetry equal in size to that of
most of our poets. But it is true that Thompson's health was
wretched from first to last. It is true also that he doctored himself disastrously with laudanum from almost the early days of
his medical studentship in Manchester. When he came to the
streets of London, the drug delivered him in a manner from their
horrors, and, besides, was, I think, some palliation of the disease
of which he finally died—consumption. . . .

" Again, Thompson was an uncertain worker ; but his friendly
editors did not hustle him. And they could always count on him
to keep time with even a ' commissioned ' poem. The Odes on the
Nineteenth Century and on the Victorian Jubilee did not get late
to the editor of the *Daily Chronicle ;* and even if they had been
late, nobody else could have sent them so quickly, for nobody else
could have sent them at all. Every week, in the *Academy,* under
Mr. Lewis Hind, Thompson's articles made fine reading—his essay
on Emerson marking the high-water mark of that manner of
criticism ; and I am certain that the editor of the *Athenæum,*
for whom he was in harness almost until the last week of his life,
and who treated him with a consideration never to be forgotten
by his friends, is in sorrow that Thompson is dead.

" Such, in brief, was my friend :—a moth of a man, who has
taken his unreturning flitting ! No pen—least of all, mine—can
do justice to him : to his rectitude, to his gentleness, to his genius.
. . . . If he had great misfortunes, he bore them greatly ; they
were great because everything about him was great. It is my

The Closing Years

consolation now, amid tears for Thompson from eyes that never thought to shed so many again, to know that he knew and accepted his fate and mission, and that he willingly ' learned in suffering what he taught in song.' But I have spoken too much. I did not mean to do more than make the writer in the *Times* aware that somebody loves his life less because Thompson is dead."

The argument of the poet's sanctity is in his poems ; and it were tiresome to take the oath in the discredited witness-box of biography in denial of any particular accusation. But the circumstances that made imputation of evil likely and credible form part of the literary history of the period. The Mid-Victorian respectability which Patmore lifted to Parnassus in the "Angel in the House," and which lifted Tennyson to the Peerage, had given way to reaction. Swinburne's showy metres had persuaded the young that bad morality could be good art. Instead of Burns's heavy drinking and light loves, Verlaine and absinthe served for a new argument to confound the squeamish. Verlaine made a fashion, and his tragedy came easily, even to minor poets, and was not altogether impious. The young men anxious to fall as he fell were anxious also to share in the depths of his contrition. The duet about commission of sin and contrition for sin had great vogue, and accounts for a deal of the poetry of self-accusation, made, not seldom, in regard to imaginary offences. Contrition was, after all, the main force at work, and, in the naked, truthful, and intense moments of death, this was the ruling passion. The reaction had, after all, been merely a reaction, and not a little genius had been spilled in barren soil. The Church and the Sacraments were at the service of men who had fondly believed that their chief strength was in rebellion, and that they had strayed into ways of loss and salvation peculiar to themselves, but who ended by being sorry.

Religion seems always to be setting its beneficent

A Certain Group

ambush for those who thought themselves most securely on another road; but in the case of the victims of abnormal and distressful phases of experience there was something more than the splendid accident of reconciliation and forgiveness. One after another of the leaders of æsthetic disaffection and disease confessed to an almost involuntary inclination to seek the arms of the Church. The devil, prowling like a lion, might leap upon them, "but the Lamb, He leapeth too." Christ's actual presence, His miracles, His hand, were for the sick, the afflicted, the wrongdoer: His inspiration to-day most often rests upon those intellectual sinners who have seemed in their misfortune to be puffing out the light of the world. And this was not only a death-bed reconciliation. What English artist for fifty years has made a "Madonna and Child?" Aubrey Beardsley made one. What poet had sung of the last sacraments? Ernest Dowson's most beautiful verses are on the Extreme Unction. Lionel Johnson, whom Thompson knew, had not been a rebel, and he did not seek a death-bed reprieve. Nevertheless his name connects one form of failure with the literary life of his day and with an ardent adherence to Religion. Another type of a school that had set out to use bad language but could say nothing finally but its prayers, is he who then sang in company with Baudelaire, but whose poet, now he has become a priest, is Jacopone da Todi. So, too, with Simeon Solomon, as his reputation and his clothes became more ragged, who, as he grew "famous for his falls" but otherwise obscure, found a co-ordinating central inspiration for his work, and found it before the altars of the Carmelite Church in Kensington. Francis may well have jostled elbows with him there, or on the pavement.

The copper-plated Death of the sixteenth century is a caution no more gruesome or extreme than the picture of these poets and painters in their pains. Two or three to a lunatic asylum, one to death that smelt of suicide, and three at least to death hastened by drink— that is the hasty record of a certain group. Francis never met Wilde, the wit who stumbled and gasped the dull man's daily words of repentance, even before his audience was well aware of his jest; nor Beardsley the artist who found death's quill at his heart before he had time to destroy the drawings, which, in his agony, he learnt some devil rather than himself had made. To the hospitals, asylums, and prisons of London and Paris, to the Sanatorium of the Pacific or the Mediterranean, to the slums, and to starvation, Literature contributed numbers out of all proportion.

Francis knew none of them; but he had made a name in the 'nineties, had lived in the streets (the last resort of several of them), had died a Catholic (most damning evidence!), had written passionately (the divinity of his passion was not noted): there was circumstantial evidence enough. He was exalted: how should the obituary writers know the exaltation was not feverish? His poetry he laid upon altar-steps; was it for them to guess he had chased no satyrs from his cathedral before he set himself to pray? His view of Dowson is characteristic:

"... A frail and (in an artistic sense) faint minor poet. ... The major poet moulds, rather than is moulded by, his environment. And it may be doubted whether the most accomplished morbidity can survive the supreme test of Time. In the long run Sanity endures; the finest art goes under if it be perverse and perverted art, though for a time it may create life under the ribs of death."

Like the legend that seeks to give an evil or a sad account of men, is the easier legend of their laziness. All who have known joy and written vastly have been accused of inertia and despondency.

Idleness and Industry

It is true that Francis was apprenticed to Idleness of wits, as well as Industry; but, finding both hard masters, and Idleness (of the common sort) the harder, he much sought to avoid it. As for his work (save in poetry) he knew few moments at which he could with Coleridge declare a happiness in difficulties, "feeling in resistance nothing but a joy and a stimulus." With Coleridge's other mood ("drowsy, self-distrusting, prone to rest, loathing his own self-promises, withering his own hopes —his hopes, the vitality, the cohesion of his being") he was acquainted. But not long; the meaning of his inactivity would burst on him, until the thought of it was labour. But with Wordsworth he says :—

". . . for many days my brain worked with a dim and undetermined sense of unknown modes of being,"

and for his reassurance he had at hand the same poet's

> 'Tis my faith that there are powers
> Which of themselves our minds impress ;
> That we may feed this mind of ours
> In a wise passiveness.

Francis construed his own defence into a hundred aphorisms. These two are signed with his initials :—

"Where I find nothing done by me, much may have been done in me," and

"For the things to-day done in you, will be done by you to-morrow many things."

Lying abed, he was acutely aware of his duty to get up. It was a conscious and laborious laziness, akin to Dr. Johnson's, whose great bulk was shaken with almost daily repentance for its sloth. The dictionary makes our shelves creak in protest at the notion held by Johnson himself and his contemporaries that he was a lazy man ; and the pile of Thompson's papers, his letters, and the following placard he pinned upon his bedroom wall

speak of his large industries and his girding at the
spectre sloth :—

> At the Last Trump thou wilt rise Betimes !
> Up ; for when thou wouldst not, thou wilt shortly sleep long.
> The worm is even now weaving thy body its night-shift.
> Love slept not a-saving thee. Love calls thee,
> Rise, and seek Him early. Ask, and receive.

I leave unprinted other more piteous solicitations for
what, virtually, though he did not guess it, was the energy
and health he could not possess. Upon another sheet
more worldly persuasions were set to urge his waking
eye. Of a printer's request for copy on an earlier day
than that usually covenanted he writes :—

" Remember the new *Athenæum* dodge testifies against
you."

It was he who found time to be pleased with Brearley's
bowling or merry with the anticipation of the morrow ;
he, sitting in grey lodgings, who crowded into the chilly
ten minutes before 3 A.M. the writing of a long letter to
be posted, after anxieties with address and gum of which
we know nothing, and a stumbling journey down dark
stairs, in a pillar box still black in threatening dawn.
There are few such journeys of my own I can count
to my credit, and few words I can remember, written
or spoken, to set against his thronging puns and his
constant sequence of "Yours ever." At any rate he
was outdone at every turn—in kindness, attentions,
sallies, patience and wit—by one among his friends,
my father, who had to crowd his generosity to the
poet between stretches of persistent overwork, the real
thronging anxieties that were at least as pressing as
Francis's imaginary ones. In reading a series of letters
Francis wrote to me in the last years, I am sorry to
think how slovenly must have been my response to
his tenacious jesting. And it was he who troubled to

His Looks

make his notes kind and acceptable, neat and long. One marvels, among the mass of his journalism and letters, at the estimate of him that passed undisputed during his life, as a man who misspent his powers and wasted his minutes as he wasted his matches. If he was unfortunate, he was also merry. Without excuse his biographer confesses to the moodiness, the silence, the disorderliness that is imputed to the poet. The consolation for all my family is the thought of my father's incessant care for and good humour towards him.

Of the hours he kept there are many legends, all made according to Greenwich time. But it is not expected of the lamp-lighter, or the contract-winder of office clocks, or the milkman, that he should write Thompson's poetry, or even read it, and yet we started with a wholly illogical desire of constraining Francis, if not to fulfil their duties, at least to be a party to their punctuality.

Mr. Orpen desired to paint him ; sittings were even appointed ; but not till Mr. Neville Lytton found him under the same roof, at Newbuildings, was his elusive likeness caught by an artist.

To look at, as it happens, he was something between a lamp-lighter and a man of letters, but nearer the lamp-lighter ; unless, seeing him stand beneath a street gas-jet to write an overdue article, one noticed he carried a pencil instead of a pole. Thus were the flares of Brown's bookstalls in Bishop's Road used by him. On and on would he write until the last shutter was closed and the gas turned down. Then dashing off the final sentence, he would rush into the shop to sell his book, and to the pillar-box with his article.

If he is to be sought for among the old masters, it is to El Greco that one would go. He had the narrow head and ardent eye that served that painter for Saint, Beggar, and Courtier. None other recalls his presence to me, or creates an atmosphere in which he could have lived. Rembrandt's was too rich and still, Tintoretto's too invigorating. Titian recognised no such pallor, Giorgione no such slightness, and Veronese no such shabbiness. For the Florentines, they were better built; their poets' countenances were more established and secure, and their excellent young men were less nervous and restless than he.

He alludes in a letter to a belief (principally, I believe, his own) that he resembled two Personages :—

"DEAR EV.,—Character counts, even in cricket. This morning I was looking at a *Daily Mail* photo. of the South African team for the coming cricket season. One of the faces instantly caught my eye. 'Well!' said I, 'if character count for anything in cricket, this should be the bowler they say has the Bosanquet style.' . . . Since Hall Caine is no Shakespeare, Plonplon no soldier, *and neither the Tsar nor the Prince of Wales [George V] are Thompsonian poets*, great was my surprise when I found the fellow *was* the Bosanquet bowler."

Had he compared his own youthful photographs with those of the present Prince of Wales he might perhaps have been confirmed in one of his impressions.

The only faces he much pondered were the poets'. Round the walls of his room he pinned the *Academy* supplements, full-page reproductions from the National Portrait Gallery; and with these was a reproduction given him by Coventry Patmore of Sargent's drawing of A. M. The supplements he liked all the better because they illustrated a favourite theory of facial angles. On foreheads he set no value; but insisted that genius was most often indicated by a protruding upper jaw. This did not mean for him that thick lips had significance, but where the bony structure from the base of the nose to the upper teeth was thrust forward, as, notably, in Charlotte Brontë and Coventry Patmore, he found the character that interested him.

328

Francis Thompson
Drawn by the Hon. Neville Lytton 1907

His Letters

Here is another letter, written in a bad light but copious good spirits, before a visit to "the Serendipity Shop" :—

"DEAR EV.,—This to remind you I shall be at the shop, whereof the name is mystery which all men seek to look into, and in the mouth of the young man Aloysius doubtful is the explanation—yea, shuffleth like one that halteth by reason of the gout ; in the forehead and forehand of the bland and infant day, yet swaddled in the sable bands of the first hour and the *pre-diluculum.* For the Wodensday, a kitten with its eyes still sealed, is laid in the smoky basket of night, awaiting the first homœopathic doses of the morn's tinctured euphrasy (even as euphrasia once cured an inflammation of my dim lid)."

Mr. Andrew Lang has complained of de Quincey's digressions ; a further sample of F. T.'s habitual guiltiness may be taken from one of the slightest of his notes :—

"DEAR EV.,—I told your father I should come to-morrow, but I send you a line to *mak siccar*—as the lover of artistic completion said who revised Bruce's murder of Red Comyn. It is interesting to see the tentative beginnings of the James school in Bruce, already at variance with the orthodox methods upheld by his critical collaborator. The critic in question considered that Bruce had left off too soon. But to Bruce's taste evidently there was a suggestion in the hinted tragedy of ' I doubt I have killed Red Comyn ' more truly effective than the obvious ending substituted by his *confrère.* History, by the way, has curiously failed to grasp the inner significance of this affair.
"I am quite run down to-night." . . . .

"I had never your lightness of heart," he writes,

The Closing Years

forcing me to wonder what he thought of one for making such poor use, in his behalf, of the imputed characteristic; "nor was I ever without sad overshadowings of the hurrying calamity. . . . 'The day cometh, also the night'; but I was born in the shadow of the winter solstice, when the nights are long. I belong by nativity to the season of 'heavy Saturn.' Was it also, I sometimes think, under Sagittarius? I am not astronomer enough to know how far the precession of the equinoxes had advanced in '58 or '59. Were it so it would be curious, for Sagittarius, the archer, is the Word. He is also Cheiron, the Centaur, instructor of Achilles. The horse is *intellect* or *understanding* (Pegasus = *winged intellect*). He is the slayer of Taurus the Bull (natural truth and natural or terrestrial power and generation, the fire of unspiritualised sense), which sinks as he rises above the horizon. Ephraim, a type or symbol of the Word (as Judah of the Fathers and the Priesthood), was an archer, or symbolised as such. (See Jacob's dying and prophetic blessing of his sons, wherein each has a symbol proper to his character and that of his tribe, indicating his place as a type in the Old Church, and in the foreshadowing of the New.) But this is very idle chatter, and I don't know how I fell upon it when my mind is serious enough, indeed. Perhaps the mind wanders, tired with heavy brooding."

But it is always the gay word that could best bear the scrutiny of the poet himself if he were to pass the proofs of his own biography. In writing of a life that has a superficial look of disaster and pain, his biographer has a shamefaced feeling of dishonesty. Every other word is, in a sense, a misrepresentation, and worse. The memory of his smile shouts out to them, "You liars!"

There was always courtesy in his notes, mixed with haste and complaints; and even he would weary of

330

His Laugh

bulletin prose, so that his needs and ailments sometimes
came recorded in doggerel :—

> I am aweary, weary, weary,
>   I am aweary waiting here !
> Why tarries Everard ? sore I fear he
>   Has forgotten my shirting-gear !
> Ah, youth untender ! why dost thou delay
> With shirts to clothe me, an untimely tree
> Unraimented when all the woods are green ?
> But thou delay not more : unboughten vests
> Expect thy coming, shops with all their eyes
> Wait at wide gaze, and I thy shepherd wait,
> In Tennysonian numbers wooing haste . . .

Of great value is A. M.'s corrective record of his
laugh :—

" He has been unwarily named with Blake as one of the unhappy poets. I will not say he was ever so happy as Blake ;—but
few indeed, poets or others, have had a life so happy as Blake's,
or a death so joyous ; but I affirm of Francis Thompson that he
had natural good spirits, and was more mirthful than many a man
of cheerful, of social, or even of humorous reputation. What
darkness and oppression of spirit the poet underwent was over
and past some fifteen years before he died. It is pleasant to
remember Francis Thompson's laugh, a laugh readier than a girl's,
and it is impossible to remember him, with any real recall, and not
to hear it in mind again. Nothing irritable or peevish within him
was discovered when children had their laughter at him. It need
hardly be told what the children laughed at ;—say, a habit of
stirring the contents of his cup with such violence that his after-
dinner coffee was shed into the saucer or elsewhere—a habit
which he often told us, at great length, was hereditary."

His laugh it is difficult to keep alive : the legend of
his extinguished happiness is too strong. For laughter is
commonly discredited; only Mr. Chesterton, for example,
persists in making the Almighty capable of humour.
While we are all ready to allow that thorns make a crown,
we hold that bells do no more than cap us—the cap and
bells of folly. Who ever spoke of a crown of bells ?

The Closing Years

The refutation of the charge against his industry lies in his published work and in the pages of a hundred crowded note-books. The newspaper Odes alone are sufficient evidence of his power to compel even his muse to arduous and humble labours.

These Odes were pot-boiling journalism; their inspiration by the clock and the column :—

"We have no doubt whatever that inspiration will not fail you for so great a subject—the Jubilee! We must have the copy by the afternoon of the 21st,"

wrote an encouraging editor (Mr. Massingham) on June 6, 1897. The request was made on the strength of Mr. Massingham's admiration for *New Poems,* and was not refused; the ode was written within three weeks, and probably in the last three hours of them. From Mr. Garvin came another letter :—

"*June 22, '97.*

"Dear Francis Thompson,—I get the *Manchester Guardian* every day not merely by good hap, but because it is the best daily in England. Whose is the ode? I thought on the leisure of the opening and then saw. Hot Jacobite as I am for England's one legitimate laureate by native grace and right divine, I could not repress the movement of natural pity for the respectable and conscientious wearer of statutory bays, who tries so hard to fly as if the *Times* page were Salisbury Downs and he a bustard. Every flap a stanza; thirty flaps of the most desperate volatile intention; and no forrarder to the empyrean, where the Thompsonian ode sails with one supreme dominion through the azure deeps of air— vital, radiant, lovely. I told you I was your poor foster-brother of prose, in witness whereof is my thought of England's dead, and other little thoughts; in that the soul danced in me to the great pulse of your ode.—Always yours,   Louis Garvin."

Of an article on Browning Mr. Garvin had written :—

"Dear Francis Thompson,—Tell me by what native instinct or faculty acquired you so easily avoid henotheism in your critical writings. My poet of the moment, as I am drawn to his centre

The Newspaper Odes

and become enveloped in his light, seems to absorb all the radiance of all song. I know there are exterior suns, but the poet only remembered bears up with difficulty against him immediately contemplated. It is henotheism exactly. But here you take the crabbed case of Browning, you extricate him from the multitude of words and you directly declare middle justice upon him, and so he betakes him to his place. Yet if a word had been said against a certain oleaginous obesity of optimism that glistens upon the plump countenance of this well-groomed poet in easy circumstances, mayhap it had been well.

" But I went most willingly with you when you laid your finger upon Browning's Elizabethan aptitude for the dramatic form of motive analysis and critical comment. And that not because of Browning. I have long had it in my mind to say that I feel the same faculty to be latent in you somewhere. I fancy very strongly that you could handle the Elizabethan form better than anybody else these two hundred years and fifty and a little more. The Elizabethan spirit of course you have to that degree. The point about Browning's manipulation of character and circumstance is completely put. Don't you wish, though, to take the other part—volition diving at the imminent billow of life and buffeting a sea of circumstance? Indefinite potentialities I feel sure you have—especially of the drama that gives a separate voice and name to all the sides of one's own numerous personality.[1] I pine for the odes. —Always yours affectionately (if I may be), Louis Garvin."

In a letter to his sister about the Jubilee Ode, Francis says :—

" Thereon forthwith followed the severe and most unhappy cab accident about which I informed you. . . . I have had a year of disasters. You will notice a new address (39 Goldney-road, Harrow-road, N.W.) at the head of this letter. I have been burned out of my former lodgings. The curtain caught fire just after I had got into bed, and I upset the lamp in trying to extinguish it. My hands were badly blistered, and I sustained a dreadful shock, besides having to walk the streets all night. The room was quite burned out."

[1] Note by F. T.: " That is not drama, but lyric."

The Closing Years

This letter he never posted, so that his sister writes out of her unwearied solicitude two years later :—

" MY DEAR FRANK,—Doubtless you will be surprised to receive a letter from me after so long a silence. But the apparent negligence is not my fault, for I have been trying for twelve months past to obtain your address, and only succeeded about a fortnight ago. You see, my dear brother, I have no one to give me any information of you, and as *you* never write to me the consequence is I am utterly in the dark. My life is very uneventful, therefore my letters to you must, I know, be very uninteresting ; but they must just show you that you have still got a sister who loves you and thinks of you and also prays much for your well-being here and hereafter."

Later the old century was " sung on her way " in an ode appearing in the *Academy*, at the beginning of 1901 ; and in the death of Cecil Rhodes (March 26, 1902) his editor saw the occasion for another paper ode. Mr. Hind describes the hasty manner of its composition, and when it appeared in the *Academy* for April 12, 1902, it bore the marks of a trumped-up emotion's inspiration. In May 1902 Mr. Fisher, now of the *Chronicle*, asked F. T. for a Peace Ode, to be pigeon-holed against the conclusion of the South African War.

Very often F. T. would decide for an eight-hour day, and offer himself, through my father, to the journals. Like most men who find work irksome when they have it, and delay all commissions, he imagined, when he had none, that the difficulty was in the getting. "The *Academy* should not and shall not have a monopoly of me," he writes, without any provocation from the *Academy*. "Take this chance for me now." (W. M. had mentioned the *Daily Chronicle* as an opening) " Bite a cherry while it bobs against your mouth." Nor were his reasons for complaint against his journalistic fate always ungrounded. The *Academy* demanded no monopoly, being willing to accept his unpunctual copy whenever it arrived, and in almost any quantity ; but

Journalistic Flurries

elsewhere minor reverses were made the most of. F. T. writes :—

"I have just got home. The *Imperial and Colonial Magazine* asked me to submit 'one or two poems' of an Imperialist nature. I sent them one, as you know. They have rejected it. If the poem sent through you is also rejected (as I expect) I shall give up. I cannot go on here—or anywhere else—under these circumstances. Try as I will, all doors are shut against me. If your poem miscarries that is the end.—Yours ever, F. T."

Thus were his fears communicated to the person who made them futile and absurd. But Thompson would never forgo them.

Commissions, however, when they came, were rejected in silence, or accepted and neglected—

" DEAR SIR,—I shall be greatly obliged if you can send me the articles you kindly agreed to write for the Catholic Encyclopædia in the letters B and C "

is a note I find among his papers, and others came, were ignored and lost. "Having done an article for the *Chronicle*," he writes, " I have still seventeen volumes of poetry undone for it." When Mr. Hind left the *Academy* the poet was in some flurry and distress ; having called on the new editor, Mr. Teignmouth Shore, he writes :—

"The interview last Friday landed me on a doubtfully hospitable Shore. All articles to be cut down to a column. Immediate result, fifteen shillings for this week. . . . Therefore am waiting most anxiously for your return, when I may explain all the complexities of the situation. At present most perplexed and anxious. Do not cut short your holiday ; yet I do need to see you."

He continued fitfully on the *Academy*, but gradually

335

transferred his allegiance to the *Athenæum*. In the meantime my father arranged that a publishing house whose literary adviser he was should supply him with work that could be done at any time and be paid for at any moment. *The Life of St. Ignatius* was commissioned. He delivered every few pages as he finished them—three were passport to a pound—and, so final was his method of composition, he neither desired nor needed to see a single page of the manuscript again. The reviewing my father obtained for him on the *Athenæum* he did with success till within a month or two of his death. Letters from Mr. Vernon Rendall illustrate the courtesy of his editors:—

"ATHENÆUM OFFICE, *December* 20, 1905.

"DEAR MR. THOMPSON,—I am very sorry to hear of your illness, which may have been aggravated I fear by our clerks. I will try to make them send things correctly in future. Do not hurry now about anything you have. You are sure to be in need of rest and recreation—which, indeed, is supposed to be the fair perquisite of all at this season.—Yours very truly, VERNON RENDALL."

And again :—

"ATHENÆUM OFFICE, *March* 14, 1906.

"DEAR MR. THOMPSON,—I was very glad to hear of your recovery, and hope you will now enjoy established health. We were clearly as much at fault as you in the delay of the notices you mention. I quite agree with you about Morris. Generally, I try to send you books worth reading, and, tho' we never have too much space to spare, I am sure that you know as well as anybody the value of a book, and I hope you will not restrict your notice of what you think really good.—Yours very truly,
V. RENDALL."

And, later, from another office :—

"THE NATION, *April* 9, 1907.

"DEAR MR. THOMPSON,—Mrs. Meynell will have sent you a letter of mine about the beautiful poem ["The Fair Inconstant"] which you wrote for us last week, and about the more elaborate work, which, in continuance of old *Daily Chronicle* days, you might

His Plays

be willing to do for us. I have always retained the utmost admiration for your poetic genius, and regard with much warmth its association with a paper like the *Nation*.—Yours very truly,

H. W. MASSINGHAM."

Of another literary enterprise which, like his journalism, shews that he could be diligent, he writes :—

"DEAR WILFRID,—I have summoned up pluck to send my little play [1] (which Mrs. Meynell and you have seen) to W. Archer, asking him whether it afforded any encouragement to serious study of writing for the stage. His answer is unfavourable—though he refrains from a precise negative. This sets my mind at rest on that matter. None the less, I wanted to read you one or two bits from my chucked-up *Saul*, since they seemed to me better than I knew."

"I never yet missed my Xmas wishes to you, and it seems uglily ominous if I should do so now. But I have been working desperately at a poem for the *Academy*. . . . When I met Whitten this morning he looked uneasy, repeatedly advised me to 'get something.' I explained I already had 'got' some tea (with my breakfast). 'Yes, but — get something more,' he said, and alleged that I was looking shrunk with cold.

---

[1] This play was again unfavourably received when, in 1903, he submitted it to *T. P.'s Weekly*. It is thus set forth on his MS. title page:

NAPOLEON JUDGES

A Tragedy in Two Scenes

DRAMATIS PERSONÆ

NAPOLEON.
GENERAL AUGEREAU.
MADAME LEBRUN (*an opera-dancer, Augereau's Mistress*).
PRESIDENT OF THE COURT MARTIAL.
A FRENCH DESERTER.
OFFICERS. SOLDIERS.

Place.—Augereau's Camp. *Time.* — The Italian Campaign of 1796. During the first scene Napoleon is absent from Augereau's Camp.

Of another class is a modern comedy, full of laboriously smart give and take, called "*Man Proposes, but Woman Disposes*. Un Conte sans Raconteur. In Two Scenes."

The Closing Years

"Of course I will come in to-morrow night. Did I not, you might be sure I was knocked off my legs altogether, and I should feel that the world had gone off its hinges. I have never missed seeing you at Christmas save when I was at Pantasaph. Every happy wish to you, dear Wilfrid, and may God be as kind to you as you have ever been to me."

CHAPTER XVII : LAST THINGS

FRANCIS'S health often dismayed him, and his terrors both in regard to sicknesses and politics covered many pages of threatening letters. The mere streets became more and more an oppression. Even Elgin Avenue grew (in 1900) as ugly to him as it always is to men less happily indifferent. At such times he could write to W. M. in the strain of the following letter :—

" I designed to call in on Wednesday, but was sick with a horrible journey on the underground. To-day, though better, I am still not well. I hope I may manage to-morrow. I have been full of worry, depression, and unconquerable forebodings. The other day, as I was walking outside my lodgings, steeped in ominous thoughts, a tiny child began to sing beside me in her baby voice, over and over repeating :—

' O danger, O danger
O danger is coming near ! '

My heart sank, and I almost trembled with fear."

He prophesied of war, and was tormented whole days by complications in the East, and the notion of a Yellow invasion. And even West Kensington, when small-pox was announced there, seemed to come marching on him, a Birnam forest of bricks. It was illness, with fear for a symptom. " Disaster was, and is, drawing downwards. . . . There are storm-clouds over the whole horizon, and I feel my private fate involved. I am oppressed with fatality," he writes in one letter (1900), and on the next page is involved in jokes which were

Last Things

heavy, not with fatality. Other letters contain complaints of dreams akin to Coleridge's :—

"A most miserable fortnight of torpid, despondent days, and affrightful nights, dreams having been in part the worst realities of my life."

On the engagement in 1903 of Monica of "The Poppy," of "Monica Thought Dying," and of *Sister Songs*, Francis wrote to her :—

"28 ELGIN AVENUE,
Saturday.

"DEAR MONICA,—I would have answered you long since if I had not been so worried with work that I do not know how to get through it. Having got rid of my poem, I have taken a little rest from work, to which I had no right, and my neuralgia seems happily to have got better—though I am almost afraid to say so, for I still feel very weak and jaded, so that it might easily return. Therefore I take this moment to write to you.

"Most warmly and sincerely I congratulate you, dear Monica, on what is the greatest event in a woman's life —or a man's, to my thinking. . . . Extend to him, if he will allow me, the affection which you once—so long since—purchased with a poppy in that Friston field. 'Keep it,' you said (though you have doubtless forgotten what you said) 'as long as you live.' I have kept it, and with it I keep you, my dearest. I do not say or show much, for I am an old man compared with you, and no companion for your young life. But never, my dear, doubt I love you. And if I have the chance to show it, I will do.

"I am ill at saying all I doubtless should say to a young girl on her engagement. I have no experience in it, my Monica I can only say I love you ; and if there is any kind and tender thing I should have said, believe it is in my heart, though it be not here.—My dear, your true friend, FRANCIS THOMPSON."

He Quotes "The Poppy"

At her bidding, he went, on her marriage day, to the Church of St. Mary-of-the-Angels in Bayswater. He had never, in all probability, failed a tryst before by coming to it too early, but to all her commands he was obedient, and his mistake was but the symptom of his anxiety to be present. The poppy that she picked and gave him, with " Keep it as long as you live," was found in the leaves of his own copy of *Poems*—the only volume of his own works that he kept by him. So were all her injunctions observed. Having gone too early to Church, he left too early, and wrote :—

" WESTBOURNE GROVE, 12.30 P.M.
Wednesday, June 14, 1903.

" DEAREST MONICA,—You were a prophetess (though you needed not to be a sibyl) to foretell *my* tricks and manners. I reached the church just ten minutes after twelve, to find vacancy, as you had forewarned me. A young lady that might have been yourself approached the church by the back entrance, just as I came away ; but on inspection she had no trace of poppy-land. There must have been other nuptial couples about, I think.

" It seems but the other day, my dearest sister (may I not call you so ? For you are all to me as younger sisters and brothers — to me, who have long ceased practically to have any sisters of my own, so completely am I sundered from them), that you were a child with me at Friston, and I myself still very much of a child. Now the time is come I foresaw then—

Knowing well, when some few days are over,
You vanish from me to another.

" You may pardon me if I feel a little sadness, even while I am glad for your gladness, my very dear.

" I was designing to call in to-night, till I learned from you that you would be occupied with your wedding-party. Then I hoped I might have got to you last night

341

instead, but could not manage it. So, to my sorrow, I must be content only to write. Had I known before, I would have called in on Sunday, at all costs, rather than defer it to (as it turns out) the impossible Wednesday.

"I shall be with you all, at any rate, in spirit.—Yours ever dearly, my dear,   FRANCIS THOMPSON."

A few years before his death his manner had changed. His platitudes, now, were merely a means of getting through an evening without making a demonstration of the trouble he was in. That his ills might not be exposed he kept covering them up with talk, as constantly as a mother tucks in a child restless in fever. The man who always takes laudanum is always in need of it, and when he is in need he is ill. He is too ill to think, too uncomfortable to meditate or be wise.

Whenever he postponed his dram, and spent his day instead with his friends, he would say an easy thing once, and finding it easy, would say it over and over again. While he spent an evening explaining that last August was hot, but this hotter, his cry really was, "Where is my laudanum?" Nor was his need only physical: his soul, too, was crying, "Where is my God, my Maker, Who giveth songs in the Night? Who teacheth us more than the beasts of the earth, and maketh us wiser than the fowls of Heaven?" I am told by a doctor that one of the greatest pains of relinquishing opium is the sense of the reason's unfitness. Thought is thrown out of joint, and hurts like a dislocated shoulder.

"Nature," says Emerson, "never spares the opium or nepenthe, but wherever she mars her creature with some deformity or defect, lays her poppies plentifully on the bruise." And even for the bruises made by poppies she has her salve. Some redress, a rebate of the price paid, was made to Francis Thompson for the agony of the opium habit. That he seldom spoke of it meant that it was a thing too bitter to speak of ; meant, too, that it was at times a thing too little to speak of, that Nature minimised its terrors. There is mercy for the slave of a bad habit : the more confirmed, the more often must there be periods during which its mastery is forgotten, even in its presence. The sorriest drunkard is not necessarily the drunkard oftenest sorry. The opium-eater is sometimes persuaded of his own invented theory of the causes of his weakness, of its uses and necessity. Francis, who would have loathed himself to the point of extinction, or redemption, if he had been an ordinary sinner, who would have found life with himself intolerable had he sullied life with common offences against the Law, was provided with some sort of protection against remorse for his own particular failing. Nature gave him poppies to set against poppies.

Periods of misery and dejection came to him, as to his fellows. With Coleridge he could in certain moods have written :—" The stimulus of conversation suspends the terror that haunts my mind ; but when I am alone, the horrors that I have suffered from laudanum, the degradation, the blighted utility, almost overwhelm me." And again in words very like de Quincey's, Coleridge speaks of " fearful slavery," of being " seduced to the accursed habit ignorantly." From the starker visitations of remorse Coleridge, too, was justly sheltered. His son has said for him :—

" If my Father sought more from opium than the mere absence of pain, I feel assured it was not luxurious sensations or the glowing phantasmagoria of passive dreams ; but that the power of the medicine might keep down the agitations of his nervous system, like a strong hand grasping the strings of some shattered lyre."

His own " my sole sensuality was not to be in pain " is sufficient for himself and for others.

Last Things

F. T.'s comments on Coleridge's case are valuable, since they rebound in his own direction :—

"Then came ill-health and opium. Laudanum by the wine-glassful and half-pint at a time soon reduced him to the journalist-lecturer and philosopher, who projected all things, executed nothing ; only the eloquent tongue left. So he perished—the mightiest intellect of the day, and great was the fall thereof. There remain of him his poems, and a quantity of letters painful to read. They show him wordy, full of weak lamentation, deplorably feminine and strengthless."

And again :—

"It is of the later Coleridge that we possess the most luminous descriptions. A slack, shambling man, flabby in face and form and character ; womanly and unstayed of nature ; torrentuous of golden talk, the poet submerged and feebly struggling in opium-darkened oceans of German philosophy, amid which he finally foundered, striving to the last to fish up gigantic projects from the bottom of a daily half-pint of laudanum. And over the wreck of that most piteous and terrible figure of all our literary history shines and will shine for ever the five-pointed star of his glorious youth ; those poor five resplendent poems, for which he paid the devil's price of a desolated life and unthinkably blasted powers."

Even if Francis spilled brown laudanum on his paper as he wrote those superlatives, he did not fit the cap of disaster to two heads.

In 1906 he again visited the monastery at Crawley, where his friends had offered him hospitality over many years, and helped him to keep an occasional feast. I take a sample at random of Prior Anselm's courtesy :—

"HOLY SATURDAY.

"DEAR FRANCIS,—The Alleluias have been sung, and I echo them to you, dearest friend, hoping they bring you joy and peace and blessings."

To the memory of
FRANCIS THOMPSON, POET
1859–1907
STUDENT OF OWENS COLLEGE
1877–1884
Whatso looks lovelily
Is but the rainbow on life's weeping rain.
Why have we longings of immortal pain.
And all we long for mortal ? Woe is me.
And all our chants but chaplet some decay.
As mine this vanishing — nay, vanished day.

Memorial at Owens College, Manchester

Carved by Eric Gill

At Crawley

Again :—

" DEAR FRANCIS,—Could you give me and the community the great pleasure of your company on the Feast of St. Anthony, when the Bishop of Southwark will assist ?   I do hope you will come, as it is the last feast I shall have before the Chapter, an event that may scatter us all to the four winds of heaven."

And again :—

" The community and particularly myself would be delighted to have the pleasure of your company on Oct. 4th, the Feast of our holy Father St. Francis and your name-day.   I am looking forward to some long talks.   How I long for a return of the happy days at Pantasaph, when we discussed all things in heaven and on earth and in infernis."

Before his departure to Crawley Francis wrote to me :—

" . . . I feel depressed at going away from you all— it seems like a breaking with my past, the beginning of I know not what change, or what doubtful future. Change *as* change is always hateful to me ; yet my life has been changeful enough in various ways. And I have noticed these changes always come in shocks and crises after a prolonged period of monotony. In my youth I sighed against monotony, and wanted romance ; now I dread romance.   Romance is romantic only for the hearers and onlookers, not for the actors.   It is hard to enter its gates (happily) ; but to repass them is impossible.   Once step aside from the ways of 'comfortable men,' you cannot regain them.   You will live and die under the law of the intolerable thing they call romance.   Though it may return on you in cycles and crises, you are ever dreading its next manifestation. Nor need you be 'romantic' to others ; the most terrible romances are inward, and the intolerableness of them is that they pass in silence. . . . One person told me that my own life was a beautiful romance.   'Beautiful' is not my standpoint.   The sole beautiful romances are

345

the Saints', which are essentially inward. But I never meant to write all this."

All this, and much unwritten trepidation, because he had to travel three-fourths of the railroad to Brighton! Of all places Sussex, he had said, was the place where he preferred to live ; but the getting him there was as difficult as a journey to Siberia. And from Crawley he wrote : —

"I am a helpless waterlogged and dismasted vessel, drifting without power to guide my own course, and equally far from port whichever way I turn my eyes. I can only fling this bottle into the sea and leave you to discern my impotent and wrecked condition."

The flung bottle was stamped and caught the post!

In the following year (1907) it became evident that F. T. was again in urgent need of change. He was thinner, even less punctual, more languorous when he fell into fits of abstraction ; less precise when he would have assumed the pathetically alert step and speech by which he had been used to respond to introductions and the calls of the very unexacting establishment he still visited sometimes twice, sometimes thrice, and always once a week. He had grown listless and slow, and it was proposed he should go to the country. "Certainly, Wilfrid," he responded, coming the next evening to explain it was impossible ; his boots, which looked stronger than himself, would not travel, he said ; the coat covering his insufficient shoulders was insufficient. Boots and shirts were bought. It was arranged that we should call for him the next day at eleven. Accordingly my father and I and a friend presented ourselves in a motor at his dwelling, prepared to wait his dressing-time. But he was already out ; nor could his land-lady, who had not seen him abroad at such an hour in all her experience, say why or where. When at last

He Goes to Newbuildings

he came, he carried a paper bag with food purchased at a shop far distant. No gourmet could have been at greater pains to secure the particular pork-pie, and no other, that he wanted.

At first he and I had sleeping quarters in an independent pavilion among fern and young oaks, as guests of Mr. Wilfrid Blunt at Newbuildings. Breakfast and a log-fire used to be prepared for us by David, a genius among odd-men, who came through the dew before we were awake, and disturbed us with the fragrance of his toast and coffee. Francis would get up quite early, but at night he was late. I used to see him in his room, propped against pillows, with candles burning and his prayer-book in his hand far into the night; and his light would still be bright when the stars had begun to grow faint in the plantation.

Later, he was moved to David's cottage, whence he was fetched every day to Newbuildings, half a mile away, for luncheon and tea. David and Mrs. David had gained the unwilling confidence of the invalid, and Mr. Wilfrid Blunt, adept in everything, himself saw that medical help was necessary. In September a doctor was consulted, but if no effective treatment followed it was probably because Francis's evasions successfully prevented a satisfactory diagnosis.

To the care he received in Sussex there was no end. On September 6, 1907, a companion of Mr. Blunt wrote :—

" Mr. Blunt paid Mr. Thompson a long visit last evening, and I hear to-day that he is better. He told Mr. Blunt that he will stay here for the present. The doctor is going to see him again. Mr. Thompson liked him, which is something gained, and he is also pleased with David and his wife. Mr. Thompson has not come to-day, but we have sent twice, and the boy will enquire again this evening."

His little tragedy at Newbuildings was a wasp-sting. Enmity had started some days before, when a wasp fell into his wine-glass. It got out and was staggering on the table when I came upon the scene. Francis stood still, watching with fire in his eye. "You *drunken* brute," he said with loud severity. But no wasp, drunken or respectable, would he kill, though he could be bitter. The next day he was stung, and Mr. Wilfrid Blunt holds it of faith that for all that summer, after the poet's malediction, no wasps buzzed in Sussex. "Sir, to leave things out of a book merely because people tell you they will not be believed, is meanness," says Mr. Blunt in the words of Dr. Johnson. For all that (since a biographer's unbelief must count for something) I do not here record the lesser miracles remembered by Mr. Blunt. But the following (an earlier experience) is of Francis's own telling, in *Health and Holiness* :—

" In solitude a poet underwent profound sadness and suffered brief exultations of power : the wild miseries of a Berlioz gave place to accesses of half-pained delight. On a day when the skirts of a prolonged darkness were drawing off for him, he walked the garden, inhaling the keenly languorous relief of mental and bodily convalescence, the nerves sensitised by suffering. Passing in a reverie before an arum, he suddenly was aware of a minute white-stoled child sitting on the lily. For a second he viewed her with surprised delight, but no wonder ; then returning to consciousness, he recognised the hallucination almost in the instant of her vanishing."

Father Gerrard, who met him in Sussex, afterwards wrote :—

" Only a few weeks ago, I was chatting with Francis Thompson in his cosy retreat at Southwater, whither he had gone as the guest of Mr. Wilfrid Blunt, to see if haply he might pull together his shattered frame. But the phthisis fiend had caught him in a tight grip. He was a dying man, and an old man, although only forty-eight years of age. Still, even in his extremity the characteristics of his life were manifest, a shrinking from fellowship, a keen perception and love of the Church, a ready and masterful power of

In Hospital

language. I could not say that conversation with him was ever an easy thing, if by conversation one means unceasing talk. Besides talk there were thoughtful silences. Then, after the thought, came the outpouring of its rich expression. The doings of the outside world had little interest for him, but the messages which I had for him from his little circle of friends set him all aglow."

He returned weaker than he went. In his extremity of feebleness any hurt seemed grievous to him. Upon an umbrella falling against him in the railway carriage, he turned to me with a tremulous : " I am the target of all disasters ! " And when a busy-body of a fellow asked him, on account of his notable thinness : " Do you suffer with your chest, sir ? " Thompson, who had but one lung, and that diseased, answered sharply, " No ! " Even then he did not know the extent of his trouble.

In error he attributed all his ills to one cause. My father, seeing him on his return, said to him, " Francis, you are ill." " Yes, Wilfrid," he answered, " I am more ill than you think " ; and then spoke a word from which both had refrained for ten years. " I am dying from laudanum poisoning."

My father asked him if he were willing to go to the Hospital of St. John and St. Elizabeth. The fact that my sister—the Sylvia of *Sister Songs*—chanced at that moment to be lying ill there, led him to consider the institution without hostility, and the next day, my father having previously recommended him to the nuns, he went unreluctant to his death-bed. Consumption was the mortal disease, and he had grown grievously thin, and too weak to be allowed much less than his habitual doses of laudanum. Some little while before the hours at which these became due, the tax upon his remaining strength was very heavy ; but only when in acutest need of the one medicine that could keep him alive (as, indeed, it had done over a long course of years) were the last days distressing for him. During most of them (he was in St. John and St. Elizabeth's ten days) he was content with his surrounding, and knew Sister Michael, his most kind nurse.

His reading was divided between his prayer-book and Mr. W. W. Jacobs' *Many Cargoes*, neither of which attested his realisation of the end. But he was not ignorant of it. When I last saw him he took my father's hand and kept it within his own, chafing and patting it as if to make a last farewell. He died at dawn on November 13, 1907.

But, for all that friends were at hand, the nurse tender, and the priest punctual, his passing was solitary. His bedside was not one at which watchers share commingling cold, as when a widow's burning fingers, holding those of her dead, are turned to inner ice; his going not as a child's, which chills the house. The fires quenched were his own. It seemed to his friends as if it were a matter personal to himself; while their sorrow for their own loss was mixed almost with satisfaction at something ended in his favour, as if at last he had had his way in a transaction with a Second Party, who might have long and painfully delayed the issue.

Nothing improvident or improper, it seemed to those at hand, had happened in the hospital ward. Such were one's feelings beside the tall window, among nuns who smiled happily because he had received the Sacraments. His features, when I went to make a drawing of him in the small mortuary that stood among the wintry garden-trees, were entirely peaceful, so that I, who had sometimes known them otherwise, fell into the mood of the cheerful lay-sister with the keys, who said: "I hear he had a very good death." To the priest, who had seen him in communion with the Church and her saints at the moment which may be accounted the most solitary possible to the heart of man, no thought of especial loneliness was associated with his death.

He was too magnanimous to take one to his dead heart. Suffering alone, he escaped alone, and left

Death

none strictly bound on his account. He left his friends to be busy, not with his ashes, but his works. It was as if the winds that caught and checked his breath were those that blew his fame into conspicuous glows. He was laid to rest in St. Mary's Cemetery, Kensal Green. In his coffin, W. M. records, were roses from Meredith's garden, inscribed with Meredith's testimony—"A true poet, one of the small band," and violets went to the dead poet's breast from the hand of my mother whose praises he had divinely sung.

"Devoted friends lament him," wrote W. M., "no less for himself than for his singing. But let none be named the benefactor of him who gave to all more than any could give to him. He made all men his debtors, leaving to those who loved him the memory of his personality, and to English poetry an imperishable name."

Index

Index

Index

Index

Index

Index

Index

359

Index

Index